METHODS and MODELS for STUDYING the INDIVIDUAL

This book is dedicated to Marian Radke-Yarrow for her lifetime contributions to the understanding of human development and the application of that knowledge to the solution of social issues.

METHODS
and
MODELS
for
STUDYING
the
INDIVIDUAL

Essays in Honor of
Marian Radke-Yarrow

Edited by
Robert B. Cairns
Lars R. Bergman
Jerome Kagan

SAGE Publications
International Educational and Professional Publisher
Thousand Oaks   London   New Delhi

For information:

SAGE Publications, Inc.
2455 Teller Road
Thousand Oaks, California 91320
E-mail: order@sagepub.com

SAGE Publications Ltd.
6 Bonhill Street
London EC2A 4PU
United Kingdom

SAGE Publications India Pvt. Ltd.
M-32 Market
Greater Kailash I
New Delhi 110 048 India

Printed in the United States of America

Library of Congress Cataloging-in-Publication Data

Main entry under title:

Methods and models for studying the individual/edited by
    Robert B. Cairns, Lars R. Bergman, Jerome Kagan.
        p. cm.
    Includes bibliographical references and index.
    ISBN 0-7619-1451-X (cloth: alk. paper).
    ISBN 0-7619-1452-8 (pbk.: alk. paper)
    I. Cairns, Robert B., 1933–   . II. Bergman, Lars R. III. Kagan, Jerome.
    BF713.M   1997   98-019777

98 99 00 01 02 03 10 9 8 7 6 5 4 3 2 1

Acquiring Editor:	C. Deborah Laughton	
Editorial Assistant:	Eileen Carr	
Production Editor:	Diana E. Axelsen	
Editorial Assistant:	Karen Wiley	
Typesetter/Designer:	Marion Warren	
Cover Designer:	Ravi Balasuriya	

Contents

❦

Preface

*H*ow can the richness of individual lives be captured by the objective methods and statistical analyses of developmental research? Several years ago, Marian Radke-Yarrow and her colleagues answered this question by observing that "the child's day-to-day experiences contribute significantly to his behavior and development and are in many respects the essence of developmental theory" (Radke-Yarrow, Campbell, & Burton, 1968, p. 152). The translation of this observation into effective research methods continues to challenge, perplex, and beguile developmental investigators.

As colleagues and friends of Marian Radke-Yarrow, we thought we could best celebrate her distinguished career by joining together to address this central problem of the science. This volume is the outcome of those attempts. The common ground has been twofold: (a) our concern with the problem of how to create methods that focus on the individual in developmental research and (b) our admiration of the insights and contributions of Radke-Yarrow. We, in turn, have been honored by her comments and incisive criticism of the ideas offered here.

We are indebted to many persons for helping us prepare this volume for publication. In particular, we thank Philip C. Rodkin for his several contributions and C. Deborah Laughton for her support and encouragement in the preparation of this volume.

Robert B. Cairns
Lars R. Bergman
Jerome Kagan

Acknowledgments

Chapter 3: This study was supported by grants from the Swedish Council for Social Research and the Swedish Council for Planning and Coordination of Research. The author thanks Lars R. Bergman, Robert B. Cairns, and John R. Nesselroade for valuable comments on the manuscript.

Chapter 4: This research was supported by grants from the John D. and Catherine T. MacArthur Foundation and from the National Institute of Mental Health, MH47077. The authors thank Donna Steinberg, Eric Peterson, and Anna Costes.

Chapter 5: The research reported in this chapter has been supported by grants to the author from the Swedish Council for Planning and Coordination of Research, the Bank of Sweden Tercentenary Foundation, and the Swedish Council for Social Research. Valuable suggestions have been given by R. B. Cairns, B. M. El-Khouri, K. Harnqvist, D. Magnusson, I. Munck, and P. C. Rodkin.

Chapter 7: The writing of this chapter was supported by a National Science Foundation Graduate Fellowship, a Chancellor's Dissertation Fellowship (University of California, Berkeley), and NIMH Grants MH49255, MH49414, and MH45548. The Pittsburgh Youth Study was supported by the Office of Juvenile Justice and Delinquency Prevention, Office of Justice Programs, U.S. Department of Justice (Grant No. 86-JN-CX-0009). Points of view or opinions in this document are those of the authors and do not necessarily represent the official position or policies of the U.S.

Department of Justice. The authors thank Samuel Gosling and the editors for their helpful comments on an earlier draft.

Chapter 9: The authors are most grateful to the staff of the Pittsburgh Youth Study for the careful data collection and for making these analyses possible. The authors are indebted to Magda Stouthamer-Loeber, Welmoet B. Van Kammen, David P. Farrington, and Wim Slot for their advice with the chapter and to JoAnne Fraser for her help in finalizing the manuscript. The research was undertaken under grant No. 86-JN-CX-0009 from the Office of Juvenile Justice and Delinquency Prevention, Office of Justice Programs, U.S. Department of Justice, and Grants MH48890 and MH50778 of the National Institute of Mental Health. In addition, financial support for the analyses was given by the Pedological Institute, Amsterdam, Netherlands. Points of view or opinions in this document are those of the authors and do not necessarily represent the official position or policies of the U.S. Department of Justice.

Chapter 10: The authors are grateful to Debra Bekerian and Stephen Ceci for helpful suggestions used in this chapter. Our research reported here was supported by a range of grants from the Medical Research Council, Foundation for Child Development, John D. and Catherine T. MacArthur Foundation, Economic and Social Research Council ALCD programme [H519-25-5031], U.S. National Institute of Mental Health [MH45268] [MH48604], and other organizations.

Chapter 11: The authors thank Beverley D. Cairns for her multiple contributions to this chapter and to the research on which it is based. This research was supported by funds from the National Institute of Mental Health and the Spencer Foundation.

~ *1* ~

Lawfulness in Individual Development

Robert B. Cairns

University of North Carolina
at Chapel Hill

Jerome Kagan

Harvard University

Lars R. Bergman

Stockholm University

*E*veryone agrees that parents influence their children's lives. Among social scientists, however, there is surprisingly less agreement on the nature of those influences. Marian Radke-Yarrow's distinguished scientific career has been devoted to understanding this puzzling and difficult problem. Radke-Yarrow believes in the lawfulness of individual development, but given the complexity of the family and cultural influences, the coherence and integration of individual development can be obscured by standard psychological methods and analyses. Thus, the meaning of every statement about the relations of parental actions to children's development or, indeed, about the relations of any variable is a function of the source of evidence. This insight she had early, but it is still not characteristic of most work of the social sciences in the 20th century.

Radke-Yarrow's methodological contributions have consistently pointed to the importance of examining the linkages among concepts, operations, and conclusions. For example, she demonstrated early that a mother's constructions of her own and her child's behavior changed over time and that, hence, recollections provided an imperfect picture of what an observer might have seen in the home several years earlier. Seemingly strong linkages between the past and the present may reflect the correlated constructions of the mother in the present. Radke-Yarrow understood that each informant had a potentially unique view of the child. These points reflect her broader concern that students of socialization have been handicapped by the modest standards for methods and measures that have been adopted in research on parenting and child development.

She recognized early that investigators are vulnerable when variable criteria are used to judge the validity of empirical observations. If a discrepancy appears in results that used different methods or that were collected across different time intervals, a few a priori guides help a psychologist resolve the discrepancy or guide a judgment of the significance of the differences. Consequently, counterintuitive findings are susceptible to displacement by intuitively reasonable ones. Because there are few guides to the evaluation of the methodological merits of different strategies, real progress is difficult to achieve—or to recognize even when it is achieved.

Is the study of parenting and child development such an elastic discipline? Radke-Yarrow and her colleagues provided an uncompromising answer in their 1968 volume *Child Rearing: An Inquiry Into Research and Methods*. At the end of the volume, they wrote:

> Childrearing research is a curious combination of loose methodology that is tightly interwoven with provocative hypotheses of developmental processes and relationships. The compelling legend of maternal influences on child behavior that has evolved does not have its roots in solid data, and its precise verification remains in many respects a subject for future research. The findings from the preceding analyses of data make it difficult to continue to be complacent about methodology, and difficult to continue to regard replication as a luxury. The child's day-to-day experiences contribute significantly to his behavior and development and are in many respects the essence of developmental theory. An exact understanding is important to science and society. In attempting to build on this knowledge, each researcher is a methodologist and as such has a responsibility for excellence. (p. 152)

Child Rearing was a brilliant and courageous appraisal of research on social development. Marian Radke-Yarrow and her colleagues challenged the discipline on three counts. First, they observed that the accepted standards for socialization methods and measures were inadequate, and they warned against the casual stance taken with respect to replication. The use of reports of mothers to describe both their actions and the behaviors of their children was particularly targeted. Second, they signaled that the problems could lie as much in the explanations that were offered as in the methods that were employed because "the compelling legend of maternal influences on child behavior that has evolved does not have its roots in solid data" (p. 152). Third, they argued that the field must reach a better fit among developmental theory, developmental methods, and the concrete events of lives in context.

These challenges apply with equal force today. But the possibility that current methods and statistics of psychology are inadequate for developmental study has been a difficult message for researchers to accept.

Radke-Yarrow and her colleagues have called for a reevaluation of the logic and standards by which systematic analyses of socialization can proceed. They have spoken to the need to evaluate rigorously "provocative hypotheses of developmental processes and relationships" (p. 152). *Child Rearing* criticized one of the most widely employed methods of child-rearing study: the semistructured interview pioneered by R. R. Sears and his colleagues in the 1950s and 1960s (e.g., Bandura & Walters, 1959; Sears, Maccoby, & Levin, 1957; Sears, Whiting, Nowlis, & Sears, 1953; Whiting & Whiting, 1963).

It is appropriate to ask, given the repeated confirmation of Radke-Yarrow's discoveries, why developmental psychologists have resisted many of her basic conclusions. The reasons have to be multiple. Convenience and logistic ease have to be one important reason. One can gather interview and questionnaire data on 100 mothers and their children in a fraction of the time required for direct observations of the parent-child dyad. And psychologists recognize that they could not be present when formative or critical events were occurring. We conjecture, however, that a more fundamental reason is the premise, religious in its zeal, that the parents themselves have the most accurate understanding and representation of their actions and their children's characteristics. Each person is an infallible witness to his or her own behaviors and beliefs and to those of his or her children.

That is why, in her most recent work in her studies of depressed mothers and their relationships with their children, she established a seminatural setting where interactions could be observed in laboratory-like conditions. Results of the extensive investigation, which will soon be published, point to unique and sometimes counterintuitive explanations that could not have been discovered if usual self-report methodologies had been employed. This recent work highlights Radke-Yarrow's continuing concern with how researchers can bridge the gap between methods and models in developmental research. Contemporary researchers now broadly support the idea that an integrated perspective is required if the discipline is to achieve progress in understanding the nature of human and animal development (e.g., Magnusson & Cairns, 1996). In every developmental phase, organismic and maturational changes coalesce with changes in the child's social and physical contexts. Accordingly, pathways of individual development should not be divorced from the concrete features of changing social contexts and social ecologies in which the child is embedded. These ecological concepts, enriched with a concern with developmental change, are compatible with the dynamic psychology of her mentor, Kurt Lewin.

But this is not the first time a provocative theoretical idea has captured the enthusiasm and commitment of socialization researchers. Similar levels of acceptance were given to earlier proposals on socialization and maternal-child relations. Throughout this century, psychoanalytic theory in one form or another has dominated accounts of socialization, either directly or indirectly, through its variants in early social learning theory and attachment theory. Unless rigorous methods are employed to assess the model in its own terms, the discipline may simply exchange one compelling myth for another.

Because the developmental framework presupposes that fresh ways are required to organize information about individuals over time, it almost succeeds in immunizing itself against challenges by conventional methods. The obvious hazard is that any exemption from detailed empirical assessment may invite researchers to reject one compelling legend and to accept another. So a large assignment confronts researchers who subscribe to an integrative developmental framework. The task is to establish procedures that permit researchers to determine empirically whether propositions derived from the developmental model are true or false.

As colleagues, friends, and students of Marian Radke-Yarrow, we believe that we can honor her by addressing this seminal issue, each from his or her own perspective, because we agree that "each researcher is a methodologist and, as such, has a responsibility for excellence" (Radke-Yarrow et al., 1968, p. 152). To achieve a common ground, we ask how developmental research can retain a focus on individuals over time. This was the theme of a conference in which we participated in late 1994, following Radke-Yarrow's concerns, and most of the chapters in this volume address this issue.

Although this celebratory volume focuses on methodological themes, it is relevant to mention her substantive contributions. Her studies of empathy and prosocial behavior in young children have motivated a whole generation of scientists to study the positive contributions of conscience development that come from the child, rather than to continue the traditional emphasis on parental punishments for misdemeanors. David Hume would have smiled to have read Radke-Yarrow's studies of empathy and its role in monitoring the actions of the 2- and 3-year-old child.

Her forthcoming monograph on the children of unipolar and bipolar depressed mothers reports different profiles for the two syndromes and generates a dramatically new set of questions about the relation of pathology in parents to the development of their children. A recurrent theme in Radke-Yarrow's work is the essential integration of emotional phenomena with the behavior and cognitive structures that permit the actualization of the holistic personality. However, neither a Watsonian or a Piagetian can explain the civil behavior of children unless one adds the affective components that Radke-Yarrow probed.

One significant change that occurred during the span of Radke-Yarrow's research career—a change she helped initiate—is the incorporation of a concern with social perceptions and their multiple roles in individual development. As she observes (personal communication, 1997), when she completed her dissertation, "Lewin wanted to talk about perceptions that parents had, and you didn't dare talk about perception at Minnesota." But perceptions and stereotypes were unavoidable in the studies she conducted on the development of prejudice in young children. This work proved to be influential in the 1954 *Brown v. Board of Education* (347 U.S. 483) Supreme Court decision on school integration.

A central issue of methodology that transcends content domains is her concern with the study of individuals across time. Radke-Yarrow appreciated that the child and the child's contexts change over time and therefore that longitudinal investigations are mandatory to understanding individual development. For instance, we now know from investigators both in the United States and abroad that less than 15% of extremely aggressive and fearful children retain their extreme characteristics two decades later. Radke-Yarrow understood that psychological ontogeny is, like phylogeny, dynamic and receptive to new events and changing conditions: "The child's day-to-day experiences contribute significantly to his behavior and development and are in many respects the essence of developmental theory" (Radke-Yarrow et al., 1968, p. 152). One can only praise Radke-Yarrow's willingness to recognize the complexity of development without being intimidated by it.

∽ OVERVIEW OF THIS BOOK

Robert Hinde (Chapter 2) observes that categorizing children on several variables permits greater insight into the natural types of personality organization. He affirms Radke-Yarrow's principle that the concept of the individual must be related to specific social contexts. Hinde outlines four ways in which categories may be formed: (a) by theoretical distinctions, (b) by classificatory or categorical analyses, (c) by empirical groupings, and (d) by identifying extreme cases. Hinde clarifies how empirical procedures can be employed in a stepwise progression to permit a focus on individual children.

Chapter 3 elaborates the advantages of focusing on individual profiles that retain a holistic view of the person. As with taxonomies of species, no one variable defines a species. The more useful strategy includes a pattern of characteristics. David Magnusson insists that individuals, not variables, are or are not stable over time. He uses data from the Individual Development and Adjustment (IDA) longitudinal program to illustrate how a person-oriented analysis can be employed to track the emergence of criminality and alcohol abuse in adulthood. The cluster of childhood characteristics captures information that is otherwise obscured in the focus on single variables or their linear combination.

Chapter 4, by Jerome Kagan, Nancy Snidman, and Doreen Arcus, demonstrates the value of focus on extreme groups of fearful and extremely exuberant children. Only a very small proportion of a large cohort of children displayed a profile of very low reactivity in infancy, minimal fearfulness, and extremely high positive affect in childhood combined with a very low heart rate and a broad facial skeleton.

Lars Bergman (Chapter 5) identifies the assumptions by which a pattern-oriented approach can be employed to study individual development over time. He provides a precise account of the

theoretical and operational definition for terms that have histori-
cally beguiled the discipline (e.g., *type* and *antitype*, *pattern* and
configuration, *taxonomy* and *classification*). He also outlines some
key technical details and illustrates the choices that confront
researchers in the application of these procedures to longitudinal
data sets. Consistent with Kagan et al., Bergman recognizes that
not all individuals can be classified by standard clustering and
configural procedures. Rather than view these extreme cases as a
liability or "error," Bergman identifies them for separate focus and
analysis.

Joan Stevenson-Hinde (Chapter 6) reports, consonant with
Kagan et al., that a small group of young children are consistent in
their extreme levels of shyness. These children differ from nonshy
children in their relationships with their mothers and in behavior
problems. Stevenson-Hinde reminds us that we must sample
across contexts and to be sensitive to the exclusion/inclusion of
extreme children.

Richard Robins, Oliver John, and Avshalom Caspi (Chapter 7)
provide a contrapuntal posture to the Baconian style of the prior
chapters. These authors, with proper reservation, make the bold
suggestion that future theories of personality will have to account
for the fact that three major types frequently emerge from the
analysis of adult personality data. About two thirds of adults seem
to be able to deal with stress in a resilient way, with neither
excessive anxiety nor anger and aggression. Some resilients are
autonomous; some prefer a more communal or affiliative style.
About 20% resemble the syndrome called *externalizing* and are
called "undercontrolled" by these authors. Some undercontrollers
are impulsive; some are antisocial. The remaining 14%, called
"overcontrolled" by Robins and his colleagues, display shyness,
restraint, anxiety, and inhibition as their salient traits.

Lea Pulkkinen's longitudinal study of Finnish children tracked
to adulthood does not disconfirm Robins et al.'s analysis but, in
accord with most earlier chapters, reminds the science of the
importance of gender, age of subject, and source of data. Pulkkinen
(Chapter 8) finds support for a hypothesis of heterotypic continuity. She also demonstrates that the predictive correlations she
discovered might be a result of the continuities in a few extreme
cases, consistent the observations of Kagan, Hinde, Magnusson,
and others.

Rolf Loeber, Mary Smalley DeLamatre, Kate Keenan, and
Quanwu Zhang (Chapter 9) point to the need to have a clear
concept of what is meant by developmental pathways. The inclu-

sion of a concern with developmental dynamics is a significant advance over the traditional methods employed in psychiatric nosological classifications. By focusing on pathways of disruptive behavior, these investigators demonstrate how it is possible to combine the strengths of variable-oriented and categorical procedures to achieve a focus on individuals.

Michael Rutter, Barbara Maughan, Andrew Pickles, and Emily Simonoff (Chapter 10) return us to Radke-Yarrow's seminal monograph on retrospective reports. These authors assess the degree of agreement between children's contemporaneous reports of parental hostility at 10 years of age and the same individuals' retrospective reports obtained at adulthood. In their recall of childhood, the best adjusted adults underestimate the problems that they perceived as children. Rutter and colleagues argue that the experience between childhood and adulthood generate new constructions of childhood experience. "The main problem with retrospective recall does not lie in interview techniques, but rather in the ways memory processes operate. . . . That has been a hallmark of Marian Radke-Yarrow's approach to research . . . and . . . illustrates the manifold strengths of her investigative approach."

Robert Cairns and Philip Rodkin (Chapter 11) address how developmental methods can be brought into line with developmental models. They outline the variety of ways configuration solutions can provide a bridge to the study of individual pathways. They emphasize the importance of making explicit the role of timing in this process and how the action of correlated constraints in development bring order, organization, and continuity to individual lives despite the inevitable fluidity in contexts, persons, and relationships. The correlated constraints also provide a stepping stone from configurations of groups to the distinctive pathways of persons over time.

Georges Clemenceau, the French statesman, once said that war is too serious a matter to be left to the generals. Likewise, the development of methods for understanding the growing child is too serious a matter to be left to pure methodologists and statisticians. The lead must here be taken by developmental researchers with their understanding of the issues and concepts encountered in the concrete realities of living. Statistical procedures and measurement models are not masters; they are tools to be masterfully used. On this score, we believe that active researchers play a critical role in pointing to areas required for method development. To use Radke-Yarrow's words once again, "Each researcher is a methodologist and as such has a responsibility for excellence" (Radke-Yarrow et al., 1968, p. 152).

∾ FINAL WORDS

We invited Marian Radke-Yarrow to comment on the proposals contained in each chapter of this volume. Her insights have proven invaluable for the discipline throughout her distinguished career. The volume provided an opportunity for us to invite her to evaluate the proposals that have been offered to provide focus on the individual in developmental research. Accordingly, we organized this book so that Radke-Yarrow would have the final word for each chapter. The editors and authors were honored when she accepted the assignment.

~ 2 ~

Through Categories Toward Individuals

Attempting to Tease Apart the Data

Robert A. Hinde

St. John's College, Cambridge

D evelopmental psychology—indeed, psychology in general—deals with extraordinarily complicated phenomena. That is a truism, but it is easy to forget how it has influenced the development of psychology as a science. Because many issues with which it is concerned occur only under certain conditions or in a proportion of individuals, psychology has come to depend more and more on statistical techniques. Their importance cannot be minimized: Through their use, psychology has become a science. Yet, they can bring with them a temptation to gloss over complexity.

The great majority of studies in developmental psychology involve comparisons between or across groups. It is not necessary here to point out the advantages of such an approach: it permits the identification of the effects of independent variables and the demonstration that such effects are unlikely to occur because of chance. However, effects that are unlikely to occur because of chance may yet account for only a small proportion of the variance, and it is tempting to deem a statistically significant result satisfactory, however little of the variance it accounts for. Individual differences too easily become submerged in group means, and the special factors that are crucial for individuals who are extreme or special in one way or another readily go unnoticed. Furthermore, different statistical techniques may yield different pictures of "truth": for example, the application of Pearson correlations, multiple regression, continuous discriminant analysis, and discrete discriminant analysis to the same data set yielded different types of relations between dependent and independent variables (Hinde & Dennis, 1986). But, as Marian Radke-Yarrow (1991) has stressed, if research is to help us understand the development of individuals, then we must overcome these problems and come to terms with the multitudinous factors that influence the individual case. Furthermore, ultimately it must be the individual going about her or his ordinary business in her or his ordinary environment. This is not to undervalue experimental studies in the laboratory; they are often essential to reveal the nature of the factors acting. But our aim must be to understand the behavior of individuals in their everyday lives. This must include understanding why particular individuals find themselves in particular situations (which is not always a matter of chance), how they respond to those situations, and the extent to which an individual's behavior may change with the situation.

One approach involves studying individuals from the start. This can involve a clinical approach, attempting to identify the issues that "matter" or have "mattered" in the individual's life. Although such an approach can be experimental, involving changes consequent upon changes in an individual's situation, it is likely to involve the abandonment of statistical analysis and, thus, an inability to specify the replicability of the findings (but see, e.g., Barlow & Hersen, 1984).

A second approach involves focusing on individuals who lie at the extreme of one or more dimensions. Kagan (1994) has shown how revealing can be the study of children at the ends of a continuum of behavioral inhibition (see below).

A third approach involves the use of statistical techniques to distinguish groups of individuals on the basis of their behavioral profiles. The chapters by Bergman (Chapter 5), Magnusson (Chapter 3), and Cairns and Rodkin (Chapter 11) in this volume exemplify this approach.

A fourth approach, and the one discussed here, is to identify groups of individuals by theory- or problem-related criteria and then to attempt to identify differences between them and others. The approach of attachment theorists (e.g., see Stevenson-Hinde, this volume, Chap. 6) exemplifies the use of theory-related criteria to categorize children into groups according to the nature of their attachment to their mothers. Radke-Yarrow, Richters, and Wilson (1988) distinguished mother-child dyads according to the stable versus chaotic nature of the family and found that the mother-child relationship was linked differently to outcomes in the two cases. Each of the last three approaches involves the categorization of individuals. The two studies discussed later in this chapter both show how categorization can help and expose some of its dangers. Because these studies involve comparisons between behavior in two different situations, a word about the situation dependence/ independence of behavior is first necessary.

∞ THE NATURE OF INDIVIDUAL CHARACTERISTICS

The earlier view that individual differences in behavior could be ascribed to individual differences along several trait dimensions was seen to be not wholly satisfactory because of the relatively poor cross-situational consistency of the traits (e.g., Mischel, 1973). As a result, person variables came to be somewhat neglected, and situational determinants emphasized (Block, 1977). Further progress came from studies evaluating the importance of Persons, Situations, and Person × Situation interactions for the variance in behavior (e.g., Endler & Magnusson, 1976). Individuals may not be consistent about all things, but at least some people are consistent some of the time about some things (Bem & Funder, 1978).

Some data illustrating this cross-situational flexibility in the behavior of 4-year-olds are shown in Table 2.1. Children were observed in both home and preschool and their behavior recorded by running commentary on audiotape. The record was subsequently analyzed in the form Subject-Verb-Object-Qualifier (e.g., mother-commands-the child-initiating an interaction). The rank orders of the children on each verb (e.g., *commands*) or qualifier (e.g., *initiating an interaction*) were compared across the two situations, and the table shows the proportion of correlation coefficients that were significant. The cross-situational consistency was quite low, and lower in boys than in girls (Hinde, Tamplin, & Barrett, 1995).

If individuals behave differently according to the situation, then we must face the important conceptual question of what we mean by individual characteristics. Such data do not mean that the

TABLE 2.1 Cross-Situational Differences in Rank Order on
Behavioral Items

Situation		Number of Coefficients Calculated	Percentage of Coefficients Significant (p < .05, one-tailed)			
			Girls		Boys	
Within situation	Mother/sibling	21	21 ⌐		5 ⌐	
				31		13
	Teacher/peer	16	44 ⌐		25 ⌐	
Across situation	Mother/peer	18	28 ⌐		17 ⌐	
	Mother/teacher	20	5		0	
				13		4
	Sibling/peer	10	10		0	
	Sibling/teacher	9	11 ⌐		0 ⌐	

NOTE: Children observed with mother and sibling at home, teachers and peers in school. The number of coefficients calculated is the number of items (e.g., speaks, comments, noncomplies) relevant to both partners. The percentage of rank order coefficients that were significant is shown in the last two columns.

search for basic personality factors is unimportant, but it does indicate that the links between such factors and behavior in particular contexts pose further problems. And personal characteristics must concern also the extents to which the individual is consistent across situations with respect to each of the several types of behavior that he or she might show (see Block & Kremen, in press).

Several languages, none wholly satisfactory, can be used for describing this cross-situational flexibility. One is to treat it as a simple stimulus-response matter. Different situations elicit different behaviors in a given individual. This, however, does not allow for the active role of the individual.

A second language is that of needs: individuals satisfy different needs, or the same needs to different extents, in different situations. The difficulty here is lack of agreement on how many basic needs are to be postulated: some argue for two (e.g., McAdams, 1988), others for half a dozen (e.g., Weiss, 1974), and others for 20 or more (e.g., Murray, 1938).

A third language is that of the symbolic interactionists (e.g., Goffmann, 1959; McCall, 1974), in which each individual is described as having a repertoire of role identities, defined as the way she or he likes to think of her- or himself as the occupant of a particular social position. Each role identity is seen both as emerging as a consequence of interaction and causing behavior and as providing both plans for action and the criteria by which action is evaluated. In an interaction, each individual tries to perceive the "character" underlying the set of role identities that the other employs and to devise a role for her- or himself that can best make use of them. The processes involved can be seen as involving negotiations as to who each person is. This approach is valuable in calling attention to the complex and active processes whereby individuals adjust their behavior to the social situation: how far those processes are present in young children is a developmental question that has not yet been addressed. In any case, the approach fails in that it does not specify the differences between individuals that affect whether individual and context fit each other.

This discussion of different ways of approaching cross-situational flexibility does not take us very far, but it does emphasize a crucial background matter. The important elements in a situation are usually social issues, and these are not just givens, but are actively influenced by the individuals as they interact. The individual characteristics affect the social situation, and the social situation affects the individual characteristics that are displayed. Thus, we are always dealing with a dialectic, and we must always think in terms of the individual-situation complex. This dialectic has especially important consequences for developmental psychologists because the characteristics of individuals may be changed by the situations that they experience not only in the short term but also more permanently. In any case, we must be clear whether the characteristics we postulate are situation-specific or more general: clearly, data relating to more than one situation are necessary if we are to come to terms with the nature of individual characteristics. Instruments to assess personality are, of course, devised with this in mind, but this necessarily makes the resulting dimensions more remote from behavior in specific situations.

To repeat, none of this is in contradiction with the view that individuals differ and differ along dimensions that can be specified, although those dimensions include cross-situational flexibility of different sorts. But it does mean that the concept of an individual is not so simple as it appears at first sight. Nearly every study deals with individuals in situations that they, in part, create.

∞ CATEGORIES, SUBCATEGORIES, AND INDIVIDUALS

We have seen that one route toward approaching the individual is by extending conventional statistical analyses of groups of individuals. Investigators (e.g., Coie, Dodge, & Kupersmidt, 1990; Hinde & Dennis, 1986; Kagan, 1994; Radke-Yarrow et al., 1988; Rubin, 1982; Rubin, LeMare, & Lollis, 1990) have shown that it is often profitable to categorize individuals in terms of their positions on one or more behavioral dimensions rather than to apply statistical techniques across the whole spectrum of individuals studied. A similar approach, but involving more qualitative assessments, is intrinsic to attachment theory, the application of which depends on dividing mother-child relationships into three or four categories and several subcategories. There is no need to emphasize the merits that may flow from such approaches. Here, we ask whether it is possible to take it further. Suppose we categorize subjects by one or other means (see below) and use standard statistical techniques for showing differences between them. The differences may be significant, but it is likely that some individuals will be outliers or do not fit. Our procedure should then be not to sweep these exceptions under the carpet, but rather to see in what other ways they differ from the members of their category. If the number of similar-looking outliers is sufficient, they may form a new category about which we may again make generalizations and perhaps look for further exceptions, and so on until we approach the individual. The first example to be discussed followed this procedure.

Three samples of 4-year-olds, about 20 boys and 20 girls in each, were observed with their mothers at home and with peers and teachers in preschool (Hinde, Tamplin, & Barrett, 1993a). We then tried to relate their aggressiveness in preschool to aspects of the mother-child relationship as observed at home. Taking the three samples as a whole, no significant correlations were found between aggressiveness in preschool and aspects of mother-child interaction at home. Categorization of the children in each sample into those who were in the upper, middle, or lower third on aggression in preschool, however, provided a more profitable approach. Taking our cue from Baumrind (1971) and Maccoby and Martin (1983), we plotted these individuals on axes of maternal warmth and maternal strong control as observed during the home observations. Figure 2.1 presents the data from the first sample and shows that most of the low-aggressive children lay in a diagonal area in which maternal strong control and maternal warmth could be seen as more or less balanced. The lines in Figure 2.1 were drawn by eye, but the two further samples provide confirmation. Lines drawn in exactly the same places with respect to the z scores again provided a considerable degree of separation between aggressive and less aggressive children. Following Baumrind, we labeled the areas on the graph as shown in Figure 2.1 *authoritarian* (high strong control and low warmth), *permissive* (low strong control), *authoritative* (balanced strong control and warmth), with very few children falling into an *indulgent* area (very strong warmth and very little strong control). This categorization of the children involved the relations between two dimensions, rather than children extreme on particular dimensions, as in most previous studies cited above. For the three samples together, the difference in aggression between these areas was significant for both boys and girls independently, with $p < .001$ overall. Individual exceptions are considered below.

The fact that aggression in preschool seems to be related to a sort of balance between maternal warmth and maternal strong control does not necessarily mean that these are the crucial or only variables involved. The mother-child relationships of children falling into these areas may have differed in many other ways. That that was, in fact, the case is shown in Table 2.2. Pooling the three data sets, ANOVAs were performed on the scores of the children falling into each Baumrind area on each aspect of mother-child interaction, followed by pairwise comparisons between the areas. Data show that children falling into the authoritative area had relationships with their mothers that differed in many other ways, in addition to maternal warmth and maternal strong control, from those in the authoritarian and permissive areas. These other aspects of the mother-child relationship, or indeed the relationship as a whole, may also be relevant to the incidence of aggression in preschool.

This provides us with a way of approaching the exceptions. If we compare the less aggressive with the more aggressive individuals in each of the three areas, we find that the less aggressive individuals scored more highly on positive aspects of mother-child interaction and less highly on the more negative aspects (Table 2.3). Had our sample been larger, we could perhaps have followed this analysis of exceptions one stage further, through smaller groups to individuals.

In this example, the individuals were categorized on a single dimension (aggression in preschool), and mother-child relation-

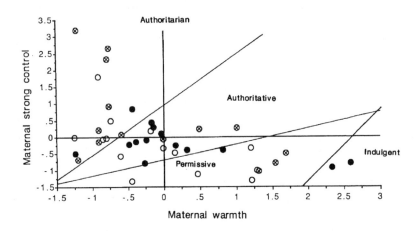

Figure 2.1. Relation Between Aggression in Preschool and Two Dimensions of Mother-Child Interaction—Namely, z Scores on Maternal Strong Control and Maternal Warmth. Filled Circles Indicate Children in the Bottom Third on Aggression in Preschool; Crosses in Circles, Those in the Upper Third; and Open Circles, the Intermediate Children.

ships differentiated initially by eyeballing the data when plotted on the two dimensions of maternal warmth and maternal strong control suggested by previous studies in the literature. The categorization procedure provides us with some insight into the principal home correlates of aggression in preschool and into the nature of exceptions to the initial generalization. It will be apparent that, following such a procedure, one could soon be led into a mass of detail about individual cases, so editors need some persuasion to accept such studies. Nevertheless, if understanding how individuals behave is the goal, this is one direction that must surely be followed.

In the next example, which concerns "social isolation" in preschool, teasing apart the data reveals both benefits and shortcomings in a categorical approach and leads us into an even greater mass of detail (Hinde, Tamplin, & Barrett, 1993b). As described for the preceding example, the children were observed at home with their mothers and in freeplay in preschool. Attention was focused on three dimensions of their behavior in preschool supposedly related to social isolation: (a) how much they were alone, (b) how much time they spent unoccupied, and (c) how frequently they interacted with other children. These three dimensions were chosen

TABLE 2.2 Comparisons Between Baumrind Oblique Areas of Items of Mother-Child Interaction and Individual Characteristics

	ANOVA Significant With p <	ATR vs. ATT	PER vs. ATT	ART vs. PER	PER vs. IND	ATR vs. IND	ATT vs. IND
Total verbal	.01	ATT**		PER**		IND*	
M. Initiates	.03	ATR**		ATR*			
Ch. Initiates	.06	ATR*					
Ch. Answers	.04	ATT*		PER*			
Ch. Friendly	.01	ATT**		PER**			
M. Friendly	.001	ATT***	PER*	PER***	IND***	IND**	IND**
Neutral Speech	.02	ATT**		PER**	IND*	IND**	IND*
M. Solicitous	.001	ATT*	PER*	PER**		IND**	IND*
M. Disconfirm	.01	ATR*	ATT*	ATR**		ATR*	
M. Negative	.01	ATR*		ATR**		ATR*	
Ch. Negative	.04	ATR*		ATR*			
M. Strong Control	.001	ATR*	ATT***	ATR***		ATR**	
M. Non-Comply	.03	ATR*		ATR**			
Ch. Non-Comply	.005		ATT*	ATR**		ATR**	
Self-Esteem	.02		PER**	PER*			
Shy					IND[1]	IND*	

NOTES: *The table includes only those comparisons for which the overall difference was significant and each of the three data sets showed a difference in the same direction. The symbols ATR (authoritarian), ATT (authoritative), PER (permissive), and IND (indulgent) indicate the higher group in each comparison. In comparisons of the indulgent area with others, differences significant with $p < .10$ have been included.

M. = Mother; Ch. = Child.

1. $p < .10$.

* $p < .05$; ** $p < .01$; *** $p < .001$

TABLE 2.3 Differences Between High and Low/Mid-Aggression
in Authoritarian and Permissive Areas, and
Between Low and High/Mid-Aggression in the
Authoritative Area[1]

	Authoritarian: High vs. Low/ Mid Aggression	Permissive: High vs. Low/ Mid-Aggression	Authoritative: High/Mid vs. Low Aggression	Gender Showing Differences
Ch. Answers			H/M*	F
M. Friendly	L/M*			F
		L/M*		M and F
Ch. Friendly	L/M*			F
M. Solicitous			L*	M
Ch. Dependent			L**	M and F
M. Gentle Control	L/M*			M
			L*	F
Ch. Controls	L/M*			M
M. Disconfirms			L*	F
Ch. Disconfirms			H/M*	M and F
Mother Initiates	L/M*		H/M*	F

1. Letters indicate the group with the higher score, and the last column the gender for which
the difference was present.
* $p < .05$; ** $p < .01$.

as aspects of children's behavior that often provoke anxiety in
preschool teachers. Linear correlations between these dimensions
of social isolation and items of mother-child interaction yielded
very little of interest, but once again a categorization procedure
provided insights into the relations between these aspects of social
isolation and the mother-child relationship.

The children were categorized into the upper, middle, and
lower thirds on the three dimensions of social isolation. From a
sample of 123 children, the number falling into the top third in
each of these categories is shown in Figure 2.2. Because the
frequency of interactions was moderately highly correlated with
time spent alone ($-.61$***), whereas both had lower correlations
with the time spent unoccupied ($-.20$* and $.31$***), the children
were initially categorized into four groups on time spent alone and
time spent unoccupied (Hi alone Hi unoccupied, Hi alone Lo
unoccupied, Lo alone Hi unoccupied, and Lo alone Lo unoccupied). *Hi* and *Lo* here refer to the top and bottom third in the
variable in question. A second analysis was carried out by using
eight groups, to include high or low frequency of interaction: Here,
to preserve an adequate sample size reasonably similar between

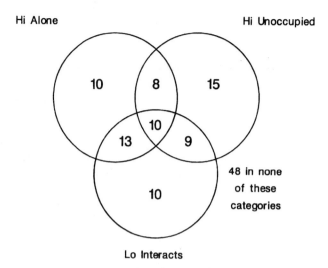

Figure 2.2. Numbers of Children in the Upper Third on Alone in Preschool, the Upper Third on Unoccupied, and the Lower Third on Frequency of Interaction

groups, it was necessary to contrast the top third (Hi) with the lower two thirds (Not Hi) or the bottom third (Lo) with the upper two thirds (Not Lo) in most cases. Measures of interactions with the mother at home and with peers and teachers in school were compared between these groups. Using two and three dimensions, the categories used, with their principal characteristics, are shown in Tables 2.4 and 2.5.

The first point to be made is that categorization immediately shows the inevitable inadequacy of attempts to find simple correlations between the isolation variables and aspects of mother-child interaction. For instance, those children who were in the top third on frequency of interaction with their mothers at home might be in the top or bottom third on alone in preschool (Table 2.5). We are reminded of the situation dependence of behavioral variables (Table 2.1).

Second, categorizing into eight groups leads to different conclusions from categorizing into four. For instance, children who were Lo alone and Hi unoccupied in the four-group analysis were Hi on friendly to peers (Table 2.4), but when this group was subdivided according to frequency of interactions, the minority who were Lo on frequency of interactions were also Lo on friendly to peers (Table 2.5). As a second example, children who were often

TABLE 2.4 Four-Group Analysis; Summary of Principal
Differences From Overall Means

	N	*Alone*	*Unoccupied*	
Withdrawn	18	Hi	Hi	Low intense, compliant, but high on mother and child initiates. Negative to disconfirm and seldom friendly to peers.
Unsociable	12	Hi	Lo	Negative to mother, who initiated relatively often. Gave and received aggression, negative behavior and disconfirmation with peers.
Sociable/ Unaccepted	9	Lo	Hi	Somewhat high intense mother and child compliant, few initiations, interact seldom. Seldom negative to mother. Aggressive and friendly to peers, who are negative but do not disconfirm or control.
Sociable	17	Lo	Lo	High intense. Mother and child interact often with few initiations. Mother compliant. Peers not aggressive, negative, or disconfirming.

NOTE: Hi and Lo indicate the upper and lower thirds on the variable in question.

both alone and unoccupied and seldom interacted with peers in preschool tended to interact often with their mothers at home, whereas those who were similarly often alone and unoccupied but interacted more often with peers tended to interact seldom with their mothers (Table 2.5). Thus, not surprisingly, the conclusions that one draws depend on the criteria for categorization that one uses. "Social isolation" is not a homogeneous category. No doubt, finer subdivisions using more criterial dimensions would yield yet more finely differentiated conclusions.

By proceeding in this way, we arrive at groups fairly homogeneous with respect to the three isolation variables and differing significantly from each other in some other aspects of peer interaction and of mother-child interaction at home. Each group is by no means wholly homogeneous, however, with respect to these other variables. To assess further the validity of the procedure, we may ask whether the home variables found to characterize the groups defined in terms of the isolation variables actually predict

TABLE 2.5 Summary of Principal Differences for Overall Means

	N	Alone	Interacts	Unoccupied	
Withdrawn	10	Hi	Lo	Hi	Initiate and interact often with mother, but in school seldom friendly and often automanipulative.
Withdrawn/ Rejected	8	Hi	Not Lo	Hi	Low on intense. Initiates often but interacts seldom with mother. Mother noncompliant. Peers aggressive.
Unsociable/ Neglected	13	Hi	Lo	Not Hi	Not Shy. Mother noncompliant. Seldom friendly and often disconfirmed by peers.
Rejected	10	Hi	Not Lo	Not Hi	Often initiates but seldom answers mother. Disconfirmed and receives aggression from peers.
Shy/ Unaccepted	9	Not Hi	Lo	Hi	Low intense, high shy. Low on initiates and neutral speech with mother. Not friendly to peers. Automanipulative.
Sociable/ Wandering	15	Not Hi	Not Lo	Hi	Mother compliant. Friendly to peers
Shy/ Accepted	10	Not Hi	Lo	Not Hi	High shy. Low on initiates and neutral speech with mother, but high on answers. Mother compliant. Below mean on friendly to, not disconfirmed by, peers.
Sociable/ Friendly	14	Lo	Hi	Lo	High intense. Interacts often with compliant mother. Friendly to peers, who seldom disconfirm or show aggression.

NOTE: Hi and Lo indicate the upper and lower thirds on the variable in question. Not Hi and Not Lo indicate the lower/upper two thirds.

the latter at the individual level. As an example, we consider first the most sociable group (Lo alone, Hi interacts, Lo unoccupied). This was found to be characterized by frequent interactions with the mother, low maternal noncompliance, and a high score on the temperamental characteristic "intense" (see Table 2.5). We identify all the children in the whole sample who were > .3 SD from the mean on these variables (which corresponds closely to the upper or lower third) and ask whether they fell into the sociable group or whether children in the sociable group actually scored high on total interactions with the mother and the temperamental characteristic intense and low on maternal noncompliance. Insofar as they did not, can any sense be made of the exceptions? We may consider three groups of individuals:

1. Three, and only three, individuals met the criteria for the sociable group in being in the lower third on Alone, upper third on Interacts with peers, and lower third on Unoccupied, and were also in the upper third on interactions with the mother and on intense, and in the lower third on maternal noncompliance.
2. Four individuals who fell into other social isolation groups nevertheless had the appropriate characteristics of mother-child interaction and intense. Two only just missed the criteria of the sociable group (Lo alone, middle third on the other two; and Hi interacts and middle third on the other two). Two, however, were Lo on interacts and in the middle third on the other two. We may ask whether these were peculiar in any other way. Both were >1.0 SD above the mean in maternal positive interactions but also high on either maternal negativity or control: however, the significance of this is quite unclear.
3. Eleven individuals met the social isolation criteria but did not satisfy the home characteristics. These are shown in Table 2.6. (The home variables shown involve variables on which at least one of these children had a score >1.0 SD from the mean.) Two of these children lacked two of the home characteristics, the other nine only one. We may ask whether these children, grouped according to the home characteristics they lacked, showed any consistency within the groups so formed.

    a. Three children interacted relatively seldom with their mothers. They had rather similar profiles, with small proportions of initiations and answers, few positive

TABLE 2.6 z Scores on Selected Variables of Individuals Who Were Seldom Alone, Often Interacted, and Were Seldom Unoccupied Yet Did Not Meet the Criteria of the Sociable Group Indicated in the First Three Columns

Individual Number	Gender	Total Interactions	M. Noncompliant	Intense	M. Initiates	Ch. Initiates	M. Answers	Ch. Answers	M. Friendly Physical	M. Positive	Neutral Talk	M. Solicitous	M. Disconfirms	M. Negative	M. Total Control	Ch. Controls
18	F	-.10	—	—	-.76	-.81	-1.11	-1.02	-.57	-.74	-1.01	-1.10	1.39	-1.24	.86	1.25
22	M	-.90	—	—	-.94	-.45	-1.02	-.90	.55	-.79	-1.49	-.60	-.84	-1.06	.10	.28
140	M	-.68	—	—	-.80	-.36	-.33	-1.55	-.14	-.66	-.75	-1.53	-.38	-.87	.61	1.75
118	F	.06	.11	—	.19	-.86	1.55	.71	-.36	-.49	.19	1.49	.39	-.75	-1.83	-.82
38	M	—	-.06	—	1.68	.63	1.53	1.10	1.24	-.40	.73	-.86	-.52	-.34	-1.04	-.11
46	F	—	-.15	—	-1.19	-.81	1.45	.16	-.69	-.39	.25	.04	-.90	.53	.11	-.03
53	F	—	.37	—	-1.34	-.65	1.03	-.22	-1.03	2.33	.88	1.85	-.61	-1.34	-2.24	.02
79	M	—	-.08	—	.16	-.22	.60	.85	2.00	.15	-.12	-.64	-.55	-.64	.36	.37
128	F	—	—	-.50	-.28	1.13	-1.58	1.51	-.85	2.49	1.59	.77	1.06	-.41	-1.61	1.65
144	M	—	—	-.72	.37	.51	-.30	-.05	3.72	-.53	.03	.55	-.37	.90	-.51	2.22
14	F	.22	—	-.62	-.19	-.33	-.72	.85	3.19	.66	1.65	-1.23	-.63	.47	-.55	-.84

NOTE: A dash (—) indicates the criterion was met.

interactions, neutral speech, maternal solicitude, and little maternal negativity but fairly high frequencies of control by both partners.

To understand the significance of these data, a slight digression is necessary. An initiation was scored if no previous interaction with the partner in question had been made for 30 seconds. Thus, a low proportion of initiations to total interactions implies long sequences of interactions. Conversely, a high proportion of answers to total interactions indicates long sequences. In the sample as a whole, answers were the most frequent sequelae to initiations, and initiations and answers were negatively correlated (Hinde et al., 1993b). However, initiations could be responded to not only by answers but also by responses in extension of the previous utterance, by complies/noncomplies if the previous statement had been a control statement, or by disconfirmation if the response were inappropriate or absent. Thus, a low frequency of answers may not signify short sequences if a high proportion of the interactions involve control. This was certainly the case for two of these individuals (nos. 18 and 140), as controls by both mother and child were high. In the third individual (no. 22), the sequences involved much physical friendliness, which was scored as not requiring a response.

Thus, all three of these individuals tended to have long sequences of interactions with their mothers, which although involving few of the more positive types of interactions, also involved little maternal negativity and frequent child controls with which the mother complied. One (no. 18) had a surprisingly high frequency of disconfirmations by the mother.

b. Four individuals failed to reach the appropriate low level of maternal noncompliance. These had fairly high frequencies of maternal answers and low levels of maternal control, implying long sequences of interactions. In two cases (nos. 46 and 53), this was supported by low relative frequencies of initiations. That the mothers were generally responsive is shown by the low frequency of disconfirmations. In addition, one mother gave an exceptionally high frequency of (verbal) positive interactions, and two of physical ones. None of these were true for number 46, however, whose mother, though seldom disconfirming, was often negative, so this girl remains rather a mystery.

c. One individual (no. 118) failed to reach the appropriate levels of either interaction or maternal noncompliance. Data in Table 2.6 suggest that her low levels of initiations and high levels of answers imply long sequences of interactions with little maternal negativity or control but much maternal solicitude.

d. Two individuals were not high on intense. Again, one was exceptionally high on mother friendly physically and the other on mother (verbal) positive. One was seldom disconfirmed, and both were high on child controls with which the mother complied.

e. One individual was not high on either maternal interactions or intense but was high on both mother friendly physically and positive verbally, and low on disconfirmation and control.

Thus, of these 11 children who met the social criteria but whose mother-child interactions did not conform to those significant for the group as a whole, reasonably good evidence supports long sequences of interaction in nine (nos. 18, 22, 140, 118, 38, 46, 53, 79, and 128). In addition, 9 were in the lower third on maternal disconfirmation, and 8 were in the top third of either mother physically or verbally positive or solicitous, with 7 of these being exceptionally high ($z > 1.23$).

It will be apparent that this procedure indicates that the characteristics of temperament and mother-child interaction found by the group analyses to differentiate the social isolation group must be treated with caution: they are only partially fulfilled by the individuals in the group and shared by some individuals outside it. At the same time, close examination of the data is beginning to indicate some regularities in the exceptions: all had indications of a positive mother-child relationship, although the positivity was revealed in different aspects of the interactions.

We may now consider the other extreme group, the least sociable one, with individuals in the upper third on alone and unoccupied and in the lower third on interacts. These were characterized as a group by high scores on total interactions with the mother but involving frequent initiations and answers by the child and much neutral conversation. Again, we may consider three categories:

1. Two, and only 2, of the 10 individuals met the criteria for social isolation and were in the upper third on the four items of mother-child interaction mentioned above.

2. Two individuals who did not fall into this social isolation group nevertheless met the characteristics of mother-child interaction. In temperamental characteristics, these two seemed to have little in common: One was more than 1 SD below the mean on the characteristic active and the other was 2.7 SDs above. The data do suggest, however, that both had rather intense relationships with their mothers. Both were in the upper third on frequency of interactions with the mother, maternal and child initiations and answers, and neutral conversation, and in the lower third on maternal disconfirmation and negativity.

3. Eight individuals who did fall into the social isolation group were not in the upper third on all four items of mother-child interaction, and only one of these could be said to be a near miss. These individuals, though homogeneous in the criterial school variables, were heterogeneous in the measures of mother-child interaction. Although the mean of the group as a whole was in the upper third of interactions with the mother, four were in the lower third. Nor could they readily be grouped according to the criteria of mother-child interaction they did meet. Seven of these eight, however, like both of those who did meet the criteria of mother-child interaction, were below the mean on child noncompliant with mother, six of them being in the lower third. (Although low child noncompliance scores characterized nearly all the children in this extreme isolated group, it did not come up as one characteristic of their relationships with their mothers because the ANOVA on the sample as a whole had not been significant.) And six of the eight were below the mean on the temperamental characteristic active, in this case unlike those who met the mother-child criteria, five being in the lower third. Of the two who were not low on active, one had a very controlling mother (2.8 SDs above the mean), and the other's mother was also in the top third on control and was also exceptionally high on physically friendly (2.3 SDs above the mean).

In general, then, we can say that these unsocial children tended to interact frequently with their mothers and that this was nearly always primarily on the mothers' initiative. The children were compliant and mostly low on activity, but it remains unexplained why two of these children had generally positive mother-child relationships not too dissimilar from those that characterized the markedly sociable children discussed first.

∞ CONCLUSION

Conventional statistical procedures, though essential for identifying factors acting in development, can distract attention from the complexity of the individual case. Categorization procedures may be more valuable than attempts to make generalizations about whole groups or populations.

We have seen that the concept of the individual must be related to the social context in question, and that usually means the relationship context. Individuals behave differently according to whom they are with, the nature and extent of the lability in each individual's behavior being themselves characteristics of the individual. This means that attempts to study individual characteristics must involve more than one situation.

The two data sets cited involve attempts to establish coherence between the characteristics of an individual's behavioral interactions in one situation and those in another. In each case, the children were categorized, in the first by following Baumrind's precedent, eyeballing the data and justifying the separation in terms of significant differences between means, and in the second by using three aspects of behavior often seen as problems in children of this age. In both cases, the categories used initially for grouping individuals were found to yield statistically significant generalizations about the corresponding mother-child relationships at the group level but to have only limited validity for individuals.

The conclusions reached about the exceptions in this chapter involve post hoc arguing, and the extent of their validity is a matter for discussion. It is clear that a given type of child behavior (e.g., degree of social isolation) can be associated with a variety, but not an unlimited variety, of patterns of mother-child interaction and that the general quality of the mother-child relationship may be a more important predictor of behavior in preschool than the frequencies of a few types of interaction. To that extent, it can be said to expose a shortcoming in molecular studies. In any case, the data did not suggest even post hoc explanations of why some children with generally similar home relationships should behave differently in preschool. Presumably, further analysis should pursue the fit among the child's characteristics, the mother-child relationship, and the characteristics of the preschool.

It may be concluded that categorization procedures with these data sets yielded insights when linear correlations failed, but even they were inadequate for some individual cases. In general, it would seem important to assess the validity of such procedures not just for the group as a whole but also for the individuals.

∞ↄↄ∞

COMMENTS ON CHAPTER 2

Robert Hinde has had a profound and very special influence on the study of behavior—on the questions investigated, the methods of search, and the integration of findings into broad domains of knowledge.

I remember first meeting Robert Hinde at a conference in Munich. A colleague and I had presented a paper on altruism in very young children. From a member of the audience came some fascinatingly penetrating questions. I did not know the questioner, but I was impressed. Fortunately, he pursued his questions after the session. Back at home, I went to the library to research his publications. I was puzzled. How, I wondered, had his research on parent-offspring relationships of birds equipped him with such sensitivity to child development? I read on. It was not long before I had become a "fan."

In this chapter, Robert Hinde proposes research procedures that will further an understanding of the individual "going about his ordinary business in his ordinary environment." Robert Hinde presents a series of analyses that take us from comparisons of groups to almost-the-individual.

In this process, he reminds us of the nature of the individual. The concept of the individual, he cautions, "is not as simple as it appears." We are always dealing with the influences of the social context on the characteristics that the individual displays and on the effects of these characteristics on the contexts. Moreover, individuals differ in the degree to which the situational context influences their characteristics. The implication for measurement procedures is somewhat awesome. If the investigator's purpose is to determine the individual's behavior in a specific situation, then measurement in that situation will suffice. If, however, the objective is to grasp the nature of the individual, then behavior in more than one context is necessary. From this perspective, Robert Hinde would, I believe, cast a critical eye on many research procedures in frequent use. Also, he leaves us with the disturbing question of where and how do we find the individual.

Robert Hinde puts his principles to the test in two research examples in which his objective is to understand the coherence of the individual child's behavior in different (home and preschool) contexts. He does so through patient and insightful descriptive analysis, beginning with correlations, through a series of categorical classifications, establishing generalizations and exceptions to generalizations, and determining generalizations within the exceptions—"until we approach the individual." This process represents a wholly different respect for the data from a swift summary of "significance" or "nonsignificance" of findings.

I take away several thoughts. Behavioral data are deserving of multiple levels of analysis. By moving from one level to another, we acquire different kinds of information that together form the basis for understanding the findings. The individual is not always our absolute goal in research. We need to be aware in our analyses, however, of just how near or far our data are from the individual.

Marian Radke-Yarrow

~ 3 ~

The Logic and Implications of a Person-Oriented Approach[1]

David Magnusson

Stockholm University

The way an individual person functions and develops can best be described as a dynamic, complex process. A characteristic feature of this process is the continuous interaction among mental, biological, and behavioral aspects of the individual and physical, social, and cultural aspects of the environment with which the individual has to deal. This view implies a holistic view on individual development and functioning (cf. Magnusson, 1995; Magnusson & Stattin, 1998; Magnusson & Törestad, 1993).

In brief, a modern holistic view emphasizes an approach to the individual as an organized whole, functioning and developing as a totality. The totality derives its characteristic features and properties from the interaction among the elements involved, not from the effect of isolated parts on the totality. Each aspect of the structures and processes that are operating (e.g., perceptions, plans, values, goals, motives, biological factors, conduct) takes on meaning from the role it plays in the total functioning of the individual.

The holistic principle holds for all systems of interest in research on human ontogeny regardless of the level at which the system is operating. It holds at the cellular level; at the level of subsystems, such as the coronary system, the immune system, the cardiovascular system, the cognitive system, and the behavioral system; as well as at the level of the individual as a total system.

It also holds for the environment and its subsystems, such as the peer system among youngsters or the family system.

In effective research on individual functioning and development, a holistic view should form the theoretical frame of reference for the formulation of the specific problem, the choice of research strategy and methodology, and interpretation of results. Of course, the application of a holistic model as the theoretical framework does not imply that all aspects of the functioning and development of an individual have to or can be investigated in one and the same study. The fact that specific studies in nuclear research and research in astrophysics, for example, are planned and interpreted in the same general model of nature does not imply that each study has to include the whole universe. The common general theoretical framework, however, enables researchers from these disciplines to communicate with and learn from each other in an effective way. Similarly, a common theoretical, holistic framework for the formulation of specific problems and interpretation of empirical results in research on individual functioning and development is a prerequisite for meaningful and successful communication among researchers from different subdisciplines in psychology—perception, cognition, motivation, personality, development, and others—and among researchers from psychology and neighboring disciplines such as neuroscience, sociology, and anthropology (Magnusson, 1996a, 1996b).

Conceptualizing the individual as the organizing principle in explanation of individual functioning has ancient roots, for instance, in the distinction between four basic temperaments. In psychology, the tendency to reduce psychological structures and processes into the smallest possible elements was discussed and criticized by James (1890) and Binet and Henri (1895). Dewey (1896), following James's criticism of the atomistic approach to mental thought processes, warned that the S-R approach could imply a new form of atomism. The general principle that the whole is more than the sum of the parts was the fundamental proposition for the Gestalt psychologists (see Brunswik, 1929, for a discussion). The proponents of typologies, as well as those arguing for a clinical view on individual functioning, mainly adhered to a holistic principle. In personality research, a holistic approach has been discussed in general terms for some time (cf. Allport, 1937; Lewin, 1935; Magnusson, 1990; Russell, 1970). A holistic view on individual development has been advocated by Cairns (1979, 1983), Lerner (1984), Magnusson (1988, 1995), Magnusson and

Allen (1983), Sameroff (1982), Sroufe (1979), Wapner and Kaplan (1983), and Wolff (1981), among others. Cairns and Cairns (1994) apply a holistic approach to the study of the socialization process; and Fogel and Thelen (1987) and Lockman and Thelen (1993) offer examples of the fruitfulness of applying this broadened perspective to research on specific topics—expressive and communicative behavior, and motor development, respectively.

A holistic, interactionistic model for individual functioning and development has received new blood from four main sources, the combination of which has infused the holistic model with the substantive content that was lacking in older approaches (Magnusson, 1995). The first enrichment comes from cognitive research. During the last decades, research on cognitive processes has been one of the most rapidly developing fields in psychology. Research on information processing, memory, and decision making has contributed essential knowledge for the understanding and explanation of individual development and functioning.

The second source stems from the rapid development of research in neuropsychology, endocrinology, pharmacology, developmental biology, and other disciplines in the life sciences that are concerned with the internal biological processes of an individual and their interaction with mental, behavioral, and social factors (Damasio & Damasio, 1996; Hockey, Gaillard, & Coles, 1986; Rose, 1995). Research in these areas will contribute much to our understanding of the ways individuals function and develop as totalities. Knowledge from these disciplines has helped fill the "empty box" in S-R models with substantive content and has contributed to bridging the gap between contrasting explanations of behavior in terms of mental factors, biological factors, and environmental factors. For example, Kagan (1992) ascribes the strong renewed interest in research on temperament to the extraordinary advances in neuroscience.

The third source lies in modern models for dynamic, complex processes, such as chaos theory (Barton, 1994; Crutchfield, Farmer, Packard, & Shaw, 1986; Gleick, 1987), general systems theory (Laszlo, 1972; Miller, 1978; von Bertalanffy, 1968), and catastrophe theory (Zeeman, 1976). These theoretical perspectives, particularly chaos theory, have had a strong impact on theory building and empirical research in scientific disciplines that focus on multi-determined, complex, dynamic processes—that is, in meteorology, biology, chemistry, ecology, and others (Bothe, Ebeling, Kurzhanski, & Peschel, 1987; Hall, 1991). Chaos theory has been evaluated as one of the most powerful theories of this century in the natural sciences. The application of chaos theory to brain functioning (Basar, 1990) is an example of application that is relevant to research on individual development.

The models for dynamic, complex processes were originally developed for the study of such processes in the natural sciences. In many important respects, the processes of individual functioning and development differ from the characteristic features of processes that are the concern of the natural sciences. However, one central proposition of the models is applicable and fundamental also for the processes that are the concern of psychological research: A total, dynamic, complex process cannot be understood by summing the results of studies on single aspects, taken out and studied in isolation from other, simultaneously operating factors. The totality has properties that cannot be derived from the investigation of one variable after the other. Thus, the old formulation from Gestalt psychology is relevant: The totality is more than the sum of parts.

At the same time, the total system and its subsystems of biological, mental, and behavioral structures involved in individual functioning and development have properties that imply they are less chaotic than the processes studied in meteorology, in which chaos theory was first developed. Each biological system functions and develops in a process in which two forces balance each other: on the one hand, maturation and experiences, which work for change, and on the other hand, the principle of resistance to change. In the face of environmental challenges, physiological systems maintain a dynamic balance. Referring to stability through change, the concept of *homeostasis* has been replaced by the concept of *allostasis* (Schulkin, McEwen, & Gold, 1994). Each biological system defends itself against inappropriate causes of change, which might lead to malfunction or destruction of the system. For example, in the normal functioning and development of the brain, several events that might have led to a detrimental butterfly effect are ignored, and only those that contribute to effective current functioning and to the development of functional new structures are accepted.

The fourth main source for enrichment of a holistic perspective on individual development lies in the revival of *longitudinal research*. Some of the most comprehensive longitudinal programs have been planned and implemented with reference to a holistic view (e.g., see Cairns & Cairns, 1994; Magnusson, 1988). A major motive for longitudinal research is that it enables the researcher to study causal mechanisms in developmental processes in a way not possible in cross-sectional research. In tracking individuals over time and context, the inadequacies of the piecemeal or variable-oriented approach to the study of developmental issues become obvious because operating factors necessarily shift over time. Only the organism remains distinct and identifiable. A manifestation of the importance of longitudinal research is the fact that the first scientific network established by the European Science Foundation in 1985 had the title Longitudinal Research on Individual Development (see Magnusson & Casaer, 1992).

Contributions from cognitive research, from the neurosciences, from modern models for dynamic complex processes, and from longitudinal research have enriched the old holistic view of individual functioning and development in a way that makes it a fruitful framework for planning, implementing, and interpreting empirical research. The modern holistic view offers a stable platform for further scientific progress, enabling us to fall into step with what happens in other scientific disciplines in the life sciences.

∞ INDIVIDUAL FUNCTIONING AND DEVELOPMENT: LAWFUL, ORGANIZED PROCESSES

A fundamental basis for the scientific analysis of individual functioning and development is the proposition that processes go on in a lawful way within structures that are organized and function as *patterns* of operating factors. *Lawful organization* is a characteristic of individual structures and processes at all levels; it is a characteristic of mental structures and processes, of behavior, and of biological structures and processes. The lawfulness of the processes within functionally organized structures is reflected in the development and functioning of all subsystems, as well as in the functioning of the organized totality. Organs and systems of organs constitute functional units of the total organism. The building stones of all biological organs are the cells. Behind the fact that the individual develops as a functional totality from a single cell is the process of interaction among cells. Each cell develops, functions, and dies as a result of cell-cell interaction, in which information is received from and sent to neighboring cells. By the application of techniques from molecular biology and biophysics on unicellular model systems and nowadays even on transgene organisms, new ways have been opened for understanding the mechanisms that regulate the growth, division, and development of new forms of cells.

In the development of biological systems, a basic, well-documented principle is their ability for self-organization. *Self-organization* is a characteristic of open systems and refers to a process by which new structures and patterns emerge (Barton, 1994; Eigen, 1971; Hess & Mikhailov, 1994; Kaplan & Kaplan, 1991; Kauffmann, 1993; Nicolis & Prigogine, 1977; see also Thelen, 1989, for a discussion of self-organization in developmental processes). From the beginning of the development of the fetus, self-organization is a guiding principle. "Finality in the living world thus originates from the idea of organism, because the parts have to produce each other, because they have to associate to form the whole, because, as Kant said, living beings must be 'self-organized' " (Jacob, 1989). Within subsystems, the operating components organize themselves to maximize the functioning of each subsystem with respect to its purpose in the total system. At a higher level, subsystems organize themselves to fulfill their role in the functioning of the totality. We find this principle in the development and functioning of the brain, the coronary system, and the immune system. The principle can also be applied to the development and functioning of the sensory and cognitive systems and to manifest behavior (see Carlson, Earls, & Todd, 1988).

To conclude, the developmental processes of an individual cannot be understood by studying single variables in isolation from other, simultaneously operating variables. A fundamental principle is that subsystems as integrated totalities, and the individual as an integrated totality, function and develop.

INDIVIDUAL DIFFERENCES

The above analysis leads to the conclusion that the important information about an individual is in the special organization of operating mental, biological, and behavioral factors at all levels of individual functioning in terms of patterns reflected in configurations of data. As an illustration of this principle as a background to some comments, an empirical study on a biological subsystem is presented here. Individual patterns of behavior are presented later.

Studying cardiovascular responses in a stressful situation, Gramer and Huber (1994) found that the subjects could be classified into three groups on the basis of their distinct pattern of values for systolic blood pressure, diastolic blood pressure, and heart rate (see Figure 3.1). A similar study on cardiovascular responses was reported by Mills et al. (1994).

The data presented by Gramer and Huber (1994) demonstrate how individuals differ in terms of patterning of basic factors operating in the cardiovascular system and how they can be grouped into homogeneous clusters on the basis of pattern similarity. The data present a momentary picture of individual functioning in terms of patterns.

How individuals differ with respect to their distinctly different biological processes has been demonstrated by Packer, Medina, Yushak, and Meller (1983), among others. To study the hemodynamic effects of captopril in patients with severe heart problems, serial right heart catheterizations were performed in 51 patients who were treated over a period of 2 to 8 weeks. (Captopril has the effect of lowering blood pressure, among other things.) Results are summarized in Figure 3.2.

As Figure 3.2 shows, the patients differed but not in a linear way with respect to how they reacted to the drug across time. For 28 patients, the drug had effects that were sustained after 48 hours and after 2 to 8 weeks. Nine patients had minimal responses initially; 6 of them failed to improve during long-term treatment, and 3 showed delayed hemodynamic benefits. In 14 patients, first doses of captopril produced marked beneficial responses. For 7 of them, the responses became rapidly attenuated after 48 hours, but continued therapy for 2 to 8 weeks led to spontaneous restoration of the hemodynamic effect of first doses of the drug (three phasic response type). For the remaining 7 patients, attenuation of the initial response was not reversed by prolonged captopril therapy. The authors drew the following conclusion: "Although first dose effects of captopril are frequently sustained, the occurrence of delayed, attenuated, and triphasic responses indicates that a complex and variable relationship may exist between the early and late hemodynamic effects of vasodilator drugs in patients with severe heart problems" (Packer et al., 1983, p. 103).

The empirical examples presented in Figures 3.1 and 3.2 illustrate two aspects of the organization of biological, mental, and behavioral structures in individual functioning and development that are fundamental for the discussion in this chapter.

First, *within subsystems individuals differ to some extent in the way operational factors are organized and function. Individuals also differ in subsystem organization and function.* These organiza-

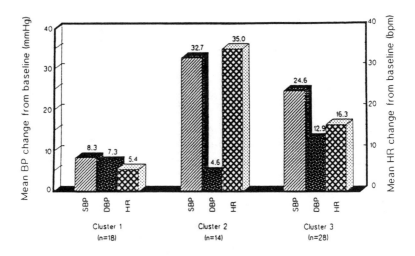

Figure 3.1. Magnitude of SBP, DBP, and HR Reactivity in Cardiovascular Response Clusters During Preparing a Speech

SOURCE: From "Individual Variability in Task-Specific Cardiovascular Response Patterns During Psychological Challenge," by M. Gramer and H. P. Huber, 1994, *German Journal of Psychology, 18*(1), pp. 1-17. Copyright 1994 by Hogrefe & Huber Publishers. Reprinted with permission.

NOTE: SBP = systolic blood pressure; DBP = diastolic blood pressure; HR = heart rate.

tions can be described in terms of patterns of operating factors within subsystems and in terms of patterns of functioning subsystems. Weiner (1989) suggested that even the oscillations produced by the natural pacemakers of the heart, the stomach, and the brain are patterned. *Thus, at all levels of organization, individual development is manifested in patterns of operating factors.* This view leads to the conclusion that individual differences are to be found in the patterning of operating factors within subsystems and in the patterning of subsystems in the totality—for example, in the way the perceptual-cognitive system, the behavioral system, and the physiological system work together in the total functioning of the individual.

Second, *the following are restricted: (a) the number of ways in which operating factors in a certain subsystem can be organized in patterns to allow the subsystem to play its functional role in the totality and (b) the number of ways in which subsystems can be organized to form the total pattern for the total organism* (cf. Gangestad & Snyder, 1985, who argued for the existence of distinct personality types, with reference to shared sources of influence). Only a limited number of states are functional for each subsystem

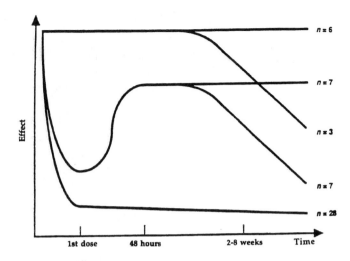

Figure 3.2. Hemodynamic Patterns of Response for Five Different Groups of Individuals During Long-Term Captopril Therapy for Severe Chronic Heart Failure ($N = 51$)
SOURCE: Based on data from Packer, Medina, Yushak, & Meller (1983).

and for the totality (cf. Sapolsky, 1994). This view suggests that each individual can be referred to one of a limited number of pattern-homogeneous categories of individuals.

Theoretically, the developmental background to these statements is the following proposition: As emphasized above, an individual develops in terms of systems of operating factors at different levels. Over time, this means a process of *personality crystallization;* that is, the developmental process of individuals whose systems organizations differ at a certain point in time as a result of different constitutional factors, maturation, and experiences will take partly different directions in the next step. Each step confirms future developmental alternatives, and eventually more stable "types" than at the beginning will emerge. If this view is correct, it should show up in clearer homogenization within categories of individuals and clearer differentiation among categories of individuals across time.

Comments. To summarize the conclusion of the above analysis: Individuals can be conceptualized, for each studied system, as belonging to different categories, each with its characteristic properties. In terms of data, each category can be described by a characteristic pattern of values for factors for the variables relevant for the study of the problem under consideration. Individuals can readily be categorized into subgroups or sub-subgroups on the basis of pattern similarity. This conclusion forms the basis for the application of pattern analysis within the theoretical framework of a person approach.

With reference to the above analysis, the task for empirical research on individual functioning and development in terms of patterns is, in each specific case, twofold: (a) to identify the possible operating factors in the system under consideration (factors that have to be considered in the particular pattern) and (b) to identify the ways these factors are organized (the actual working patterns). So far, most empirical research has been devoted to the first task.

∞ THE MATCH BETWEEN PSYCHOLOGICAL AND STATISTICAL MODELS

The basic goal of empirical research on biological organisms is to explain and understand the principles and mechanisms guiding the processes underlying current functioning and development of individuals (cf. Crick, 1988). A necessary condition for empirical research to reach that goal and to contribute not only figures and theories but also real knowledge is a strong link between the methodology applied for elucidation of the problem, on the one hand, and the character of the structures and processes involved, on the other (cf. Magnusson, Bergman, Rudinger, & Törestad, 1991). This implies that the statistical model must match the psychological model for the phenomena under consideration. The appropriateness and effectiveness of the statistical model, applied for the study of a specific problem, depends on how well the properties of the psychological model are reflected in the statistical model.

The empirical study of the relation between individuals' latent aggressive dispositions (aggressiveness) and actual aggressive behavior may serve to illustrate the issue (cf. Magnusson, 1976). The assumption of a statistical linear regression model for the relation is presented in Figure 3.3A. The statistical model matches and is appropriate for the study of the problem with reference to a linear psychological model that assumes that the stronger the latent disposition, the stronger the manifestation in actual aggressive behavior along the whole range of the latent disposition. However, the statistical model does not match and is not appropriate for the study of the problem in the framework of a possible psychodynamic psychological model that makes the following assumption: For low to medium aggressiveness, a monotonic positive relation says that the stronger the individual's latent disposition, the stronger his or her aggressive behavior will be. When latent aggressiveness becomes very strong, the aggressive impulses are repressed and aggressive behavior inhibited. The stronger the aggressive impulses, the stronger the defense mechanisms, and the psychological model for the relation will take the form shown in Figure 3.3B. Thus, the statistical linear model is appropriate for the study of the psychological model shown in Figure 3.3A but not for the empirical analysis of data for the psychological model shown in Figure 3.3B.

During the last decades, a distinction has been made between two approaches in empirical research on individual functioning, and they are discussed with particular emphasis on the match between psychological models, on the one hand, and the statistical models, on the other, in each of the two approaches.

THE VARIABLE APPROACH

Much psychological research, including research in the field of developmental psychology, is concerned with the relation among variables studied across individuals by the application of statistical methods (Wohlwill, 1973). The focus of interest is on a single variable or combination of variables, their interrelations (R-R- and S-R-relations), and their relations to a specific criterion. The problems are formulated in terms of variables, and the results are interpreted and generalizations made in such terms. The approach can be seen in many contexts—for example, in studies of the relations among variables, in studies of the stability of single variables across time, in studies of the links between environmental factors and various aspects of individual functioning, and in studies on the developmental background of adult functioning. Commonly used statistical models include comparisons between means, correlation and regression analysis, factor analysis, and structural equation modeling. For instance, most traditional re-

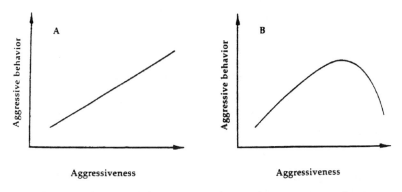

Figure 3.3. The Assumed Function of Actual Aggressive Behavior on Latent Aggressiveness for (A) the Trait Measurement Model and (B) the Psychodynamic Measurement Model
SOURCE: From "The Person and the Situation in an Interactional Model of Behavior," by D. Magnusson, 1976, *Scandinavian Journal of Psychology, 17,* p. 256. Copyright 1976 by Blackwell Publishers. Reprinted with permission.

search on the relation between various aspects of individual functioning and environmental upbringing conditions, on the one hand, and the development of adult alcohol abuse and criminal behavior, on the other, has applied a variable approach. One manifestation of the dominance of a variable approach is the widespread application of structural equation modeling in the search for causal relations (e.g., Hoyle, 1995).

Because the aim of empirical research is to contribute to the understanding of individual functioning mentally, biologically, and behaviorally, a basic assumption for the relevance of studies in this approach is that the measures of the relations among variables studied *across* individuals are valid for the relations among the variables *within* the individual.

A fundamental theoretical assumption underlying the use of a variable approach was discussed by Coleman (1986). He argued that causal modeling applying statistical techniques using a variable orientation is built on the assumption that individual functioning can be explained by various individual and contextual "determinants." *Variables* are regarded as the actors in the processes being studied. In a sociological framework, Coleman reflects on the implication of the change from the traditional community studies: "One way of describing this change is to say that statistical association between variables has largely replaced meaningful connection between events as the basic tool of description and analysis" (pp. 1327-1328). This formulation has relevance also for research in psychology.

Treatment of Data-Statistics

In a variable approach, the lawfulness of structures and processes in individual functioning and development is studied in terms of statistical relations among variables. The basis for this treatment of empirical data is a statistical model with certain specifications. "At the most basic level, a model is a statistical statement about the relations among variables. Models take on different forms in the context of different analytical approaches" (Hoyle, 1995, p. 2). Statistical models have been developed for different cases. Here, the implications for psychological analysis of the application of the most frequently used statistical model, *the linear model*, is discussed. The linear model forms the basis for the application of several statistical methods, such as Pearson correlations, multiple correlations, ANOVA, and LISREL (see Bergman, 1988a; Nesselroade & Ford, 1987).

In two interrelated ways, the demand for a match between the statistical model applied in the study of a specific problem, on the one hand, and the characteristics of the phenomena under study, on the other, is often violated in research that uses a variable approach. First, psychological individual-related problems are being formulated and discussed in terms of statistical relations among variables—that is, with reference to a statistical model, with little or no reference to an explicitly formulated view regarding the nature of the phenomena to which the data refer (Cairns, 1986; Magnusson, 1992). Such is often the case, for example, in discussions and applications of causal models and causal relations (e.g., see Hellvik, 1988; von Eye & Clogg, 1994). Second, the statistical models are tested with reference to data sets, the relevance of which is taken for granted without reference to the character of the real phenomena. An example can be found in the literature on structural equation modeling (e.g., Hoyle, 1995).

Basic Assumptions in Statistical
Linear Regression Models

The proper application of linear statistical models in the search for lawfulness of individual functioning presupposes that the following interrelated assumptions are valid.

1. Individuals can be compared on a nomothetic, continuous dimension in a meaningful way.
2. Individuals differ only quantitatively, not qualitatively, along the dimension for a certain variable.
3. Relationships among variables and their way of functioning in the totality of an individual is the same for all individuals. For example, in a multiple regression equation, each variable has the same weight for all individuals and reflects what is characteristic of the average person.
4. The interrelations among variables studied in nomothetic analyses can be used to make inferences about how the variables function within individuals.

In analyses of developmental issues, for example, in analyses of the problem of stability and change in a developmental perspective, a fifth assumption should be valid.

5. The psychological significance and meaning of positions on the nomothetic scale should be the same quantitatively and qualitatively across ages.

How compatible are these assumptions of the statistical model with the psychological model describing individual functioning and development in terms of dynamic, complex processes? A careful analysis of the characteristics of psychological processes with reference to a holistic, dynamic model demonstrates that assumptions of the statistical model are valid only under very specific conditions. The number and range of cases in which the linear statistical model is applicable in a relevant way are far more limited than their frequency in empirical psychological research would indicate.

Let me refer particularly to one basic characteristic of the psychological model that invalidates the application of a linear model in many cases in a decisive way: the assumption that the psychological significance of a single factor, in the individual or in the environment, is not to be found in each factor itself in isolation. A certain value on a quantitative dimension does not derive its meaning for the totality from its position on that dimension in relation to other individuals' positions on the same dimension. At all levels of a nomothetic dimension, each individual position gets its psychological significance by its role in the individually specific constellation of operating factors. That is, what distinguishes one individual from the other is his or her specific constellation of positions on several latent dimensions, not the relation to other positions on the same dimension.

An Empirical Example

A certain field in which the linear regression model is frequently applied is developmental psychology, in investigations of the role of early antisocial behaviors and of factors in the early environment for behavior at adult age. The aim is often formulated in terms of the predictive value of one or several early factors. An empirical example, in which the variable approach is used to elucidate the relation between early problematic behavior in boys and later problematic functioning in terms of alcohol problems, forms the background to some comments on the application of the linear regression model in that kind of research. A comprehensive presentation of the study was given by Magnusson, Andersson, and Törestad (1993).

Data

The data come from a longitudinal research program, Individual Development and Adjustment (IDA; Magnusson, 1988; Magnusson, Dunér, & Zetterblom, 1975). The group studied consists of all boys who attended Grade 6 in the school system at the end of the spring semester in one community in Sweden ($N = 540$). The average age of boys at that level of the school system in Sweden is about 12 years and 10 months.

As early antecedents of later alcohol problems, seven variables were chosen: (a) aggressiveness, (b) motor restlessness, (c) concentration difficulties, (d) lack of school motivation, (e) disharmony, (f) school achievement, and (g) peer rejections. The basis for the choice of these variables was that each has been reported in the literature to be an early indicator of later antisocial problems (see Andersson, Bergman, & Magnusson, 1989; Cloninger, Sigvardsson, & Bohman, 1988; Donovan, Jessor, & Jessor, 1983; Hesselbrook et al., 1984; Jones, 1968; McCord & McCord, 1960; Robins, Bates, & O'Neill, 1962). Data for the first five variables were obtained by teachers' ratings; data for peer rejection were obtained by sociometric ratings; and data for school achievement were obtained by summing the grades in literature/reading and mathematics.

Alcohol problems in adulthood were studied in terms of data from official records. Data were collected from the police, the social authorities, and open and closed psychiatric care (Andersson, 1988). The data are complete for all subjects and represent the age period of 18 through 24 years of age. The information refers to arrests for public drunkenness, conviction for drunken driving, measures taken in accordance with the temperance law, and the *DSM-III-R* diagnosis alcohol abuse and alcohol dependence (American Psychiatric Association [APA], 1987). In total, 80 subjects were registered for alcohol abuse during this period.

Statistics and Results

The statistical criterion of adult alcohol problems was dichotomized, yielding two groups of males: those with and those without alcohol records. The dichotomization was undertaken because the distribution of criterion values was skewed.

The first column of figures in Table 3.1 displays the coefficients of correlation for the relationship between each of the independent variables, on the one hand, and the dependent variable, on the other, obtained as point biserial coefficients. The semipartial correlations are presented in the second column of figures. Each semipartial coefficient reflects the linear relation between the variable under consideration and the criterion, when the "effect" of the other independent variables is partialled out from the independent variable.

Each independent variable has a significant, linear relationship with the dependent variable except one: peer rejections. So far, the significant coefficients for the correlation between single, early indicators of problem behaviors and adult alcohol problems are in line with results from many earlier studies using the same methodology.

No one of the semipartial correlations exceeds .10, however. This means that data for each of the independent variables explains less than 1% of the total variance for registered alcohol abuse at adult age, when the variance, common with all the other variables, has been controlled. Thus, the *specific* contribution of each single variable to prediction of alcohol problems at adulthood is very limited.

Comments. The empirical study briefly described is an example from a domain of developmental research in which a variable approach dominates—namely, studies on early antecedents of the later outcome(s). The results demonstrate some features of the ap-

TABLE 3.1 Point Biserial Correlations and Semipartial
Correlations Between the Independent Variables
and the Dependent Variables (Registered Alcohol
Abuse Ages 18-24)

	Correlation	
Independent Variables	Point Biserial	Semipartial
Aggressiveness	.221	.025
Motor Restlessness	.236	.036
Concentration Difficulties	.262	.048
Lack of School Motivation	.259	.030
Disharmony	.248	.079
School Achievement	−.180	.018
Peer Rejections	.055	−.049

SOURCE: From "Methodological Implications of a Peephole Perspective on Personality,"
by D. Magnusson, T. Andersson, and B. Törestad, 1993, in D. C. Funder, R. D. Parke,
C. Tomlinson-Keasey, and K. Widaman (Eds.), *Studying Lives Through Time: Personality and
Development* (p. 211). Copyright 1993 by American Psychological Association. Reprinted with
permission.

propriateness of the linear statistical model for empirical research
in this and similar domains.

1. Of particular interest are the low semipartial coefficients,
reflecting the "pure" role of each variable, applying a linear statistical model. *Statistically,* at the data level, the low semipartial
coefficients are only a necessary consequence of the colinearity,
reflected in sometimes high intercorrelations among the variables
involved in the process under investigation (e.g., Darlington,
1968). *Substantively,* the size of the semipartial coefficients are
understandable in light of a holistic view on individual functioning as a dynamic, multidetermined, and complex process. At the
individual level, the variables in the analyses only reflect different
aspects of the dynamic functioning of one and the same organism,
functioning as a totality. This implies that many particular elements are operating jointly and simultaneously in forming individuals' functioning and malfunctioning. Thus, it is not surprising
that data pertaining to one variable will also contain information
about other, simultaneously operating variables in the process that
is the object of interest. The high correlations often found at the
group level, for example, among various aspects of manifest behavior such as aggression and motor restlessness reflect the fact that

they largely overlap with respect to content at the individual level. As a consequence, measures of single variables will, sometimes greatly, overestimate the unique contribution of single factors to the total current functioning of the individual and in the process of developmental change, as well as the unique role of specific aspects of the environment in these processes. In empirical research, the risk for overestimation is common, as a consequence of the fact that rarely more than one or a few variables that together form the operating constellation of factors are studied simultaneously.

2. The example also illustrates the fact that many, if not most, variables studied in empirical analyses of developmental phenomena are just labels. This implies that each label represents a fuzzy concept without clear boundaries and reflects a limited aspect of what is a total, multidetermined, complex, and dynamic process. Hypothetical constructs of this kind, in which developmental psychology abounds, run the risk of reification—that is, of being regarded as tangible, concrete entities. This risk is augmented by using sophisticated statistical models containing latent variables such as structural equation modeling.

3. A limiting factor in the application of linear regression models and in interpretation of results from such studies, such as the coefficients in Table 3.1, is the fact that the models do not consider the existence of interactions, which is a consequence of the dynamic interaction among mental, behavioral, and biological factors within individuals and between individuals and their environments (cf. Hinde & Dennis, 1986). To a certain extent, interactions can be handled within structural modeling, for example, but these possibilities are limited (see Bergman, 1993).

Conclusion

Everything is exactly what it is—no more, no less. There is nothing wrong with any statistical model. The specific properties and assumptions of a statistical model are clear and cannot be disputed. The problem arises when it is applied for the study of phenomena that do not meet the assumptions. The above analysis leads to the conclusion that the match between the linear statistical model and the psychological model is weak, not to say very weak, in most cases where the statistical linear model is usually applied.

∞ THE PERSON APPROACH

The term *person approach* was coined by Block (1971) as the theoretical framework for his application of Q-sort technique for studying individual differences in terms of ipsative data. The approach as a framework for empirical research in personality and development was discussed by Magnusson and Allen (1983) and Magnusson (1985, 1988). Relevant for the following discussion are the discussions by Filsinger and Karoly (1985) about a typological approach in health psychology and Meehl's (1992) analysis of the notion of "types" and a taxonomic approach in personality assessment. Among others, Cairns and Cairns (1994) in their research on adolescence, Kagan (1994) in his studies of temperament, and Pulkkinen (Chapter 8, this volume) have emphasized and illustrated the importance of a person approach to developmental problems.

The theoretical basis for person-oriented research, which statistical models have to match, is the holistic, integrated view briefly summarized in the introduction; the person is conceptualized as an integrated, hierarchically organized totality, rather than as a summation of variables. The goal is to discover the distinctive configurations of operating factors, which characterize each individual's functioning and development, at different levels of the total hierarchical system. The characteristic feature of a person approach is that the specific problem under consideration is formulated in person terms and is operationalized and studied empirically in terms of patterns of values for variables that are relevant to the problem under consideration.

With reference to the goal for psychological research—namely, to understand and explain how and why individuals think, feel, act, and react as they do in real life—a great advantage of the person approach is that generalizations of empirical results refer to persons, not to variables.

The holistic, integrated model, which forms the theoretical framework for the person approach, does not imply that the entire system of an individual must or could be meaningfully studied in every research endeavor. The essential function of the model is to enable us to formulate specific problems at different levels of the total functioning organism, to implement empirical studies, and to interpret the results within a common theoretical framework. Thus, the theoretical framework and its application serve the important function of enabling researchers interested in different aspects of individual functioning and development to communicate with each other.

Treatment of Data: Pattern Analysis

The basic difference in terms of data between a person approach and a variable approach is in the view on the interpretation of the number indicating an individual's position on a latent trait. As discussed earlier, in a *variable* approach, each single datum derives its psychological meaning from its position relative to positions for other individuals on the same dimension. In a *person* approach, each single datum derives its psychological meaning from its place in a pattern of data for the same individual representing her or his positions on the latent dimensions under study. This difference in the view on a single datum follows from the different theoretical models underlying the two approaches.

The conclusion of the above discussion is that, in a person approach, individual differences are empirically investigated in terms of patterns of data for relevant operating factors. Several methods can more or less naturally be used for this purpose: cluster analytical techniques (Bergman, 1993; Bock, 1987; Manly, 1994); Q-sort technique (Block, 1971; Ozer, 1993); latent profile analysis (LPA; Gibson, 1959); configural frequency analysis (CFA; Krauth & Lienert, 1982; von Eye, 1990a, 1990b); latent transition analysis (Collins & Wugalter, 1992); log-linear modeling (Bishop, Feinberg, & Holland, 1975); and multivariate *p*-technique factor analysis (Cattell, Cattell, & Rhymer, 1947; Nesselroade & Ford, 1987). The characteristic features of these and other methods are discussed by Bergman (this volume, Chap. 5).

These methods for pattern analysis have been applied in many studies (see, among others, af Klinteberg, Andersson, Magnusson, & Stattin, 1993; Andersson et al., 1989; Asendorpf & van Aken, 1991; Bergman & Magnusson, 1983, 1984a, 1984b, 1987, 1991; Bergman & Wångby, 1995; Block, 1971; Gustafson & Magnusson, 1991; Lienert & zur Oeveste, 1985; Magnusson, 1996b; Magnusson & Bergman, 1988, 1990; Mills et al., 1994; Mumford & Owen, 1984; Pulkkinen & Tremblay, 1992; Stattin & Magnusson, 1990; van Aken & Asendorpf, 1994).

A common characteristic of the methods mentioned above is that they are applicable for statistical analyses of individual functioning in terms of patterns (Magnusson & Törestad, 1993). For the study of developmental issues, the approach has primarily been applied in studies linking patterns observed at one age to patterns observed at another. Relatively few attempts have been made to develop and apply methods for the empirical analyses of dynamic, developmental processes in terms of patterns. For further progress in research on human ontogeny, an important challenge is to develop and apply process-oriented methodological tools.

An Empirical Example

An empirical pattern analysis contains the following steps:

1. *Identification of the system to which a pattern analysis is to be applied.* This implies specification of the level of analysis—that is, if the interest is in the patterning of variables in a subsystem at a microlevel, such as a subsystem of the brain, in the patterning of variables at a more general level, such as in the system of manifest behavior, or in the patterning of subsystems forming a system of higher order.
2. *Identification of possible operating factors at the specified level of analysis to constitute the pattern to be studied.*
3. *Application of a statistical method for pattern analysis*—for instance, grouping the individuals in categories that are homogeneous with respect to their patterns of values for the variables included in the analysis.

In Figure 3.1, an empirical illustration of a person approach was presented, concerned with the patterning of factors in a biological system—namely, the cardiovascular system. Another demonstration that can throw further light on the issue of this chapter can be fetched from Magnusson and Bergman (1988). They used a person approach to investigate early problem behaviors in boys as precursors of adult adjustment problems based on data from the same group as the one for which the results presented in Table 3.2 were obtained. Three empirical parts of this study are shortly presented to illustrate basic principles of the person approach.

Pattern Analysis of Early
Problem Behaviors

With reference to the above identification of the steps in a pattern analysis, the following information is of interest:

TABLE 3.2 Clusters of Boys at Age 13, Based on Data for Overt Adjustment Problems

Cluster Number	Size	Average Coefficient*	Aggressiveness	Motor Restlessness	Lack of Concentration	Low School Motivation	Underachievement	Poor Peer Relations
					*Cluster Means***			
1	296	.12	—	—	—	—	—	—
2	23	.30	—	—	—	—	—	2.4
3	40	.28	—	—	—	—	2.6	—
4	61	.39	1.3	1.4	—	—	—	—
5	41	.39	—	1.5	2.3	1.9	—	—
6	12	.56	1.7	1.8	2.3	1.9	2.6	—
7	37	.37	2.3	2.3	1.9	1.3	—	—
8	22	.48	2.2	2.7	2.6	2.4	—	1.9
Residue 8			1.5	1.4	1.3	1.3	1.3	2.3

NOTES: * Average coefficient means average error sum of squares within the cluster.
— indicates that the cluster mean of a variable is less than 1 in the 4-point scale coded 0, 1, 2, 3 (from Magnusson & Bergman, 1988).

1. The data that form the basis for the pattern analysis refer to the behavioral level of individual functioning at age 13.

2. The decision about variables that were identified as possible operating factors in the developmental process underlying adult maladjustment was made with reference to the scientific literature in the area.

3. For the grouping of individuals on the basis of pattern similarity, a cluster analytical technique was applied.

The patterns in Table 3.2 are based on data for six variables covering different aspects of problem behaviors: (a) aggressiveness, (b) motor restlessness, (c) lack of concentration, (d) low school motivation, (e) underachievement, and (f) poor peer relations. Data for each variable were transformed to a psychological scale with values 0 to 4, reflecting levels of seriousness of problem behaviors for boys at age 13. The methodology and results of the pattern analysis are discussed in detail in Magnusson and Bergman (1988). Here, only a few comments pertinent to the discussion in this chapter are made. (The procedure used for the cluster analysis allows for the existence of misfits, those boys who do not fit into any of the clusters. They are presented in Table 3.2 as "residues." They are removed from the data set before classification and are analyzed separately. For theoretical and methodological discussion of this aspect of the procedure, the reader is referred to Bergman [1988b].)

Table 3.2 demonstrates that the boys could be grouped into eight distinctly different groups with reference to their pattern of values for the variables under study. The results have some features that are interesting with reference to the holistic, psychological model. First, only underachievement and poor peer relations are sole characteristics of single groups of boys. Second, conduct problems in their strong manifestations appear to occur together in multiproblem syndromes with or without the simultaneous occurrence of underachievement and poor peer relations.

*Pattern Analysis of Adult
Problem Behaviors*

As the criterion on adult maladjustment, data for three aspects were used: (a) criminal offenses, (b) alcohol problems, and (c) psychiatric problems. Data for these aspects of maladjustment for the age period 18 to 24 were obtained from official records and were collected for all those for whom data were presented in Table 3.1.

A pattern analysis of criterion data was performed with *configural frequency analysis (CFA)*. CFA tests whether an observed pattern occurs significantly more often—a *type*—or significantly less often—an *antitype*—than expected by an independence model (Lienert & zur Oeveste, 1985). The result of the pattern analysis is presented in Table 3.3.

In terms of patterns of maladjustment indicators, Table 3.3 shows two significant types of individuals with adult problems: (a) those males who appear in both criminal and alcohol registers and (b) those males who appear in criminal, alcohol, and psychiatric registers. It is noteworthy and in line with the theoretical perspective of this chapter that occurring in only one of the three registers is a significant antitype; that is, it is significantly less frequent than could be expected that an individual appears in only one of the registers.

This observation is not only of theoretical interest; it demonstrates important research strategy implications of the person approach. Most single studies in research on the developmental background of adult criminal activity, adult alcohol problems, and adult psychiatric illnesses are performed by using a variable approach, concerned with one of these aspects with neglect of the others. Despite the fact that the individuals who are their subject of interest in many cases are the same individuals, criminologists study them as criminals, alcohol researchers study them as alcoholists, and psychiatrists study them as psychiatric cases. Effective research on criminality, alcohol problems, and psychiatric illnesses should be planned, implemented, and interpreted, taking into account that these problems most often appear together in a person who functions as a totality. An analysis of this kind was reported in Magnusson and Bergman (1990).

Longitudinal Analysis

For illustrative purpose, a study by Magnusson and Bergman (1988) is reported here, relating individual belongingness to one of the conduct problem clusters at age 13 to belongingness to each of the three registers at adult age. The result of the analysis is shown in Table 3.4. The statistical analysis showing the significance of each percentage has been performed by using configural

TABLE 3.3 Cross-Sectional Configurations of Data From
Records for Criminality, Psychiatric Care, and
Alcohol Abuse

Configuration				
Criminality	Psychiatric Care	Alcohol Abuse	Observed Frequency	Expected Frequency
No	No	No	504[t]	443.10
No	No	Yes	22[at]	66.50
No	Yes	No	25[at]	41.22
No	Yes	Yes	6	6.19
Yes	No	No	71[at]	117.73
Yes	No	Yes	48[t]	17.67
Yes	Yes	No	13	10.95
Yes	Yes	Yes	16[t]	1.64

SOURCE: From Magnusson & Bergman (1988).
NOTE: t = Type, significant at the 5% level after Bonferroni correction.
    at = Antitype, significant at the 5% level after Bonferroni correction.

frequency analysis (Lienert & zur Oeveste, 1985). This analysis
shows which percentages are lower than could be expected from
a random model (antitype) and which percentages are higher than
could be expected from a random model (type).

Some observations of special interest for the purpose of this
chapter can be made. First, a significant positive relationship exists
between belonging to a conduct problem cluster at age 13 and
appearing in one of the registers at age 18 to 24 only for the two
most severe clusters and only for appearing in records for criminality and alcohol abuse. Second, belonging to one of the two
clusters characterized by only one conduct problem at age 13—
underachievement or poor peer relations, respectively—does not
indicate a long-term problem as reflected in appearing in the
records at adult age.

In variable-oriented research, many studies have demonstrated empirically, mostly in studies applying linear regression
models, a statistically significant relation between each of several
conduct problems at an early age and adult maladjustment. The
results presented in Table 3.4, interpreted in the theoretical framework of a person approach, lead to the following question: Can the
frequently reported pairwise significant correlations between single aspects of individual functioning, on the one hand, and adult
functioning, on the other, be accounted for by a limited number of

TABLE 3.4 Relation Between Adjustment Clusters at Age 13 According to School Data, and Criminality, Psychiatric Care, and Alcohol Abuse at Age 18-24 (Males, $N = 538$)

	Cluster at Age 13	N	Criminality	Psychiatric Care	Alcohol Abuse
			Percentages That Appear in Records for		
1	No problems	295	13.6[at]	6.4	7.5[at]
2	Poor peer relations	23	13.0	13.0	4.3
3	Underachievement	40	10.0	5.0	12.5
4	Weak aggression, weak motor restlessness	61	18.0	0.0	13.1
5	Lack of concentration, low motivation	40	30.0	15.0	27.5
6	Multiproblems— severe under- achievement and lack of concentration	12	33.3	0.0	8.3
7	Hyperactivity with aggressiveness	37	48.6[t]	16.2	37.8[t]
8	Severe multiproblems	22	50.0[t]	13.6	36.4[t]

SOURCE: From Magnusson & Bergman (1988).
NOTES: t = Problem *type*, significant at the 5% level after Bonferroni correction.
at = Problem *antitype*, significant at the 5% level after Bonferroni correction.

boys who are characterized by several conduct problems (by syndromes)? To elucidate this issue further, additional calculations were performed, the results of which are presented in Table 3.5.

One of the most frequently studied variables at an early age as a precursor of adult maladjustment is aggressiveness. In Table 3.5, (a), the relation between ratings of high aggressiveness at age 13 and appearing in records for criminal offenses and in records for alcohol abuse, is presented. As can be seen from the table, this relation is rather strong; it is significant at the promille level. In Table 3.5, (b), the relation between being rated as highly aggressive and appearing in the records for criminal offenses and alcohol

TABLE 3.5 Longitudinal Relationship Between Aggression at
Age 13 and Criminality or Alcohol Abuse at Age 18
to 24

			Age 18 to 24			
			Criminality		Alcohol Abuse	
			No	Yes	No	Yes
Age 13 (all males)						
		No	383	69	405	47
(a)	Aggression		(84.7)	(15.3)	(89.6)	(10.4)
		Yes	50	36	62	24
			(58.1)	(41.9)	(72.1)	(27.9)
			$p < .001$		$p < .001$	
Age 13 (males minus multiproblem cluster)						
		No	373	67	395	45
(b)	Aggression		(84.8)	(15.2)	(89.8)	(10.2)
		Yes	22	5	24	23
			(81.5)	(18.5)	(88.9)	(11.1)
			ns		ns	

SOURCE: From Magnusson & Bergman (1988).
NOTE: The significance of a relationship was tested by using a chi-square with one *df*, corrected
for continuity.
a. For all males ($N = 538$).
b. For males after removal of those belonging to severe multiproblem clusters at age 13 ($N = 467$).
Frequencies (row-wise percentages within parenthesis)

abuse, is presented for those boys who do not belong to one of the
three most severe clusters as they are presented in Table 3.2. As
can be seen, when those boys characterized by the syndromes of
conduct problems in which aggressive behavior forms a strong
element are removed from the analysis, no relationship remains
between being rated early as aggressive and appearing in one of
these two records at adulthood.

Thus, the answer to the question is yes: The results of the
calculation point to the possibility that the correlation coefficients
frequently presented for the relation between single early problem
behaviors and adult maladjustment can be explained by the existence of a limited number of boys whose behavior has a broad
register of problems.

∞ CONCLUSIONS AND COMMENTS

1. The empirical studies presented above illustrate the first basic proposition of the theoretical basis for a person approach to the study of individual functioning and individual development: The complex, dynamic process of individual functioning and development cannot be understood by summing results from studies of single variables taken out and investigated in isolation from the context of other, simultaneously operating variables. A certain factor, say aggressiveness, does not have a significance of its own independent of the context of other factors simultaneously working in the individual. It obtains its significance from its context.

2. With reference to the guiding principle of self-organization in the development of biological systems and of organisms and illustrated by examples from the biological domain of individual functioning (Figures 3.2 and 3.3), two fundamental propositions were put forward: The first proposition says that individual differences are mainly to be found in the patterning of operating factors within subsystems and in the patterning of subsystems at the level of the total organism. The second proposition says that in only a limited number of ways can operating factors within subsystems and subsystems in the total organism be functionally organized. An illustration from the behavioral domain (Tables 3.2 and 3.3) supported the propositions.

The two propositions lead to the conclusion that subsystems and individuals can be understood as a complex set of categories, or what Meehl (1992) discusses as "natural classes"—that is, really existing classes or categories as distinct from "arbitrary classes." This conclusion has specific consequences for measurement, for the choice of statistics, and for research strategy.

3. In different ways, the theoretical analysis and the empirical studies demonstrate that the linear statistical model does not usually fit the psychological model of individual functioning and development as a dynamic, complex process (cf. Nesselroade & Ford, 1987). Of course, the consequence of this conclusion is not that the linear regression model should or could be abandoned in psychological research. So, what are the merits of a variable approach applying linear regression models? It depends on the nature of the problem; in some areas of psychological research it is highly appropriate. As discussed earlier, an analysis of the task for empirical psychological research as a study of dynamic complex processes has led to the identification of a 2-stage process.

The first stage is the identification of possible operating factors that should be considered in the theoretical framework for the study of a specific problem. The second stage is the identification of the principles and mechanisms guiding the process(es). The first stage lays the foundation for the second. In the 2-stage process, linear regression models can be useful tools in the first stage, the identification of possible operating factors. Such information is a necessary basis for analyses of individual current functioning and development in terms of characteristic patterns of operating factors using a person approach.

4. The measurement task becomes distinctly different in a variable approach and in a person approach. In the variable approach, measurement is basically based on the assumption that individuals take on positions on latent dimensions for the relevant factors. Thus, the task is to locate individuals on the dimension(s), and the appropriate measurement technique is the one that discriminates along the whole range of possible individual positions. In the person approach, the task is to assign individuals to categories at the appropriate level of the total system, and the measurement problem is to maximize cutting scores on the borders of each category or class.

5. The distinction between a variable approach and a person approach concerns the theoretical framework, the application of statistical models, and the research strategy. Thus, outcomes of empirical research using different approaches will have different qualities (cf. Meehl's [1992] discussion of types and prototypes). The appropriateness of each of them cannot be evaluated with reference to how well one or the other of the two approaches predicts a certain outcome: The only criterion is how well each of them contributes to the understanding of the processes of individual functioning and development, which are our main concern. An example can be fetched from research on the developmental background of adult antisocial behavior. In an often-cited article, Robins (1966) demonstrated empirically the old observation that the broader the register of antisocial behavior that characterized a boy, the greater the likelihood for adult antisocial behavior as demonstrated in multiple correlations. The empirical studies referred to in this chapter clearly demonstrate that the results of the pattern analyses yield important information beyond what the Robins study did, information that not only is statistical but also contributes to understanding the psychological problems that are focused.

6. A general assumption underlying much psychometric work in psychological research is that data for a normal sample of individuals form a normal distribution on a continuous dimension. This assumption is often well founded in theory and empirical work for the univariate case. That the assumption is valid for the univariate case, however, does not imply that it is valid in the multivariate case and that the variables jointly follow the multivariate normal distribution, an assumption often made when applying linear models. Rather, the empirical studies presented above support the assumption that individuals form clusters in the multivariate space (cf. the general assumption of latent profile analysis about "local independence" without any assumption of normality or homoscedasticity).

7. Proponents of a nomothetic, variable approach often motivate its use by the proposition that it permits generalization of results, which is a fundamental goal for empirical research. In principle and in practice, generalizations can be made with the same degree of effectiveness when using a person approach as when using a variable approach. By studying homogeneous subgroups of persons, references can be made to the appropriate population. The great advantage of the person approach is that the generalizations refer to persons rather than to variables.

8. For classifying individuals in terms of patterns, we have access to different methods and models. As emphasized earlier, however, relatively few attempts have been' made to develop and apply methods for the empirical analyses of dynamic, developmental processes in terms of patterns across time, a task that is important for further progress in research on individual functioning and development.

In the natural sciences, the formulation of theoretical models for complex, dynamic processes has led to strong activities to develop adequate methodologies for the study of such processes. One line is the revival of nonlinear mathematics and methods for the study of patterns. For further scientific progress, it is important for researchers in our field to take advantage of this development. If adequately applied, the methodologies for dynamic, complex processes have important implications for theory building and empirical research on the dynamic, complex process of individual development (see Wallacher & Nowak, 1994). There is also a growing interest in, and application of, models and methods in this direction in developmental research. An interesting example is van Geert's (1994) application of a nonlinear dynamic model for the redefinition of Vygotsky's "zone of proximal development" (1978; see also Valsiner, 1994).

Although it is important to follow what happens methodologically in neighboring sciences, it is also essential to be careful when applying methods originally developed for the study of phenomena in the natural sciences, in research on individual functioning. Certain similarities exist between the structures and processes studied in the natural sciences and the structures and processes investigated in psychological research. Essential differences also exist, however, particularly when our focus is on the functioning of the total organism. At that level, a fundamental characteristic and guiding element in the dynamic, complex process of individual functioning is *intentionality*, which is linked to *emotions* and *values*, and the fact that the individual learns from experience. These characteristic features of individual functioning and development must be taken into consideration when methods derived from the study of dynamic, complex processes, which do not have these elements, are applied in the planning and implementation of empirical research in psychology. We have to develop our own tools in a way that matches the characteristic properties of the phenomena that are the object of our concerns.

∞৻৽∞

COMMENTS ON CHAPTER 3

There is no question—David Magnusson has had a compelling influence on the holistic approach to individual functioning. In this chapter, he states the case strongly: A holistic view should provide the framework for formulating the research problem, choosing the research strategy and method, and interpreting the results.

David Magnusson gives us a systematic elaboration of this approach. He contrasts variable and person approaches in their assumptions and proceedings. With illustrative empirical data, he provides object lessons: Findings can, and do, differ from variable-oriented and person-oriented models. Distortions are inherent in the use of some analytic procedures for some research problems.

It is apparent that a person approach, by viewing individuals in terms of organized configurations of interactive factors, is both complicating and simplifying. As David Magnusson stresses, a primary goal in this approach is to respect and preserve the nature of the phenomenon being studied. A necessary first step, therefore, involves identifying similarities and differences among individuals in distinct, meaningful patterns of factors. This step may not be an easy one: How are relevant factors for a pattern arrived at? How are homogeneous subgroups of individuals determined? This is a research land relying on contributions of theory, findings from variable-oriented studies, and individual case analyses. How one can proceed in arriving at clusters depends not only on existing knowledge but also on the source of individuals being studied (whether a community or an epidemiological sample or a small clinical group). This is a critical phase of person-oriented research, both theoretically and methodologically.

A further research challenge comes in determining how factors within a pattern operate together. How do they interact to influence each other, to be more than the sum of the parts? This aspect of study has yet to receive due attention.

As David Magnusson has pointed out, a holistic approach is especially critical for problems in developmental psychology, for questions of behavioral links from childhood to adulthood. The nature of the phenomenon must, in these instances, be ready to include in "individual" configurations those factors that are larger than the individual—the dyad, the relationship, the network of relationships.

It is clear that a holistic approach to individual development has many implications. It raises questions concerning existing research information, it stirs up many old and new issues, and most important, it charts a challenging course for research.

Marian Radke-Yarrow

∞ Note

1. The work presented here was supported by grants from the Swedish Council for Social Research and the Swedish Council for Planning and Coordination of Research. I thank Lars R. Bergman, Robert B. Cairns, and John R. Nesselroade for valuable comments on the manuscript.

~ 4 ~

The Value of
Extreme Groups

Jerome Kagan
Nancy Snidman
Doreen Arcus
∞

Harvard University

*A*lthough most scientific ideas that have the privilege of a brief period of popularity vanish permanently, a small, select group enjoys one or more cycles of revival because it possesses a feature that has heuristic value. The case history, as well as small-group analyses, belong to this category. The case history was an important and frequent source of evidence in professional journals from about the second to the sixth decade of this century, when psychoanalytic theory held a dominant, ideological position in the United States and England. Freud's imaginative use of the cases of Dora, little Hans, and Schreber persuaded many of the validity of psychoanalytic hypotheses in the same way that Machiavelli's concrete examples in *The Prince* persuaded political leaders of his era of the wisdom of his insights into the management of state affairs.

The human mind finds it easy to leap from a single instance to a universal generalization and to ignore the unique features of a specific case. The student of evolution might argue that the habit of abstracting a general principle from a single event is adaptive. It would be useful for an animal that has experienced a single traumatic event in a particular place to behave as if the place were causal and to avoid it.

Single events, however, as well as rare profiles, can mislead scientists searching for generality. That is why the case history became a target of harsh criticism after World War II: in part, because graduate training in statistics became more prevalent and the unquestioning faith in psychoanalytic theory was replaced with a more critical attitude. One important exception to this secular trend are the papers on H. M., appearing in neuroscience journals, that describe the psychological consequences of bilateral removal of the temporal pole and the hippocampus in a male adult. This single case has generated important clues to the role of the brain in varied cognitive competences (Milner, Corkin, & Teuber, 1968).

The case of H. M. provides another reason why case descriptions are currently unpopular. These reports assume that the individual described represents a distinct category of person who is not on a continuum with others; an adult, like H. M., who is missing both temporal poles represents a discrete, rare category. The training of students in social science during the past 40 years, however, has maintained that all, or at least most, human qualities are continua, not categories. It was assumed that a person with a very bad memory simply had "less" of what everyone else possessed in more generous amounts.

The assumption of continuous processes permits psychologists to use covariance techniques to control for features of a particular group. For example, investigators interested in the relation between two variables that happened to be correlated with social class—for example, the relation of family size to children's academic achievement—typically used covariance techniques to control for the family's social class. The covariance strategy assumes linear relations among social class, size of family, and academic achievement, however, and is insensitive to the possibility that large, illiterate, immigrant families from the Caribbean living in New York might represent a group that is qualitatively, not just quantitatively, different from professional, Caucasian families with two children living in a small town in Wisconsin on variables that affect academic achievement.

The domination of research in both personality and development by statistical treatments that rely on analysis of covariance and regression has frustrated a small group of investigators who have had the intuition that some subjects were qualitatively different from the majority of their sample. Because the group was small in number, however, the usual inferential statistics did not reach the popular .05 level required for referee approval. Consider, as an example, an investigator, unfamiliar with Down syndrome, who was studying the relation of maternal age to children's intelligence in a sample of 600 families. The correlation between the two variables would most likely not reveal a statistically significant relation. Examination of a scatter plot, however, might indicate that two children with very low IQ scores had the two oldest mothers in the sample. Reflection on that fact would tempt the investigator to speculate that these two children were qualitatively different from the other 598 and, perhaps, that these two families provided a clue to a relation between age of mother and child's intelligence for a very small proportion of the population. Research in our laboratory provides a real illustration.

One child from a cohort of 100 infants followed longitudinally in our laboratory showed a unique developmental profile (Kagan & Snidman, 1991). While being administered a standard battery of visual, auditory, and olfactory events at 8 weeks of age, this boy frowned spontaneously six times, either during or between the stimulus presentations. Spontaneous frowns are rare among all infants and especially during the quiet interval between stimulus presentations when nothing is in the infant's perceptual field. This boy continued to frown frequently to a similar laboratory battery when he was 4 months old, retaining a sad facial expression for periods as long as 30 seconds—a rare response. He emitted a sharp scream to the presentation of a moving mobile; no other 4-month-old in the sample behaved that way. When this boy was seen at 9 months, he fretted at every stimulus presentation and remained wary throughout the 60-minute battery.

This child's profile continued to be idiosyncratic at 14 months. He maintained a sad facial expression throughout the 90-minute battery, had several uncontrolled tantrums, refused the administration of most episodes by screaming, vocalized in short explosive bursts, and often showed a pained facial expression without an accompanying cry or fret—a silent expression of angst. His mother acknowledged to the examiner that he had become more aggressive lately, noting, "He walks up and bites you."

At 3½ years of age, however, he was calmer and displayed no unusual behavior during a 90-minute session. But several weeks later, when he was observed in a play situation with one other unfamiliar boy of the same age, he showed a single act of impulsive aggression that is statistically rare: As the session started, he remained close to his mother while staring at the other boy. After 5 minutes, he left his mother, went to the center of the playroom, and began to punch a large inflated toy. Two minutes later, he seized the toy that the other boy was holding and retreated with it to his mother. About 5 minutes later—that is, 15 minutes into the session—when the other boy was inside a plastic tunnel, he picked up a wooden pole and began to strike the tunnel with force in the place where the boy was sitting. The force of the blow made the other boy cry. This unprovoked act of aggression to an unfamiliar child is a very rare event in this laboratory context, especially with both mothers present in the room.

This boy showed unique reactions on every assessment: frequent frowning at 2 months, a scream to a mobile at 4 months, extreme fearfulness at 9 months, silent expressions of distress at 14 months, unusual resistance at 21 months, and a single act of unprovoked aggression at 3½ years. Although the aggressive act is rare in this context, it was the only deviant act in that session. Most psychologists observing this child for the first time at 3½ years of age would probably dismiss the aggression as reflecting greater than normal frustration on that particular day. The mother was not concerned with her son's development and did not request any additional information. In light of the history described, however, we suspect that the impulsive act of aggression reflects a deep psychological quality that makes this boy a member of a rare temperamental category. The remainder of this chapter presents empirical data from a second, larger cohort that point to the theoretical utility of examining small groups within large samples.

∞ THE EXUBERANT CHILD

We are studying longitudinally a large group of healthy, Caucasian children from a cohort of 462 individuals as part of a general inquiry into the origins and development of inhibited and uninhibited children (Kagan, 1994). The children were observed originally at 4 months of age and were classified into one of four reactive groups on the basis of their behavior to a standardized battery that consisted of visual, auditory, and olfactory stimuli. About 40% of the 4-month-old infants demonstrated a profile characterized by low levels of motor activity and minimal crying or fretting to the stimuli. About 20% of the infants displayed a combination of very high motor activity and frequent fretting and crying. The former group is called "low reactive"; the latter group is called "high reactive." The low and high reactive infants consist of equal proportions of boys and girls.

These children were observed again in the laboratory at 14 and 21 months, and about three fourths of the original group of high and low reactive children are currently being evaluated at 4½ years of age. When the children were 14 and 21 months old, they were exposed to a variety of unfamiliar events—people, objects, and procedures—and their fear reactions were coded. *Fear* was defined as crying to an unfamiliar event or failing to approach a small number of events that had been classified a priori as discrepant (e.g., a stranger, a clown, a robot). The low reactive infants were the least fearful at 14 and 21 months. However, 20% of the low reactive girls but only 6% of the low reactive boys became temporarily timid and fearful at 21 months of age. Thus, more boys than girls remained minimally fearful in the 2nd year.

The frequency of spontaneous smiling toward the unfamiliar female examiner during the laboratory assessments at 14 and 21 months was rated reliably on a 3-point scale. Although the correlation between frequency of smiling and fearfulness in the 2nd year was negative, the magnitude of the relation was modest across all children ($r = -.29$ at 14 months; $r = -.31$ at 21 months). But the low reactive, minimally fearful boys smiled more often than any other group in the 2nd year.

Variation in initial baseline heart rate at 4 months while the infant was resting quietly in an infant seat was unrelated to reactivity, fear, or smiling across all children. The low reactive boys who both smiled frequently and had low fear scores in the 2nd year, however, had especially low baseline heart rates at 4 months (47% had a baseline heart rate > 440 msec, compared with 17% of all the other boys). (Boys generally had lower heart rates than girls at every age; Snidman, Kagan, Riordan, & Shannon, 1995.)

Finally, we noticed that the low reactive infants had broader faces than other children, and we measured both the width of the face at the bizygomatic and the length of the face and computed a ratio of width to length (Arcus & Kagan, 1995). Children with ratios less than .52 appear to observers to have narrow faces; children with ratios greater than .56 appear to have broad faces. Although a low but significant correlation was found between this ratio and the fear scores at 14 and 21 months across the 204 children with adequate data on all variables ($r = -.18, -.16, p < .05$), two thirds of the low reactive boys with low fear scores had broad faces (ratio equal to or greater than .56).

The original sample contained 99 low reactive boys—20% of the entire cohort. Of this group, 31 boys were minimally fearful (zero or one fear) at both 14 and 21 months. Of this group of low fear boys, 20 smiled frequently at both 14 and 21 months. Of these 20, 8 had a low initial baseline heart rate at 4 months (440 msec or < 136 beats per minute [bpm]). Of this group of 8, 4 had facial measures available at 14 months; 2 of these 4 children had broad faces (ratios > .56). Thus, 2 children—1 firstborn and 1 later born—met the criteria for all five of the above characteristics. This is less than 1% of the original sample of 462 children who had all of the relevant data at 4, 14, and 21 months. These low reactive, low fear, high smiling boys with low 4-month baseline heart rates and broad faces represent a rare group.

We now describe the behavior of one of these boys when he was 4 months, 14 months, and 21 months; it is atypical of most low reactive boys. At 4 months of age, this boy smiled and vocalized during the first episode of the battery when the mother looked down at him without vocalizing. These reactions are statistically unusual as the battery begins. He was unusually relaxed and showed a minimal level of arousal while listening to a recording of a woman speaking short sentences and while watching a series of colorful mobiles. Most children become motorically active to some degree to the mobiles; this boy was extremely still and relaxed to these dynamic visual events. Furthermore, he smiled during the interstimulus intervals of an episode that consisted of a recording of nonsense syllables read by a female voice. This reaction is also uncommon.

At 14 months, his atypical behaviors included no resistance and minimal arousal to the administration of drops of sweet and sour liquid; many children resist accepting the liquid on their tongues. Surprisingly, he smiled when the examiner frowned and issued a stern chastisement (using a nonsense phrase) as the boy reached for a novel toy. Most children stare at the examiner, withdraw in their chair, or cry to the unexpected chastisement. This boy's smile implies that he did not become uncertain when an adult issued signs of criticism or rejection. He approached an unfamiliar woman who had entered the playroom within 20 seconds of her entrance; most children wait at least 1 minute before approaching the stranger. When this woman later uncovered a large metal robot that was in a cabinet in the corner of the playroom, he approached this unfamiliar object before the woman invited him to do so. Most children wait until the woman invites them to approach the unfamiliar toy.

He continued to be spontaneous at 21 months. He laughed when the female examiner criticized him for failing to imitate successfully the building of a block construction—a reaction reminiscent of his behavior at 14 months when he smiled at the examiner's criticism. When a stranger entered the playroom, he approached her within 5 seconds and smiled several minutes later when an adult dressed in a clown costume entered the room. Most children freeze or retreat to their mothers when the clown enters the room. The extreme degree of spontaneity, laughter, and minimal fearfulness displayed by this boy are atypical of low reactive children, and we suspect that he is qualitatively different from the majority of low reactive infants.

∞ THE EXTREMELY FEARFUL CHILD

A comparable analysis was performed on the high reactive infant girls. Because a high baseline heart rate did not distinguish high from low reactive girls, the heart rate variable was not used in this analysis. There were 52 high reactive girls—11% of the original cohort. Of these 52, 18 (35%) were highly fearful (four or more fears) at both 14 and 21 months; 7 of these 18 girls (38%) smiled minimally at both 14 and 21 months (a rating of 1 at both ages). Only 3 of these 7 girls had facial measurements; the other 4 high reactive girls refused the procedure. All 3 had narrow faces (ratio equal to or less than .52), however. Hence, we estimate that about 1% of the original group of 462 children would have shown the combination of high reactivity, high fear, infrequent smiling, and a narrow face. These few girls were much more fearful than the remaining high reactive girls. Consider some evidence on one of these girls:

At 4 months of age, she frowned and arched her back at the presentation of the taped sentences, became highly aroused by the mobiles, fretted to the presentation of the nonsense syllables, and cried when her mother looked down at her at the end of the battery.

At 14 months, she refused to accept the sour liquid on her tongue and protested by crying. She cried in fear at the unexpected presentation of a pair of puppets and again when the examiner issued a stern chastisement in a nonsense phrase. Recall that the low reactive boy we just described had laughed to this event.

When the robot in the cabinet was exposed, she walked toward it initially, stopped, and then retreated to her mother. She froze in place when an unfamiliar woman entered the room, and she shook her head when the stranger asked her to approach.

At 21 months, she again refused to accept the liquid on her tongue and cried. When the examiner criticized her for failing to build the block construction, she fretted and added, "I don't want to do it." She refused to approach a radio-controlled robot, and when the toy began to move, she ran to her mother in fear.

The intercorrelations among the variables that define the profiles of the exuberant and the fearful child across the whole sample were modest in magnitude: Coefficients ranged between .15 and .30 (see Tables 4.1 and 4.2). No significant correlation was found between smiling and 4-month heart rate for boys or between smiling at 21 months and motor arousal or crying at 4 months. Further, a factor analysis of the corpus of data did not reveal a factor that represented the small number of low reactive boys and high reactive girls who met the criteria described above. These facts imply that these children may be qualitatively different from the majority of the sample.

∞ BEHAVIOR AT 4½ YEARS

We are currently evaluating the high and low reactive infants from this cohort at 4½ years of age. The two responses that differentiate the two temperamental groups most clearly are the number of spontaneous comments and the number of smiles displayed during a 60-minute battery administered by an unfamiliar woman who did not know the children's original classification. A *spontaneous comment* is a remark that is not provoked by an examiner's question. Both responses were scored reliably from videotape records of the session. These data support the claim that extreme scores can be informative.

Spontaneous Smiles

A nice illustration of the utility of examining extreme scores is provided by an analysis of the number of spontaneous smiles made during the interaction with the examiner. The mean for a sample of 151 children was 23.9 ($SD = 17.8$). One girl displayed 95 smiles—the highest value. The 2 children with the next two highest frequencies, also girls, displayed 81 smiles (about 1 SD lower). We now ask whether the children with very high smiles, and especially the girl with 95 smiles, might be qualitatively different from the rest of the sample on their behavioral profiles at 4, 14, and 21 months.

TABLE 4.1 Intercorrelations Among Eight Variables for All Boys

Variables	1	2	3	4	5	6	7	8
Motor behavior, 4 months	—	.16	−.08	−.16	.22	.24	−.23	−.17
Cry behavior, 4 months	—	—	−.04	−.08	.10	.07	−.30	.10
Smiling at 14 months	—	—	—	.30	−.27	−.15	.22	.05
Smiling at 21 months	—	—	—	—	−.21	−.35	.20	.14
Fear at 14 months	—	—	—	—	—	.50	−.11	−.06
Fear at 21 months	—	—	—	—	—	—	−.07	−.11
Facial width	—	—	—	—	—	—	—	.04
Baseline heart rate at 4 months	—	—	—	—	—	—	—	—

NOTE: If correlation $\geq .16$, $p < .05$.

TABLE 4.2 Intercorrelations Among Seven Variables for All Girls

Variables	1	2	3	4	5	6	7
Motor behavior at 4 months	—	.15	−.14	−.07	.21	.06	−.24
Cry behavior at 4 months	—	—	−.15	−.08	.23	.00	−.30
Smiling at 14 months	—	—	—	.20	−.30	−.24	−.10
Smiling at 21 months	—	—	—	—	−.18	−.30	.16
Fear at 14 months	—	—	—	—	—	.38	−.23
Fear at 21 months	—	—	—	—	—	—	−.23
Facial width	—	—	—	—	—	—	—

NOTE: If correlation $\geq .15$, $p < .05$.

Table 4.3 contains the scores on six early variables for groups of children displaying varying numbers of smiles. The six early variables were (a) motor activity, (b) duration of crying, (c) number of trials smiling when the infant was 4 months old, (d) number of trials vocalizing, (e) number of fears displayed to the series of unfamiliar episodes when the child was 14 months, and (f) number of fears displayed at 21 months old. The data reveal that the 6 children (4% of the sample) who displayed the most smiles at 4½ years (61 to 95 smiles) produced about twice as many smiles at 4 months as did the total sample. The correlation between frequency of smiling at 4 months and at 4 years for the entire sample, however, was only .02.

TABLE 4.3 Relation of Behavior at 4, 14, and 21 Months to
Smiles at 4½ Years ($N = 151$)

Variable	Mean SD	Smile = 0 (n = 5)	Smile 01-20 (n = 70)	Smile 21-40 (n = 51)	Smile 41-60 (n = 19)	Smile 61-80 (n = 3)
Motor Score	55.0 (38.0)	62.0	67.2	47.0	39.3	15.3
Duration Cry (Sec)	8.4 (17.8)	23.1	11.3	6.1	2.3	0
Smile (No. of Trials)	1.4 (2.1)	1.8	1.6	1.1	1.0	2.3
Vocalization (No. of Trials)	11.4 (6.4)	6.8	10.9	10.9	14.4	16.5
Fear at 14 months	2.6 (2.3)	4.8	2.8	2.4	2.3	2.3
Fear at 21 months	2.5 (2.0)	4.6	2.7	2.3	2.4	1.3

The girl who smiled 95 times vocalized on 20 trials at 4 months of age (compared with a mean of 11.4 for the total group) and did not cry at all (compared with a mean of 8.4 sec for the total group). Moreover, she had only one fear at 14 months and at 21 months, compared with mean fear scores of 2.6 and 2.5 for the entire sample. The correlations for all children between smiling at 4½ years and vocalization and crying at 4 months, however, were only .20 for vocalization and −.19 for crying ($p < .05$ for each coefficient), and between smiling at 4½ years and fear at 14 and 21 months the correlations were −.11 and −.15, respectively. The low magnitudes of these coefficients between smiling at 4½ years and most of the earlier behaviors disguise the fact that the small number of children with extreme values on smiling at 4½ years appeared to be qualitatively different from the rest of the sample. This claim is supported by the fact that after we eliminated the 5 children who did not smile at all and the 6 children with more than 60 smiles (7% of the sample), all of the correlations between smiling at 4½ years and the earlier variables, with the exception of motor behavior, dropped to nonsignificant levels. That is, 7% of the sample was responsible for the minimal, though significant, coefficients between vocalization and crying at 4 months, on the one hand, and smiling at 4½ years, on the other.

Support for the claim that the children with a large number of smiles are qualitatively different from the rest of the sample is revealed in a statistical analysis that examined simultaneously a set of eight measures on every subject (the six early variables plus spontaneous comments and smiling at 4½ years) and estimated the summed deviation of each child's scores from a weighted mean (mu) of each variable. The weights are applied to each score in a way that minimizes the extreme values. Finally, each child is assigned a score (delta) that represents the summed squared deviation of that child's scores from the mu for each variable. The distribution of delta was highly skewed, with 89% of the sample having a delta equal to or less than 16 (the mean and the mode were 4). The 3 girls with 81 or more smiles had delta values of 22.9, 21.6, and 15.5. The probability of attaining delta values that large are .08, .09, and .18, respectively, suggesting that 2 of the 3 girls are very different from the rest of the sample on their behavioral profile.

Spontaneous Comments

The distribution of the number of spontaneous comments made to the examiner ($M = 50.5$; $SD = 45.8$) was also skewed to the right; 17 children (11% of the sample) made more than 111 comments, and the 2 children with the highest number of comments uttered 199 and 203 comments, respectively. Table 4.4 suggests that these 2 highly talkative children were different from the rest of the sample on their early data. They neither cried nor smiled at 4 months, and the child with 199 comments had a very low motor score at 4 months and a very low fear score at 21 months. The delta values for the 2 children were 16.8 and 17.2. However, the correlations between spontaneous comments, on the one hand, and early crying and smiling, on the other, were low ($r = -.03$ and .03), and the correlation was only $-.17$ ($p < .05$) with the fear score at 21 months.

Because smiles and comments were positively correlated ($r = 0.4$), we created a mean standard score from the standard scores on both variables. One highly subdued boy who had been a high reactive infant had the lowest standard score ($z = -1.22$) of all high reactive children. This boy was different from the 4 high reactive infants who had the next most extreme standard scores ($z = -1.17$, -1.16, -1.15, and -1.11), as well as from the remaining 58 high reactive children. This boy had an unusually high cry score at 40

TABLE 4.4 Relation of Behavior at 4, 14, and 21 Months to
Spontaneous Comments at 4½ Years ($N = 151$)

Variable	S.C. = 0 (n = 4)	S.C. 1-27 (n = 52)	S.C. 28-52 (n = 38)	S.C. 53-111 (n = 40)	S.C. 112-167 (n = 15)	S.C. = 199 (n = 1)	S.C. = 203 (n = 1)
Motor Score	65.7	64.2	50.5	50.6	45.8	4.0	27.0
Duration Cry (Sec)	1.0	10.1	6.4	6.0	12.6	0	0
Smile (No. of Trials)	1.0	1.4	0.9	2.1	1.1	0	0
Vocalization (No. of Trials)	7.5	10.8	10.3	13.4	12.1	17.0	15.0
Fear at 14 months	2.5	2.9	2.7	2.5	1.9	2.0	1.0
Fear at 21 months	3.0	3.6	2.3	2.2	2.4	0	1.0

NOTE: S.C. = spontaneous comments made to the examiner.

months (he cried for 80 seconds), with no smiles and no vocalizations and a lower than average motor activity score for a high reactive infant. This boy's delta value was 53.0 ($p < .01$), suggesting that he was a very deviant child. By contrast, the child with the highest standard score for comments and smiles ($z = 3.3$)—the most exuberant—was the girl described earlier who smiled 95 times. As noted, she was different from most low reactive infants.

Extremes on Delay

A final analysis is persuasive of the utility of examining subjects with extreme scores. In the middle of the 4-year battery, the examiner asked each child to perform 12 simple acts; 6 of the acts did not violate norms for proper behavior (hit the table, pour water into a cup); however, the other 6 acts did violate middle-class standards (pour juice on the testing table, throw a Styrofoam ball at the examiner's face, scribble with a crayon in a new book, tear up a color photograph of the examiner). Most children performed all the acts, but some delayed a few seconds before obeying the examiner's request, presumably because of uncertainty over violating a socialized standard. These children would look at the examiner, sometimes displaying a serious face, and a few seconds later perform the act.

Most high reactive children showed delays on two or three of the six violations. Most low reactives fell at either extreme; they showed no more than one delay, or they displayed four or more delays. We compared the 17 low reactive children (8 boys and 9 girls) who showed a minimal number of delays (zero or one) with the 12 low reactives (6 boys and 6 girls) who showed five or more delays. We presume that the latter group was more uncertain than the former. The data support that expectation for the group with many delays had been significantly more fearful in the laboratory when they were 14 months old (75% of this group had two or more fears, compared with 40% of the group who showed no more than one delay). Further, the children who had many delays had a more serious mood in the laboratory at 21 months; not one child in this group smiled frequently, compared with 55% of those who showed minimal delays. However, these differences in fearfulness and smiling occurred only for these two small groups of low reactive children who were at one of the extremes on the delay variable. No relation across all children was found between number of delays and fearfulness or smiling in the 2nd year.

It appears that because the high reactives were more intimidated by the examiner than were the low reactives, the former were more likely to obey at once and less likely to delay on a large number of requests. By contrast, low reactive children are generally less intimidated by an unfamiliar adult. Only those who experience some uncertainty over violating socialized norms on behavior should pause before acting. But the relation between number of delays and earlier fear or affect was not linear; it only occurred for children whose temperaments led them to fall into a range of uncertainty that was relatively low. The relation between delays and earlier behavior did not occur for high reactive children who typically operate at much higher levels of uncertainty.

∞ DISCUSSION

Marian Radke-Yarrow would not be surprised by these data. She advised her colleagues on many occasions to ask about the individual and to resist being lost in abstractions (Radke-Yarrow & Waxler, 1979).

The concept of *emergenesis*, proposed by Lykken and his colleagues (Lykken, McGue, Tellegen, & Bouchard, 1992), may be helpful to investigators trying to understand small subgroups within large samples. Less than 1% of our large cohort consisted of low reactive boys who were minimally fearful, high smiling, and had low heart rates and broad faces. It is reasonable to assume that gender, low reactivity, low sympathetic tone on the cardiovascular system, ease of smiling, fearlessness, and the boney structures of the face are inherited independently in large populations. Thus, the probability of any one child inheriting the genes that contribute to all six features is relatively low. That is why siblings living in the same home are often different in many psychological qualities.

One 4 ½-year-old was dramatically different from the other 150 children in her behavior with the female examiner. This child's most salient quality was her aggressive behavior. On some occasions, she pinched the examiner, pulled her hair, pushed the table against her legs with vigor, and placed her face against the examiner's while uttering a loud sound. These deviant responses seemed to be under her control, however, because she was cooperative on many of the episodes. Her mother acknowledged that she was difficult at home; "wild and wonderful" was the phrase used by the mother. However, the mother does not appreciate how unique her daughter's behavior was, compared with most children.

Examination of this girl's profile at 4, 14, and 21 months revealed a unique pattern. At 4 months of age, she became extremely aroused motorically and vocally to the mobiles, but she did not cry. Further, she was in the 99th percentile for smiling on the 4-month battery and had a low initial baseline heart rate (< 135 bpm). No other infant in the sample combined high motor arousal and frequent crying with frequent smiling and a low baseline heart rate. Thus, her unique aggressive behavior at 4½ years had a parallel in a singularly distinctive profile at 4 months, suggesting that her aggressive behavior occurred, in part, because she was a member of a rare temperamental category.

She was in the top 5% of the distribution of fearful behavior at 14 and 21 months, but her profile of fears was unusual. Most children with such a high fear score usually avoid the clown and the stranger and do not approach when each invites them to play. This girl's high fear score was attained because she cried in fear to many of the unfamiliar episodes, but, surprisingly, she approached both the stranger and the clown.

This girl's complete longitudinal record was atypical, and her delta score was very high—57.5 ($p < .01$). We believe that she and the aggressive boy described in the introduction represent examples of statistically rare temperamental categories that are of theoretical interest. Typical samples in developmental psychology of 40 to 50 children, however, will probably not contain either of these children. Psychologists are unusual among natural scientists in their assumption that any set of 40 volunteers living within 10 miles of a laboratory is representative of all humans. No biologist studying fearful behavior in mice would make that assumption.

A central tension in empirical studies of individual differences derives from a controversy over whether people differ quantitatively on the same set of dimensions—therefore, each individual is best described as a set of values on factor scores—or whether some individuals belong to qualitatively distinct groups. As noted earlier, a factor analysis of the motor, cry, and baseline heart rate values at 4 months; the smile and fear scores in the second year; and facial width at 14 months did not reveal a factor that represents the boy we described earlier. Neither would the two Down children of older mothers in the hypothetical sample of 600 children discussed in the introduction emerge from a factor analysis of that corpus. We do not suggest that investigators reject currently popular analytic techniques and always favor qualitative groups. Some phenomena are probably best understood as linearly related continua, at least for certain ranges. But it will be useful for investigators to reflect on the presence of small, qualitatively distinct groups as they explore their evidence.

An understandable preference for simplicity favors continuous psychological functions over discrete categories of people. Einstein's theory of relativity implies that, in the frame of an observer, objects shorten as their velocity approaches the speed of light. To universalize this law and retain the aesthetics and parsimony of a continuous mathematical function, Einstein suggested that this shortening occurs as I swing my tennis racquet, although the velocity is so small that the apparent shortening, in the frame of an observer, is not detectable with current instruments. But many functions in nature are not linear. Water does not begin to form very tiny ice crystals as it cools from 30° to 28°C; the crystals only form when the temperature approaches 0°.

Repeatedly, psychological data show similar nonlinear functions, with categorical phenomena emerging within specific ranges. The relation of a low heart rate and frequent smiling in infants provides one example. The relation between baseline sitting heart rate in 4-month-old infants and subsequent smiling in the 2nd year was close to zero for the entire sample. However,

4-month-old boys with very low heart rates—usually attained while listening to a recording of human speech—smiled frequently in the 2nd year. Sixty-one percent of the boys, independent of their 4-month reactivity classification, who smiled frequently in the 2nd year had a very low 4-month heart rate (less than 120 bpm), compared with 25% of the boys who smiled infrequently ($\chi^2 = 8.2$, $p < .01$).

If similar nonlinear functions are common in many domains of psychology, as we suspect, current statistical procedures, including regression analyses, will fail to reveal important relations in nature. These analytic procedures assume that the forces producing the values on the measures of interest are the same at all ranges; the causal mechanisms presumably vary only in magnitude. The reluctance to acknowledge that, on some occasions, it is useful to examine extreme groups that may be qualitatively different from the rest of the sample has been slowing theoretical progress in psychology.

Nonlinear functions are common in the life sciences, and at transition points novel qualities often emerge. For example, the behavior of a single ant or a few ants appears to be random and without coherence. But when the number of ants in a colony reaches a critical density, rhythmic activity emerges; that is, a large colony of ants has distinct qualities that cannot be predicted from, or explained by, an additive model that sums the behavior of an increasing number of single ants (Goodwin, 1994).

Brian Goodwin (1994), a biologist, makes the case for qualitative categories: "The study of biological form begins to take us in the direction of a science of qualities that is not an alternative to, but complements and extends, the science of quantities" (p. 198).

∞℧∞

COMMENTS ON CHAPTER 4

Jerome Kagan, Nancy Snidman, and Doreen Arcus have given us a minihistory of the rejection of individual case studies as a scientific source of knowledge and the domination of research by statistical strategies. In this process, qualitative individual differences have yielded to quantitatively defined dimensions of individual characteristics. But a part of the history is missing; it does not mention the bold venture into the qualitative realm by Jerome

Kagan when, in the late 1970s, he began his research on behavioral inhibition. His research program was greeted critically and treated roughly by many: How could he so flagrantly ignore the canons of science, so abuse the rules! The rest of the history of his research on behavioral inhibition speaks for itself. I think that this research has done much to encourage more timid souls who have wanted to speak up for the qualitative child.

It is not uncharacteristic of Jerome Kagan to challenge firmly held themes: His arguments on temperament and attachment and his position regarding long-term effects of early experience are examples. I have wanted to ask him, however, regarding early experience, how "the tape is erased" (how can the effects of early experience be modified or eliminated in development?).

To the Harvard group goes credit for bringing attention to the children who are not like the rest of the group and for helping establish the legitimacy of directing research inquiry to them.

The Harvard team has demonstrated that some children stand out from the rest of the sample under study—most immediately visible in "extreme" scores. Although this observation is not in itself a revelation, what has happened to these children in research is of concern. They have been "brought into the distribution," the familiar solution, a practice that denies their existence. Furthermore, it has kept investigators quite blind to different configurations that "define" children and to the fact that small subgroups of children at the extremes can and do reveal "relations in nature, and mechanisms that operate in distinct ways within these groups."

It is interesting that research in developmental psychopathology has characteristically used a categorical, "extremes" approach in classifying children. The "diagnosis" is such a classification, arrived at not by a quantitative score on a single dimension of behavior, but by a pattern of qualities that coexist. This approach has been acceptable and fruitful for a long time—in contrast with its unacceptability as a research strategy in studies of "normal" development. In both fields, of course, knowledge of the full range of children establishes the firmest foundation of knowledge (see also Joan Stevenson-Hinde, this volume, Chap. 6).

The qualitative subgroups that have been challenging to investigators tend to be those presenting problems (e.g., the very inhibited or shy, the highly oppositional, the very withdrawn). The children with qualities at the opposite poles tend to be "plowed into" the group remaining. These opposites include the very spontaneous, the very compliant, and the very altruistic, among others. Which is only to say that renewed attention to subgroups of children at the extremes in the samples for whom we assess central tendencies can bring a new level of insight into the nature of individual functioning.

Marian Radke-Yarrow

~ 5 ~

A Pattern-Oriented Approach to Studying Individual Development

Snapshots and Processes

Lars R. Bergman

Stockholm University

The variable has for a long time been the main conceptual and analytical unit in research on individual development (Thomae, 1988; Wohlwill, 1973). From an interactional perspective, however, and if the interest is in analyzing the character of structures and processes involved in the total functioning of an individual, this variable-oriented approach to individual development has limitations as pointed out by, for instance, Cairns (1983) and Magnusson (1985, 1995). To summarize the criticism of the variable-oriented approach in one sentence: The modeling/ description of variables over individuals can be very difficult to translate into properties characterizing single individuals because of the variable-oriented, not individual-oriented, nature of the information provided by the statistical method used.

Individual development can be described as a multideter-mined stochastic process partly unique to the individual, a characteristic reflected in strong interactions and nonlinearity in data across individuals. From this viewpoint, it is natural to complement the variable-oriented approach with one in which the person as a Gestalt is the central object of interest. Operationally, this focus often implies that individuals are studied on the basis of their patterns of individual characteristics relevant for the study of the problem under consideration. Under the name of a person-oriented approach, theoretical formulations and some methodological solutions according to this perspective have been pursued by Bergman and Magnusson (1983, 1991), Magnusson (1988), Magnusson and Allen (1983), and Magnusson and Bergman (1988). Of course, the plea for considering persons-as-wholes and not just variables is by no means new, having been brought up, for instance, by Allport (1937), Block (1971), and Lewin (1935).

It is useful to conceptualize individual development as a process characterized by states with change taking place in continuous time. The following four assumptions about the basic properties of this process can then be made (Bergman & Magnusson, 1991):

1. The process is partly specific to individuals.
2. The process is complex and is conceptualized as containing many factors on different levels that may have complicated relations to each other.
3. A meaningful coherence and structure exists (a) in individual growth and (b) in differences in individuals' process characteristics. Assumptions (a) and (b) are similar to those made by Magnusson (1988) when characterizing an interactional approach to psychology.
4. Although there is an infinite variety of differences with regard to process characteristics and observed states at a detailed level, there will often be few rather common types if viewed at a more global level. The assumption is made both intraindividually (viewed over time for the same person) and interindividually (for different individuals at the same or different times).

The assumption of emerging types is suggested by analogies to system theoretic thinking; usually, only a few states are in some sense optimal and lead to a stable behavior of the system. For instance, in biological systems, often distinct types are found (e.g., of species, ecotypes; see Colinvaux, 1980). Within psychology, a similar point has been made by Block (1971), talking about " 'system designs' with more enduring properties" (p. 110) and by Gangestad and Snyder (1985), arguing for the existence of distinct types, each sharing a common source of influence.

The limitations of a variable-oriented approach and the power of a person-oriented approach to overcome some of these limitations have been discussed very briefly above in rather abstract and theoretical terms. Without elaborating too much, an example is given in Table 5.1 to illustrate the point. Admittedly, the example is extreme and simplified and only applies to one aspect of the variable-versus-person issue. In Table 5.1, the multivariate data structure is given of two dichotomous variables studied at two points in time (fictitious data).

It is seen that a standard variable-oriented analysis based on the correlation matrix would find no interesting structure in the data because all correlations are zero. This conclusion also holds for many applications of structural equation modeling (SEM), wherein the data input usually is the correlation matrix. However, higher order interactions in the data set have the interesting interpretation that either both variables change or none change. This is immediately seen by using a person-oriented method focusing on the individuals' complete value patterns. The example illustrates the importance of being clear about what aspects in the data are judged relevant and the limitation of many variable-oriented methods in equaling the information of interest to that provided by the correlation or variance-covariance matrix. Differently put: When the whole information structure of each individual is important and no evidence exists for believing that this information is captured by the correlation matrix, then a pattern-oriented research method is natural.

There is no generally accepted precise terminology for the issues discussed in this chapter. Terms like *pattern, configuration, taxonomy, classification, typology, type,* and *antitype* can mean different things, depending on the context. Therefore, some definitions of these are needed here (without implying that these definitions are generally valid):

A *pattern* is here meant a specific individual's value profile in the variables under study.

A *configuration* is a theoretically possible combination of values in different variables that may or may not occur for one or more individuals.

A *taxonomy* is a theory-based hierarchical categorization.

A *classification* is a division of the studied subjects into groups so that the subjects within a group are considered to be alike, whereas the groups are not.

A *typology* is a generalization of a classification.

A *type* is one class in a typology except in the context of configural frequency analysis, wherein *types* and *antitypes* refer to configurations that occur, respectively, more and less frequently than expected by chance.

TABLE 5.1 An Example of a Data Set Containing Higher Order Interactions. Two Dichotomous Variables, x and y, Studied at Two Points in Time for Eight Persons (Fictitious Data)

Data set:				Between each pair of variables, the following cross-tabulation is obtained:				

Time 1		Time 2			1	0		
x	y	x	y					
1	1	0	0	1	2	2	4	χ^2 = phi = 0. The variables are pairwise independent.
1	1	1	1	0	2	2	4	
1	0	1	0					
0	0	0	0		4	4	8	
1	0	0	1					
0	1	1	0					
0	1	0	1					
0	0	1	1					

The data set can be presented by the following multivariate tabulation:

		Time 2			
		00	01	10	11
	00	1			1
Time 1	01		1	1	
	10		1	1	
	11	1			1

Summary of multivariate structure: No change at all or change in both variables.

The theoretical aspects are not further discussed here because they are treated by Magnusson in Chapter 3 of this volume. I hope that the background has been sufficient for indicating the potential usefulness of a person-oriented approach to individual development and of then using pattern-oriented methods for studying development.

∞ PATTERN-ORIENTED METHODS FOR STUDYING INDIVIDUAL DEVELOPMENT

Overview

It could be argued that at the heart of understanding individual development is the detailed study of the single individual's development (intraindividual change) followed by a careful generalization on the basis of an integration of studies of many such single cases. In the context of studying short-term changes in behavior, this argument was put forward by, for instance, Jones and Nesselroade (1990), but it is relevant also in the context of long-term development. In practice, however, one rarely has the intensive information of a time-series type necessary for this kind of analysis. A combination of limited information from each subject and a focus on interindividual change motivates the use of other strategies of analysis. In Figure 5.1, an overview is given of common pattern-based methods for studying individual development from an interindividual perspective.

Of course, different categorizations of pattern-oriented methods are possible, and the one presented in Figure 5.1 is not complete, although it is sufficient for the present purpose. A basic distinction is made between model-based and descriptive methods, although the borderline is not always clear. An example of a model-based method with latent variables is *latent transition analysis*, which was developed within the framework of latent class analysis (Collins & Wugalter, 1992). An example of a model-based method without latent variables is *loglinear modeling* (Bishop et al., 1975); examples of tailoring this method to the study of change are given by, for instance, Clogg, Eliason, and Grego (1990). Although model-based methods are highly useful in certain situations, they are not further pursued in this chapter. We instead concentrate on descriptive methods, which are more basic and flexible. They also usually involve fewer assumptions about the properties of the data and, hence, also for this reason are more suitable as basic methods in the tool chest.

In the descriptive analysis of pattern development, the focus need not be on classification. If the variables constituting the patterns are discrete and just taking a few different values, all possible value patterns could be analyzed. A simple methodological framework for this is provided by configural frequency analysis, presented in the next section. Sometimes the interest is focused on special aspects of patterns, such as profile scatter and profile

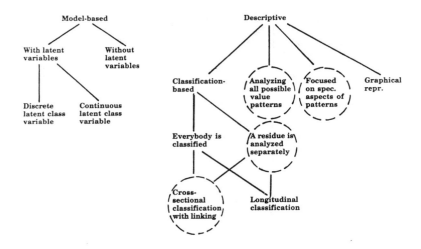

Figure 5.1. Overview of Common Pattern-Oriented Methods for Studying Individual Development From an Interindividual Perspective
NOTE: Methods that are circled in the figure are a focus in this presentation.

extremes, which we will come back to later. Graphical representations of similarities between profiles can sometimes be highly useful in developmental research—for instance, based on multidimensional scaling (Wood, 1990). Such illustrative methods, however, are not discussed here because they usually are best suited for describing a fairly small number of objects, and the interest here is on interindividual differences studied for moderate to large samples of persons.

The main emphasis here is on classification-based methods for studying the development of individuals' value patterns. A crucial distinction is, then, in which of two ways the developmental process is classified:

1. A longitudinal pattern is formed, and longitudinal types are identified directly in the classification. Ideally, this means that full account is taken of each individual's specific pattern of change.
2. At each age, a classification is made, and the results of the different classifications are linked, usually pairwise (the time i classification is linked to the time $i+1$ classification). The individuals' class membership over time is then studied.

In the sequel, both of these strategies are discussed, with a focus on the second one, which is believed to be more robust and generally applicable.

Analyzing Longitudinal Patterns

Focusing on longitudinal patterns is, in theory, attractive because they are basic in the description of individual pattern change. Two common analytic strategies are (a) direct clustering of the complete longitudinal patterns and (b) an ordination strategy wherein first the number of dimensions is reduced by using, for instance, principal components analysis and then the factor scores are cluster analyzed (e.g., Mumford & Owens, 1984).

One could argue that longitudinal classification is preferable to a snapshot and linking study because the former approach is closer to the individuals' processes of change. In practice, however, this genuinely longitudinal approach can run into problems. For instance, when applying longitudinal cluster analysis where data from all ages are included in the value profile, the clustering in many cases gives heterogeneous clusters that are difficult to interpret. Especially in cases with many measurement occasions, one might have to accept subjects being classified as belonging to the same developmental cluster although they have a different outcome or a different start-up because they were similar at the other measurement occasions.

An empirical example of the cluster heterogeneity that often is obtained when using longitudinal cluster analysis is given by Bergman and Magnusson (1986) in a study of the development of about 500 boys' patterns of extrinsic adjustment problems (six problems measured at two points in time). The researchers used a clustering procedure similar to the one described below in the section "Cluster Analysis With Linking," except that for identifying and analyzing a residue of unclassified objects, RESIDAN was not used. Instead, a different procedure, RESCLUS, was used in which the residue objects were identified only during the reallocation stage. A residue of 5% of the sample was found, consisting of boys having a developmental pattern that did not fit into any of the clusters. In the cluster analysis, an 11-clusters solution was chosen, explaining 62% of the total error sum of squares. Cross-sectional cluster analyses using the same clustering procedure were also undertaken and the results linked. In these analyses, an 8-cluster solution sufficed, and the explained variances were at both ages 71% with residues of 2% of the sample. Bergman and Magnusson's conclusion was that the longitudinal analysis gave interpretable results with a reasonable correspondence to the results obtained by the strategy of cross-sectional analyses followed by linking. The heterogeneity of the resulting longitudinal clusters, however, was fairly high. It can be argued that, in this case, the complexity of the individuals' developmental patterns was too high for summarizing the developmental paths by a reasonably small number of clusters pertaining to a single longitudinal classification.

In the case discussed above, both level and form of the profile were relevant; if only profile form is the focus of interest, however, a direct longitudinal classification might work better than otherwise because the strain on the classification system then is reduced (less information has to be summarized by the cluster membership variable). An example of the potential of a longitudinal classification strategy is offered by Block's (1971) study of longitudinal personality types. He used judges to perform Q-sorts at different ages of the saliency of a large number of personality characteristics. Ninety items were identical in junior high school and at adult age. These 180 items constituted an individual's profile to be analyzed. First, the similarity between each pair of individuals was computed by using the Pearson correlation coefficient (with the two persons as variables and the 180 Q-sort items as cases). Then Q-factor analysis was used; for boys, five factors (personality types) were extracted, and for girls, six factors were extracted. In presenting his results, Block makes these methodological observations:

∞ With his interest in studying "the whole personality," it was not relevant to measure similarity also with regard to level and scatter; only form was relevant. For this purpose, the available scores on the Q-sort items were optimal. He is critical toward the use of conglomerate measures of similarity that take profile form, level, and scatter into account.

∞ A balance has to be struck between a fine-graded classification rendering too few cases for statistical analysis for certain types and a classification with just a few types that would lead to an unwanted heterogeneity in the studied groups. In his case, cluster homogeneity was conveyed by the standard deviation of the set of factor loadings of the representatives of a type on its defining factor.

∞ Constructing classifications separately at the different ages and then connecting them would raise interpretational problems and hit beside the target that was a longitudinal typology.

∞ By including in the profile equally many and identical items from the adolescent years and from adult age, a balance is achieved and, for instance, a high degree of similarity between two individuals' profiles can be interpreted as them having undergone a similar personality development.

∞ It is important to allow for the fact that not everyone fits into any of a small number of types; hence, a residue of unclassified persons was formed.

For his purpose and with the available data, Block's strategy for constructing a longitudinal typology appears relevant and is probably useful also in certain other situations when only profile form is of interest. One should be clear, however, that his approach means that interindividual differences are only studied with regard to ipsative stability and change. One has to assume that level differences between individuals in the studied dimensions are unimportant and that the ranking of the saliency of characteristics has the same meaning for different individuals; that is, one can disregard that some persons might have dramatic differences in the expression level of different characteristics and that some other persons might be more "even" with smaller differences in the expression levels of the different characteristics. His arguments against cross-sectional classification followed by linking appear to me less convincing than his arguments for a direct longitudinal classification (see Block, 1971, pp. 109-120, for a more detailed discussion). His main argument against appears to be that the error-fitting characteristics of the Q-factor analyses he prefers will create disparities between the two ages studied that cannot be disentangled from valid disparities caused by different life stages being involved. Instead of the Q-factor analysis that Block used, a classification-oriented researcher might prefer to use one of the established cluster analysis algorithms (e.g., average linkage). The method decision depends on whether one wants to accept the assumptions of factor analysis in this for the method, unusual situation, and the decision rules for assigning subjects to types according to the factor loading pattern. It also seems a bit contradictory to rely on a linear model like factor analysis if the purpose is to study patterns and higher order interactions.

Measurement Issues in Classification

Basic to a classification analysis using cluster analysis is the matrix of (dis)similarities between all pairs of subjects. This matrix can be constructed either directly (e.g., by using subjective ratings of the similarity between each pair of subjects) or, more commonly, indirectly by first obtaining measurements for some variables and then, on the basis of these measurements, computing the (dis)similarity between each pair of subjects. Block's (1971) innovative use of the Q-sort technique represents one attempt to handle the tricky problems of measurement of variables in patterns in a longitudinal setting. He also points out the importance of taking multivariate measurement seriously and that the choice of scaling and of (dis)similarity measure must be in congruence with each other and with the purpose of the classification. To reiterate, when undertaking cluster analysis, a basic decision has to be made how (dis)similarity between each pair of subjects is to be measured. The two most common measures of (dis)similarity between pairs of subjects are the following:

1. If one is interested in both profile level and form as a basis for the comparison, an often-used measure for the dissimilarity between two subjects is the *average squared Euclidean distance,* defined as the sum over variables of the squared deviations in each variable divided by the number of variables.

2. If one is interested only in profile form, a possible measure is the *correlation coefficient* between the two subjects (with each subject treated as a variable in the computation and each variable treated as a case).

Discussions of different ways of measuring (dis)similarities between profiles are given by Cronbach and Gleser (1953) and Budescu (1980). It is important to point out that neither the correlation coefficient between subjects nor the average squared Euclidean distance is invariant or proportional to linear transformations of the involved variables (except in the trivial case when all variables are transformed by the same linear function). Simple scaling operations can change the monotone ordering according to size of the (dis)similarity coefficients and, hence, affect what clusters the analysis produce. Why it is so is perhaps least obvious for the correlation coefficient that is invariant to linear transformations of the involved variables. When computing the correlation between a pair of subjects, however, the case has an unusual definition and is what usually is called the *variable.* Hence, when we are talking about a normal variable transformation of the data set, this means, from the perspective of the correlations between pairs of subjects, a case transformation to which the coefficient is not invariant.

In the typical case, when the scales of all involved variables are arbitrary and have no absolute interpretation, they are usually best transformed to, for instance, z scores at each age separately. If such a transformation is not undertaken, it might result in totally misleading results irrespective of whether the average squared Euclidean distance or the correlation coefficient between subject pairs is used. In certain cases, however, the scales do have a more absolute meaning with, for instance, differences in standard deviations between different variables or ages containing important information. A z transformation may then not be called for because standard deviation differences in this way are obliterated. This could, for instance, have the effect that large and important differences in a variable with a large standard deviation are scaled down to the same size as small and insignificant differences in another variable with a small standard deviation. To reiterate: One has to make sure that the scalings for the different variables really are comparable in all respects; otherwise, the variables should be standardized. A discussion of this issue in relation to the measurement and classification of adjustment profiles is given by Bergman and Magnusson (1991). For their purpose, they invented a quasi-absolute scaling applied to all variables at all ages. In my opinion, this issue of multivariate scaling has not been given sufficient attention in the literature.

Not infrequently, only incomplete data are available for some subjects. This can pose a tricky problem. If a substantial part of a subject's data is missing, that subject usually should be deleted from the analysis. But if many subjects have only one or a few missing values, this is less of an attractive option. Complete data are then bought at the price of loosing many subjects and possibly creating a dropout bias. The least bad solution might be to impute missing values for subjects having almost complete data. For this purpose, it seems natural to use a twin approach in a pattern-oriented setting. A missing value is then replaced by the value in that variable of a twin subject with complete data (Bergman & El-Khouri, 1992). Other sophisticated methods are available. They often use some kind of linear model, however, and in this context, where nonlinear relationships and higher order interactions are emphasized, they might be considered less natural choices. It goes without saying that what is created by using imputation is not a new data set, but a temporary file for a specific analysis.

Cross-Sectional Analyses With Linking

In this section, methods are presented for cross-sectional analysis of profile data followed by pairwise linking of the results.

Without in any way claiming to be complete, and only discussing and presenting a limited number of methods, it is the goal of this presentation to provide a reasonably sufficient toolbox for basic analysis of pattern development from an interindividual perspective using the snapshot-linking approach. As an illustration, these methods are applied to intelligence data in the section "An Illustration of Pattern-Oriented Analysis Strategy in Analyzing Intelligence Data."

Cluster Analysis With Linking

Classification is as old as humans. The typologies within early abnormal psychology are but one application within psychology of this basic human tendency to impose structure on the phenomena we encounter (for a historic overview, see Misiak & Sexton, 1966; for a review of cluster analysis in psychiatry, see Skinner & Blashfield, 1982). During this century, classification of individuals as a main research tool within psychology has become less prominent; one reason for this is the enormous expansion of powerful methods for variable analysis and hypothesis testing within both experimental and non-experimental settings. As was discussed at the beginning of the chapter, however, the limited capacity of such methods for handling complex interactions and difficulties in translating results from variable-oriented research into statements about individuals as "wholes" has led to an interest in methods focusing on individual value patterns or structures, rather than on separate variables. A basic approach in a developmental setting, then, is classification of individuals at each age by using cluster analysis followed by pairwise linking of the classification results.

Within the framework of cluster analysis, a wide variety of methods is available for classifying objects on the basis of their (dis)similarities. We focus here on methods based on comparisons of individuals' value profiles, but, of course, other ways of obtaining (dis)similarities are possible (e.g., by using raters). Different major types of cluster analyses are hierarchical methods (agglomerate or divisive), partitioning methods, and methods that allow overlap between clusters. Within each such major category of methods, a variety of specific methods and algorithms exist. For general overviews of cluster analysis and related methods, the reader is referred to Blashfield (1980), Gaul and Schader (1986), Everitt (1974), and Gordon (1981).

Which method of cluster analysis is best also depends, of course, on the data set at hand and the specific problem under study. Methods allowing overlap between clusters are potentially attractive but may lead to various interpretational problems (Wiener-Ehrlich, 1981) and are not further pursued here. Hierarchical-agglomerate algorithms and partitioning methods are in very general use. Evaluations of the sensitivity of different clustering algorithms to error perturbation and of the ability to recover a known structure suggest that, as expected, no one method is generally superior to others. However, Ward's (1963) hierarchical minimum variance method, average linkage (sometimes called group average, UPGMA), and especially k-means relocation based on a sound start classification are reported to be well-functioning methods (Milligan, 1980, 1981b; Morey, Blashfield, & Skinner, 1983). Promising new methods based on so-called beta-flexible clustering have been proposed (Belbin, Faith, & Milligan, 1992). Ward's method and k-means relocation are included in the cluster analysis procedure suggested below. In studies based on Swedish samples, Bergman and Magnusson (1984a, 1984b, 1991) have demonstrated a satisfactory replicability of classifications using the suggested procedure.

In the following three situations, one might want to evaluate statistically the classification provided by the cluster analysis:

1. *To evaluate the quality of a resulting classification in the sense of how faithfully it reflects the basic (dis)similarity data or raw data:* A variety of internal criterion measures are available, but most appear to be of doubtful value. One reasonable index is the point biseral correlation between (a) being in the same cluster/not being in the same cluster and (b) the dissimilarity value (with each pair of subjects constituting a case). For an overview, see Milligan (1981a). If value profiles of interval scaled variables are available and if average squared Euclidean distance is chosen as the measure of dissimilarity, a simple measure of cluster heterogeneity is the error sum of squares within clusters (denoted with Ec). Ec is computed in the following way: First, for each person in a cluster, the sum of all squared deviations from the cluster centroid is divided by the number of variables. These are summed over persons in the cluster and over clusters to obtain Ec. Denote with Et the total error sum of squares when all individuals are in the same cluster. The following measure of overall cluster homogeneity can then be convenient:

$$EV = 100 \times (Et - Ec) / Et$$

EV indicates the percentage of the total error sum of squares "explained" by the cluster solution. A figure of 100 indicates a perfect cluster homogeneity; a figure of 0 indicates a total absence of cluster homogeneity. The term *error sum of squares* may cause some confusion because it is perhaps applied in a way unfamiliar to the reader. It is a logical name, however, because from a classification point of view, all variation within a cluster indicates imperfections or error in the clustering.

2. *To evaluate the similarity of two different classifications pertaining to the same sample:* Often, one classification is considered the "true" or criterion classification, and the other one's cluster recovery is to be evaluated. A measure of this recovery is called an *external criterion measure.* Based on a count of the number of subject pairs being classified as belonging to the same clusters in both classifications, belonging to the same cluster in one classification but not the other one and vice versa, and belonging to different clusters in both classifications, some agreement coefficients have been proposed. One index with certain attractive properties is the *modified Rand index* suggested by Hubert and Arabie (1985).

3. *To compare statistically the results of replication studies:* This can be done by a straightforward comparison of the ordinary results obtained for the different samples, but special evaluation procedures are also available (see Breckenridge, 1989). In the section "Classifications," a one-to-one matching procedure is presented for comparing the results obtained for two different samples.

It has long been recognized that multivariate outliers may disturb the results of cluster analysis, and it has been suggested that, in some situations, it might be useful to have less than 100% coverage (to not classify everybody; Edelbrock, 1979). For instance, the results from Ward's method appear to be sensitive to the effects of outliers (Milligan, 1980). In addition to technical reasons for this, theoretical reasons have been suggested by Bergman (1988b). There must often exist a few "unique" individuals because of extreme environmental conditions and particular genotypes, and they should not be forced into a cluster. He indicated a semiobjective procedure, *RESIDAN*, for a priori identifying and analyzing separately a residue of unclassifieds. Briefly summarized, the following four major steps are included in RESIDAN:

1. On the basis of a (dis)similarity matrix, subjects being similar to
   not more than *k* other subjects are identified (*k* is often 0 but may
   be 1 or 2 for large samples). These subjects are separated from the
   rest and are placed in a residue. The (dis)similarity threshold
   should be decided on theoretical grounds and is often related to
   the criterion for considering two subjects in a cluster to be reasonably similar. For standardized data, and with average squared
   Euclidean distance as the dissimilarity measure, a threshold value
   in the range 0.25 to 0.75 is often used.

2. The cluster analysis is performed on the sample exclusive of the
   residue.

3. The residue is analyzed separately. The size and composition of
   the residue can give valuable information about the multivariate
   structure of the sample, but the focus is on an analysis of each
   residue case, preferably by using additional information not included in the classification analysis. The goal is to identify
   whether a specific residue subject is the result of errors of measurement or represents a truly unique configuration. Unique configurations are the multivariate counterpart to extreme values and
   may teach us things about the system under study (see also Kagan,
   Snidman, & Arcus, this volume, Chap. 4).

4. After the residue has been removed, a pattern hypothesized to be
   rare or nonexistent (cf. the antitype concept in CFA discussed in
   the next section) can be added to the sample as an artificial subject
   that is then subjected to a new residue analysis. The theory then
   predicts that the artificial subject would be identified as a residue
   subject.

Linking the results of classifications from different ages can be
done by straightforward cross-tabulation techniques. Often, a linking of the results from adjoining ages is sufficient. Usually, the
number of clusters at each age are in the range 6 to 15, resulting in
large contingency tables, with several expected frequencies being
very low if the sample size is moderate. Testing for significant
cluster combinations (over or under frequented cells) is then
problematic by using ordinary chi-square-based statistics because
the normal approximations are not good enough for that purpose.
It is then advisable to use exact cellwise tests, building on the
hypergeometric distribution (Bergman & El-Khouri, 1987).

Having made the above considerations, it should be obvious
that many different procedures are possible for undertaking cross-
sectional classification analysis followed by linking and that these
are best tailored to the specific case. There is also a value, however,
in having a sort of standard method that is useful in a variety of

situations and that can serve as a reference or comparison method. Here, we restrict ourselves to the case when value profiles based on interval scaled data are to be analyzed, with both the form and level of the profile being of relevance and when it is considered important to obtain reasonably homogenous clusters. For this purpose, the method below is presented. For convenience of reference, it is named LICUR (LInking of ClUsters after removal of a Residue). The following steps are involved in LICUR:

1. First, the RESIDAN approach is used at each age separately to remove a residue that is analyzed separately.

2. Then, a cluster analysis is undertaken at each age separately by using Ward's hierarchical cluster analysis method, and an optimal number of clusters is decided upon. Four criteria can guide in this decision:

   a. The accepted solution has to be meaningful and the last cluster fusion judged not to obliterate two distinct and theoretically interpretable clusters.

   b. The number of clusters should, preferably, not be more than 15 and cannot normally be expected to be fewer than 5.

   c. A sudden drop in the explained error sum of squares of the solution may indicate that a suboptimal number of clusters have been reached.

   d. The explained error sum of squares should, preferably, exceed 67%. This demand is to ensure reasonably homogeneous clusters and might be complemented, for instance, by demands on the largest acceptable standard deviation of any variable within a cluster. Admittedly, the figure 67% or two thirds "explained" is arbitrary, but it is a figure often surpassed by "successful" classifications, in my experience. The more variables that make up the subjects' value profiles, however, the more difficult it tends to be for the clustering algorithm to find homogeneous clusters for a given number of clusters (see further the discussion in the section "Discussion").

   Of course, other criteria are possible, and no generally accepted procedure exists for deciding the number of clusters. For instance, Milligan and Cooper (1985) examined many automatic decision rules for determining the number of clusters in a data set and found that stopping when the point-biseral correlation coefficient attained its maximum value was among the four best methods.

3. When the hierarchical property of the cluster solution is important, each cross-sectional analysis stops here, but when there is a strong focus on obtaining as homogenous clusters as possible, the

Ward cluster solutions are used as start solutions in *k*-means relocation cluster analyses where objects are relocated to maximize the explained error sum of squares. When this is done, the hierarchical property is lost.

4. Finally, the results of the cluster analyses are linked by cross-tabulating adjoining classifications and testing for significant types and antitypes of cluster membership combinations, preferably by using exact cellwise tests.

The ambitious researcher would like to obtain some idea of the sensitivity of the results to the choice of method for cluster analysis and to the characteristics of his or her particular sample. For this purpose, Ward's method could be replaced, for instance, by the average linkage method or beta-flexible UPGMA clustering and the analysis repeated on an equivalent sample or, if that is not available, on a random sample of, say, 75% of the original sample. A split-half procedure is sometimes appropriate. One might also want to vary method and sample separately in a design, but for practical reasons, this might follow the finding that changing both method and sample did change the results considerably. Of course, such considerations are influenced by the inference situation in the specific case (e.g., if the studied group is the population, no split-half should be undertaken). If the studied group is a sample, considerable sampling variation can occur in the results if the sample is small. There can also be an "overfit" of the results to the specific sample, making fewer clusters, giving a more homogenous solution than would have been obtained if the population or a large sample was analyzed.

Configural Frequency Analysis

The *configural frequency analysis (CFA)* of Gustav Lienert is a set of methods for analyzing all possible value patterns. The involved variables have to be discrete, often dichotomized or trichotomized, to make manageable the number of value patterns to be examined. As with most good ideas, the basic principle is simple and not new (e.g., see Zubin, 1937). Lienert and his coworkers have developed CFA in several ways, and for a basic introduction the reader is referred to Krauth and Lienert (1982) and for a more recent overview to von Eye (1990a). The CFA rationale has also been applied in longitudinal analyses by, for instance, Lienert and zur Oeveste (1985) and von Eye (1990b) and for linking cross-sectional results by, for instance, Lienert and Bergman (1985). In the following discussion, only the basic rationale is presented.

Consider three dichotomous variables, each taking the values 1 or 0. Eight different configurations then exist: 000, 001, 010, 100, 011, 101, 110, 111. For each configuration, the observed frequency is compared with the corresponding expected frequency under some null hypothesis of no relationships in data. The simplest null hypothesis is one of complete independence. An expected frequency is then obtained by multiplying the sample size by all marginal proportions for the values in the specific pattern. An observed frequency is significantly more frequent than the expected one at Level A if, under the null hypothesis, the probability of observing a frequency as large as or larger than the one observed is less than or equal to A. This is called a *type*. An observed frequency that is significantly smaller than the expected one is called an *antitype*. The binomial distribution can be used for calculating these probabilities with the probability parameter equal to the expected frequency for the specific pattern divided by the sample size and the number of trials equal to the sample size.

The generalization is obvious to a different number of categories in the variables and to more than three variables. By cross-tabulation, all configurations at one age can be related to all configurations at another age. Sometimes it is instead useful to categorize change directly—for instance, into positive and negative change—and then subject the categorized change variables to a CFA. One must be careful with disturbances caused by errors of measurement, however, because change scores tend to be much less reliable than ordinary scores (Bergman, 1972; Harris, 1963).

It is obvious that CFA has many resemblances to other techniques for analyzing higher order contingency tables like, for instance, log-linear modeling. Compared with that technique, CFA is a simpler and more explorative method and can be used also in cases with cells containing zeros. If one ignores the special features of CFA with regard to design of configurations and measurement, it can be viewed as a special type of analysis of residuals within a more conventional method. Within the CFA paradigm, methods have been developed for handling a large variety of situations, including repeated measurement designs (von Eye, 1990b; von Eye, Spiel, & Wood, 1996).

Focusing on Specific Aspects of Profiles

Instead of considering the complete value patterns in a pattern analysis, it is possible to focus on specific aspects of the patterns. Two such analyses are mentioned here:

1. *Studying profile extremes:* It could be argued that, for some problems, the most important aspects to study are the two extremes in the subject's profile. Of course, this implies that the different variables are scaled in a commensurable way. The categorization of value profiles into the different possible maximum-minimum combinations may convey important information about the individual's status in the variables under study. For instance, a very frequent maximum-minimum combination tells us that the two involved variables tend to have that relation to each other in the Gestalt where the values in the other variables provide the background.

2. *Studying profile scatter:* Again assuming that the involved variables are scaled in a commensurable way, a basic aspect of an individual's profile is whether it is even or uneven. This can be studied in different ways, and an obvious measure of profile scatter is its variance around the mean of the values in all variables constituting the profile. Certain advantages may exist in using other measures—for instance, city block metric—but the variance has the advantage of being well-known and mathematically easy to handle. This can be important when the variables constituting the profile cannot be assumed to be error-free. Measurement errors create uneven profiles even if all true profiles are even and some estimation of the effects of errors of measurement on profile scatter can be called for.

Computer Programs for Undertaking Pattern-Oriented Analyses With Linking

Many of the above analyses can be accomplished within the major statistical packages with some juggling around. The most extensive package for cluster analysis is the *CLUSTAN* package (Wishart, 1987). The imputation, residue analysis, and cluster analyses suggested earlier can be conveniently accomplished by *SLEIPNER*, which is a new package developed especially for pattern-oriented analyses (Bergman & El-Khouri, 1995). It also contains modules for the exact analysis of single cells in contingency tables and for CFA.

AN ILLUSTRATION OF A PATTERN-ORIENTED ANALYSIS STRATEGY IN ANALYZING INTELLIGENCE DATA

Studying the Development of Intelligence Structure

The structure of intelligence has been extensively studied in a variable-oriented framework, and it is probably fair to say that the results in this field have proved to be quite useful (Carroll, 1993). The nature of the theories and concepts involved and the psychometric characteristics of the measurements that can be obtained make a sophisticated variable-oriented approach a natural choice. Using modern SEM techniques, many contributions have also been given to the understanding of the development of the ability structure (e.g., Härnqvist, Gustafsson, Muthén, & Nelson, 1994). A bit paradoxically, this state of affairs was here considered a good reason for applying a pattern methodology to that area for illustrative and comparative purposes. The clear-cut variable-oriented context would simplify an understanding of the differences in information obtained by the pattern-oriented methodology as compared with that obtained by the ordinary variable-oriented approach. An additional reason was the fact that almost the same sample that was to be used in the pattern analysis had previously been subjected to a variable-oriented SEM analysis using LISREL (Olsson & Bergman, 1977). In that way, comparisons of results between methods would be simplified.

Sample and Variables

The studied sample constituted 402 girls followed longitudinally and having complete data from both age 10 and age 13 in five intelligence-related tests (imputation of one missing value was undertaken for 10 girls). They constitute 80% of a complete school grade cohort, in a Swedish mid-sized town, that was followed from age 10 (taken from the longitudinal research program Individual Development and Adaptation [IDA Project], led by David Magnusson for more than 30 years; Magnusson, 1988). The dropout was largely caused by migration. The same type of test data were collected at both ages and are presented in Table 5.2. Reported split-half reliabilities for the five intelligence-related variables are around .90 (Bergman, 1973). In this presentation, these five variables constituted the value profiles to be studied. In all analyses, z-transformed scores were used (transformed at each age separately).

Identifying a Residue

By using the earlier described RESIDAN rationale, a residue of unclassified girls was removed at age 10 and at age 13 (11 and 10 girls, respectively). These girls were not classified and were instead studied as case histories. These results are not presented here. In addition, in the RELOCATE phase, one girl at age 10 and five girls at age 13 were removed to the residue because they were atypical and did not fit any of the clusters.

Cross-Sectional Results

Classifications

In Figure 5.2, the cluster mean profiles (= centroids) are presented that are based on a cluster analysis of age 10 intelligence and achievement data following the earlier described LICUR procedure. In Figure 5.3, the corresponding results from analyzing age 13 data are given. The age 10 and age 13 cluster analyses explained 72.2% and 76.5%, respectively, of the total error sum of squares. At both ages, the 10-clusters solution was chosen following the four criteria outlined above in the section "Cluster Analysis With Linking." The clusters at age 10 have been numbered according to an ascending overall level of performance; the clusters at age 13 have been matched on a one-to-one basis with those at age 10 according to the similarities of the centroids.

It is seen in Figure 5.2 that, at age 10, three clusters are characterized by centroids below the overall mean in all five variables (#1, #2, #3). Two of these are quite low, with #1 being especially low in V, As, and Am and #2 being especially low in I and S. Two clusters have centroids above the overall mean in all variables (#8 and #10), and #10 is generally very high and #8 is high except in S. A small cluster of 17 girls (#5) is quite low in I and below average in S but above average in the two verbally

TABLE 5.2 Variables

Name	Description
V	Verbal ability (the sum of scores on the tests Similarities and Opposites)
I	Inductive ability (the sum of scores on the tests Letter Groups and Figure Series)
S	Spatial ability (the sum of scores on the tests Cube Counting and Metal Folding)
As	The total sum score on a comprehensive standardized achievement test of Swedish
Am	The total sum score on a comprehensive standardized achievement test in mathematics
SES	Dichotomous variable based on ratings of the educational level of the parent with the highest education (dichotomized at the overall mean). This variable is only used for calculating the results presented in Table 5.6.

oriented tests, indicating a verbal specialization. Cluster #7 is higher in the three nonverbal tests, indicating a nonverbal specialization. This is also true for Cluster #4 but at a lower general level. Clusters #6 and #8 are lower in S but at different general levels.

The cluster structure at age 13 is quite similar to that at age 10 (Figure 5.3). These clusters have been matched with those at age 10 on a one-to-one basis beginning with the two most similar ones and so on. In Figure 5.5, the average squared distances between each age 13 cluster and the corresponding age 10 cluster are given. It is seen that, for most clusters, this distance is quite low (the median is .10), and only for two cluster pairs (#2 at ages 10 and 13; #5 at ages 10 and 13) the distance is moderate. Also for these two pairs, however, the form and general level of the profiles are fairly similar. One gets the impression of a considerable structural stability between the two ages in the typical patterning of the five intelligence-related tests. Whether an individual stability exists is another question, which is addressed in the section "Longitudinal Linking of Cluster Memberships."

Replication of the Classification at Age 13

To study the replication of the cluster solution on another sample, use was made of the fact that data in the same variables

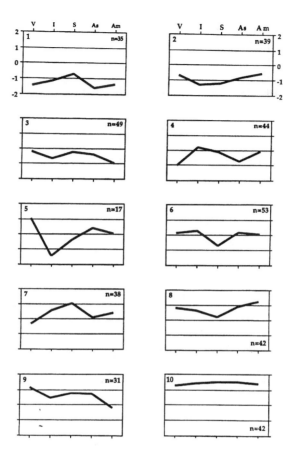

Figure 5.2. Profiles of Cluster Means for the Five Intelligence-Related Variables at Age 10 (z-transformed Scores)
NOTE: $N = 390$, and explained error sum of square = 72.2%.

were available from age 13 for a pilot group (a school grade cohort from the same town as the main group but born 3 years earlier). The pilot group, however, did not contain girls needing special schooling (about 3% of the cohort). The results of the replication are presented in Figure 5.4, and the same LICUR procedure that was applied on the main group was used on the pilot group except that a priori a 10-clusters solution was chosen to simplify comparisons of results. The centroids in the pilot group solution have been matched with those in the main group solution by using the one-to-one matching procedure described above. It is seen that the

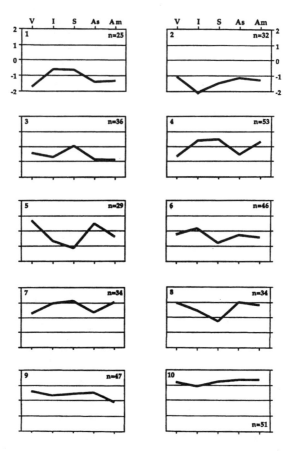

Figure 5.3. Profiles of Cluster Means for the Five Intelligence-Related Variables at Age 13—Replication of Pilot Group Data (z-transformed Scores)
NOTE: $N = 387$, and explained error sum of squares = 76.5%. The average square Euclidean distance from each cluster centroid to the corresponding main group cluster is indicated in the figure.

match is good for almost all clusters. The median of the average squared Euclidean distances of the corresponding centroids is 0.15. The large discrepancy found for #7 in the pilot group is a consequence of the one-to-one matching because that cluster fairly well fitted to #10 in the main group, which, however, already was "occupied" because it even better matched #10 in the pilot group. Because the pilot group is larger and contains more children with a high ability level than the main group, it is not surprising that a

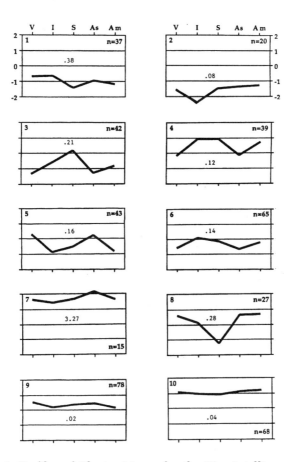

Figure 5.4. Profiles of Cluster Means for the Five Intelligence-Related Variables at Age 13—Replication of Pilot Group Data (z-transformed Scores). NOTE: $N = 434$, and explained error sum of squares = 75.2%. The average square Euclidean distance from each cluster centroid to the corresponding main group cluster is indicated in the figure.

small Cluster #7 with very high performance levels in all tests was found in that analysis. Also, #4 and #7 in the main group have the same form with different general levels, indicating nonverbal specialization, but are in the pilot group solution represented by only one cluster (#4) with the same form and a general level intermediate between that of the corresponding two main group clusters. To summarize, the results seem to indicate a reasonable degree of replicability of the cluster structure.

TABLE 5.3 Summary of Profiles That Came Out as Significant Types in Configural Frequency Analyses of Trichotomized Variables at Ages 10 and 13

Profile					Observed Frequency Age 10	Observed Frequency Age 13	
2	2	2	2	2	40*	41*	
0	0	0	0	0	28*	41*	0 = lowest third
0	0	1	0	0	13*	11*	1 = middle third
2	2	1	2	2	11*	11*	2 = highest third
1	0	0	0	0	12*	8*	
1	2	2	1	2	7	9*	variables in profile:
0	0	0	0	1	8*	2	V I S As Am
The remaining 236 profiles were not significant types, including the profile 1 1 1 1 1							

NOTES: The expected frequencies are between 1.3 and 2.1.
* $p < .05$, using a test based on the binomial distribution and adjusting for that 243 simultaneous tests were performed.

Configurations

In Table 5.3, the main results of configural frequency analyses of the five trichotomized intelligence-related variables are given. Significant pattern types obtained in the age 10 and age 13 analyses are presented. First, it is seen, as expected, that being among the highest third in all five variables or among the lowest third in all five variables are very strong types. The variable S is represented in two pattern types as the highest and the lowest part, respectively.

It is also interesting what does not come out as significant types. One would have expected it to be a significant type to be "normal" (belong to the middle third in all five variables), but this was not the case. Five girls at age 10 and seven girls at age 13 were so characterized. Of course, to some extent, a significant "middle" type found using true scores would be attenuated more by errors of measurement than "low" or "high" types because of the narrower range of true values for the "middle" type increasing the number of persons misclassified on the basis of observed scores containing errors of measurement. Reliabilities of the indicators, however, are very high (probably even higher around the mean), so this explanation appears not to be sufficient. A tentative conclusion is that there is no marked tendency for individuals' intelligence profiles to cluster around the average in all variables. Instead, in the middle range, some kind of specialization may be the norm.

Profile Scatter

Regardless of level, an important aspect of an intelligence profile is how even it is—that is, its degree of *scatter*. Do individuals predominantly have about the same value in all variables that constitute their profile? How common is it that individuals exhibit extreme differences in value levels in different intelligence-related components? For each individual, profile scatter was computed as the variance of the values in the five intelligence-related variables that constituted the profile. Profile scatter was found to be very similar at the two ages, with positively skewed distributions and about 80% being characterized by only a small or a moderate scatter (profile variance < .50). Assuming that classical test theoretical model assumptions hold with reliabilities of 0.9 and that each profile based on true scores is even (variance = 0) would lead to an expected mean scatter of 0.08 to be compared with an obtained mean scatter of 0.36 at age 10 and 0.34 at age 13. Hence, the observed scatter can only to a lesser extent be explained by errors of measurement.

Profile Extremes

It was seen in the previous section that a substantive minority of the children at both ages were characterized by a considerable profile scatter. This naturally leads to an interest in the characteristics of the scatter. For instance, do one or two variables stand out from the rest in the profile in that they most commonly are the maximum or the minimum in the profile? In the cluster analyses, a deviant value in S seemed to stand out in many clusters, and in the configural frequency analysis, two types had a deviant value in S. Considerations like this led to the study of individual profiles focusing on the extremes in the profiles—that is, on the variable with the maximum and the variable with the minimum value in the profile. The 20 possible maximum-minimum combinations are given in Table 5.4, together with their frequencies at ages 10 and 13. Under an independence model, the expected frequency of each max-min combination is 20.1. Twelve of the 20 combinations have

TABLE 5.4 The 20 Possible Profile Combinations According to the Variable With the Maximum and Minimum Value in the Profile and Their Frequencies at Ages 10 and 13

Max-Min Combination	Frequency at Age 10	Frequency at Age 13	Max-Min Combination	Frequency at Age 10	Frequency at Age 13
V max I min	27	23	As max V min	6**	4***
S min	34**	33**	I min	11*	17
As min	6**	6**	S min	21	32**
Am min	22	25	Am min	12	16
I max V min	27	19	Am max V min	22	27
S min	21	19	I min	17	16
As min	19	15	S min	24	17
Am min	14	16	As min	15	11*
S max V min	38**	37***			
I min	18	12			
As min	24	35***			
Am min	24	22			

NOTE: *, **, and *** mean that the observed frequency is significantly higher (lower) than the expected one ($p < .05$, $p < .01$, $p < .001$, respectively) using a chi-square test with one degree of freedom and the expected frequencies 20.1 ($402/20 = 20.1$) and 381.9 ($402 - 20.1 = 381.9$).

S as a maximum or minimum. All combinations being more frequent than expected by chance (all types) are such S combinations (2 combinations at age 10, and 4 combinations at age 13). All other combinations deviating significantly from the expected value include As and are antitypes (3 combinations at each age).

The larger frequency of observed profiles with S as maximum or minimum as compared with the other profile types can be seen in Table 5.4. In fact, the average number of girls with S as maximum in their profile is about 26 at both ages, and with S as minimum, about 25 at both ages. This should be compared with the number of girls characterized by any of the other variables as maximum or minimum in their profile that is on the average 16.4. Without venturing too far into speculation about possible causes of this interesting result, it was decided to do just one extra analysis to relate the profile combinations to the educational level in the home. It was believed possible that spatial ability was more linked to a "practical orientation" than to the other abilities. Some training in spatial ability is achieved by different kinds of handicrafts that are a frequent interest of practically oriented girls, often from lower socioeconomic status (SES) groups. (It must be remembered that these data are fairly old and refer to the 1960s.) If this is the case, we would expect girls with a maximum in S to come more frequently from low-SES homes and girls with a minimum in S to come more frequently from high-SES homes. This was also found at age 13. All four profile combinations with S as a maximum had means below the average in SES, and none of the four profile combinations with S as a minimum had a mean below the average in SES. The probability for this simultaneous finding is roughly .0002 under a random model. The variable-oriented reader might wonder whether this issue could be illuminated by a conventional correlational analysis—for instance, by studying the partial correlation coefficient between S and SES after partialling out the other intelligence factors. Such an analysis gives partial correlation coefficients of –.03 and .01 at Grades 3 and 6, respectively, indicating no relationship, in contrast with the results of the analysis of profile extremes.

Longitudinal Results

Longitudinal Linking of
Cluster Memberships

In Figure 5.5, the clusters of intelligence profiles are related over age. Cluster membership combinations between ages 10 and 13 that are significantly more common than expected by chance are indicated by arrows. To guard against the mass significance fallacy (because 10 tests of stability were performed), a conservative significance level was chosen ($p < .005$). The strongest individual stability was shown by the typical pattern characterizing Cluster #1, being very low in all variables except S (age 10) or except S and I (age 13). It was 5.2 times more common than expected by chance to have this cluster combination. A significant individual longitudinal stability was shown for 8 of the 10 clusters at age 10. Cluster #6 exhibited no significant stream, and Cluster #3 (below average) streamed to Cluster #5 (verbal above, nonverbal below average), indicating a verbal specialization.

Longitudinal Linking of Maximum-
Minimum Profile Combinations

Longitudinal streams of maximum-minimum combinations in profiles were also studied. Ten of the 20 possible max-min profile

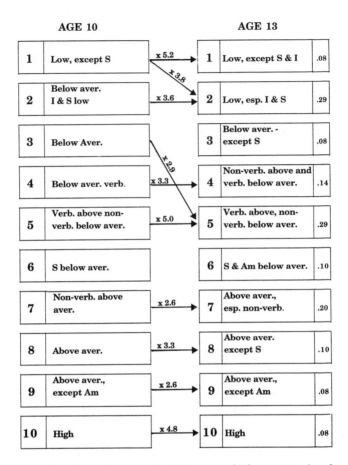

Figure 5.5. Significant Longitudinal Streams of Cluster Membership Between Ages 10 and 13 ($p < .005$). $N = 378$.

combinations exhibited a significant stability, 2 at the 0.1% level (I maximum, S Minimum; and S maximum, V minimum). Apparently, certain maximum-minimum combinations of a profile is a person characteristic exhibiting significant longitudinal stability.

Profile Scatter in a Longitudinal Perspective

It is interesting to relate profile scatter at age 10 to profile scatter at age 13. A significant relationship was found in the expected direction ($r = .35$), and a dense cluster of girls being low scatterers at both ages exists. The observed correlation is a conservative estimate of the corresponding error-free correlation, which can be assumed to be higher. Taking into consideration that the highly skewed distributions of the two scatter variables might make the Pearson correlation misleading, Spearman's rho was also computed. This coefficient was .29, which is slightly lower but still highly significant.

Comparison of the Results With Those Obtained by Structural Equation Modeling

The intelligence data for the main group have been subjected to an ambitious analysis using structural equation modeling (Olsson & Bergman, 1977). This analysis focused on the development of intelligence structure, with special reference to Garrett's (1946) theory of age differentiation in ability structure. In the SEM study, LISREL was used on eight variables from each age (the difference to the main group data set used in the pattern-oriented analyses being that the two tests of each of the V, I, and S components were used as separate variables). The sample comprised 375 girls, with those not having data from both ages and those attending special schooling excluded. Hence, the sample was very similar but not identical to the one used for the pattern analysis. The following longitudinal factor model fitted the data:

1. Four correlated factors were found at each age (a verbal, an inductive, a spatial, and a knowledge factor that related to As and Am; As was in the model also related to the verbal factor, and Am also related to the spatial factor)
2. The structural relationships over time were restricted to each factor at age 10 being related to the same factor at age 13.

The reader interested in scrutinizing the results obtained by using SEM is referred to the above-mentioned article by Olsson and Bergman (1977). Many similarities are found between the substantive interpretations of the results obtained by these two very different approaches, and these are summarized in Table 5.5. It is seen that similarities are found with regard to (a) structural stability and change and (b) individual stability and change.

However, quite a few differences also appeared (see Table 5.6). These were not mainly discrepant results, but rather an expression of the fact that results relevant to certain findings were only obtained by one or the other method.

TABLE 5.5 Similarities Between the Results Concerning
Intelligence Structure Obtained by Using SEM
and a Pattern-Oriented Approach

Finding	Result in SEM Analysis	Result in Pattern-Oriented Analysis
Very similar intelligence structures were obtained at the two ages.	Approximately the same factors emerged with similar factor correlations at both ages.	Approximately the same clusters emerged at both ages.
The accountability of the data by the structure identified increased with age.	The factors explained more of the variance of the response variates at age 13 than at age 10.	The explained error sum of squares was higher at age 13 than at age 10.
Girls being characterized by a certain intelligence status at age 10 tended to retain this status at age 13. Knowledge, as measured by the achievement tests, was at age 10, but not at age 13, almost inseparable from inductive ability.	A very strong relation exists between the corresponding factors between ages 10 and 13. The correlation between the inductive factor and the knowledge factor was .93 at age 10 and .79 at age 13.	For 8 of 10 clusters, a significant longitudinal stability was found. Seven of 10 clusters at age 10 were fairly similar in I, As, and Am; at age 13, this was the case for 5 of 10.

The overall conclusion is that the interpretations reached with
these two very different approaches were similar in many ways
with regard to the substantive issues that could be studied by both
methods. It should be noted that the verbal explications of findings
given in Tables 5.5 and 5.6 are, to a certain extent, ambiguous and
not precisely defined for the obvious reason that words alone
almost never can be exact. These results highlight the method
dependence of more precise interpretations of findings.

∞ DISCUSSION

As an illustration of a pattern-oriented methodological approach, the intelligence structure and its change were studied in a
longitudinal sample of about 400 girls (studied at age 10 and again
at age 13). In most analyses, the basic unit of analysis was the girls'
profiles in five intelligence-related variables at each of the two
measurement occasions. In the main analysis, using the LICUR
procedure, first the girls were classified at each age by using cluster

TABLE 5.6 Discrepancies Between the Results Concerning
Intelligence Structure Obtained by Using SEM and a
Pattern-Oriented Approach

Finding	Result in SEM Analysis	Result in Pattern-Oriented Analysis
Identification of knowledge, verbal, inductive, and spatial dimensions.	Identified as correlated factors at both ages.	Not studied because only composite intelligence tests were used (to minimize disturbances of errors of measurement).
Identification of typical intelligence patterns and their evolvement.	Not possible to see in model.	Classifications at each age and longitudinal streams between clusters.
The distinctive role of spatial intelligence.	Not seen in model.	More frequently maximum or minimum in individual profiles.
Being consistently "normal" in intelligence status is not typical.	Not possible to see in model.	Belonging to the "middle third" throughout is not a significant type, and no cluster was found being average in all variables.
The different intelligence dimensions can be described as developing independently.	In the model, the factor at age 13 only depended on the corresponding factor at age 10.	Not possible to see in the model.

analysis. Then, the classifications were linked to highlight typical
streams of cluster memberships. As was pointed out in the previous section, the main findings had many similarities to those
obtained by using a totally different variable-oriented approach
(SEM) on approximately the same data. For instance, in both
cases, the intelligence structures at the two ages were very similar, the accountability of the data by the structure identified increased with age, and girls having a certain intelligence status at
age 10 tended to retain this status at age 13. Differences in the
findings produced by the two approaches had largely to do with
their different perspectives: Certain aspects of reality could only
be seen by using one of the two perspectives. For instance, for
obvious reasons, findings pertaining to latent intelligence dimensions were only obtained by using SEM, and findings relating to
intelligence as a Gestalt were only seen by using the pattern
approach.

Let us look at some findings seen only by the pattern approach:

1. Typical intelligence patterns at the two ages and their corresponding longitudinal streams were identified. This is a main result produced by the chosen pattern-oriented approach.

2. It was not typical for a subject to be "normal" in intelligence throughout. From a theoretical perspective of adjustment to the norm and from the high intercorrelations of the different intelligence variables, one might have expected the contrary. This simple result from the pattern analysis instead points out not only that, in the middle range, specialization in some form is the norm but that being throughout "normal" is not even significantly more frequent than expected by chance if all the intelligence variables were independent.

3. Spatial ability appeared to have a separate role in describing a subject's intelligence status. This is seen, for instance, in profiles with spatial ability as the maximum or minimum value being much more frequent than profiles with maximum and minimum values in the other variables. In principle, in a general sense, this finding might be detectable by using a variable-oriented approach, but it was not obvious in the current data set when studying factor correlations within the SEM model (spatial ability was not consistently less correlated with the other factors than they were among themselves). However, spatial ability did have higher unique variances than verbal ability or the knowledge factor (but not higher unique variances than inductive ability).

It has been pointed out to me that using a more modern SEM analysis involving a hierarchical model would have been preferable to the longitudinal model with correlated factors that was used. There are two reasons for not doing this: (a) Although the SEM analysis presented here was published already in 1977, the LISREL method used is not out of date, and a nicely interpretable, simple, longitudinal model was obtained that fit the data well; and (b) if a new SEM analysis were undertaken, it would demand more space than is available in this chapter to present the results in sufficient detail. The researcher who questions whether the conclusions reached here are valid to other types of SEM modeling is encouraged to undertake such a reanalysis. The correlation matrix is omitted here because of lack of space but is available in the original report and can be obtained from the author.

The above discussion of the unique findings produced by a pattern approach should, of course, not be seen as a plea for throwing out variable-oriented methods when studying intelligence development. In this area, the use of variable-oriented methods like SEM are valuable because there exist psychometrically sound measurements, a reasonable grasp of the dimensions involved (believed to be essentially continuous and normally distributed), and an extensive theory building based on variables. The properties of sophisticated variable-oriented methods for model testing that can take measurement errors into account are also highly useful. But, I hope, the empirical illustration has shown that a pattern-oriented approach can provide a wealth of interesting new information, some of which, once found, can be targeted in specially designed variable-oriented analyses. In other areas where strong higher order interactions can be expected and where the theoretical focus is person oriented, not variable oriented, the roles of the two kinds of methodological approaches might well be reversed, with basic exploratory variable-oriented analyses being followed by pattern-oriented analyses.

Genuinely longitudinal pattern analyses are potentially attractive but, as discussed above in the section "Analyzing Longitudinal Patterns," may contain problems with resulting heterogeneous classifications and also weighting problems caused by possibly varying sizes of time differences if more than two measurement occasions are involved (e.g., if the same number of variables are available from all measurement occasions but two of these occasions are close in time, then the status during that time period would obtain a larger weight in deciding the cluster structure than the statuses at the other measurement occasions). Time also is sometimes not best conceived as linear in relation to chronological age; see, for instance, Stattin and Magnusson (1990) for a discussion of the importance of biological age. For further discussion of longitudinal pattern analysis, the reader is referred back to the section "Analyzing Longitudinal Patterns." For another perspective, see also Block (1971).

Within the framework of studying individuals as dynamic systems in an interactional paradigm, Bergman (1995) stressed the usefulness of the concept of *i-state*, which he defined as a specific subject's value profile at a specific point in time. From a dynamic system perspective, he is developing two types of longitudinal pattern analysis:

1. *I-state sequence analysis (ISSA)*, in which an a priori taxonomy of theoretically expected common types of individuals' developmental i-state sequences is used to structure the data set, and then,

within each set, it is looked at for typical developmental sequences (Bergman, 1995a).

2. *I-states as objects analysis (ISOA)*, in which each i-state is considered a subindividual and then subjected to classification analysis (Bergman, 1995b).

Under certain assumptions, these methods can be considerably more powerful and can extract more information than conventional methods, especially when small samples and many measurement occasions are involved. ISSA and ISOA share one important limitation: It must be assumed possible to measure the (dis)similarity between i-states pertaining to different measurement occasions. Studies covering time periods with dramatic developmental changes and where the measured variables cannot be assumed to measure "the same thing" at different measurement occasions are not suited for this type of analysis. The methods are also truly longitudinal without many of the weaknesses of the earlier described "all-in-the-pot" method, which simply classifies subjects in one step on the basis of all information from all points in time. ISSA and ISOA, however, are just beginning to be developed and cannot yet be properly evaluated.

Here one pattern-oriented methodological approach has been expounded: descriptive cross-sectional analysis followed by linking. The main procedure presented for accomplishing this was LICUR, which is a basic method and fairly generally applicable. It can be used when only limited information is obtained from each subject at just a few points in time, and it works also in cases when dramatic developmental shifts occur: There is no need for the same variables to be studied at the different points in time. The method is fairly robust, and the principle of measuring cross-sectionally is consistent with a system-state thinking with snapshots taken in continuous time. It can be used as a purely descriptive method but also for hypothesis testing. Examples of its use are given by Bergman and Magnusson (1987, 1991) and Gustafson and Magnusson (1991).

In the cluster analysis strategy suggested here (LICUR), the following two key assumptions are involved:

1. The variable profile under study adequately summarizes the information Gestalt in which one is interested. This is a crucial assumption because method studies show that even exchanging just one variable in a profile can radically change the resulting classification (e.g., Milligan, 1981a). In a pattern analysis, the question of what variables to include tends to be more crucial than

in a variable-oriented analysis. Changing just one variable in a profile changes the whole Gestalt, which is the basic unit of analysis. Changing one variable in a variable-oriented analysis usually only changes some aspects of the results obtained.

2. The values in the different variables are commensurable, and the similarity between two subjects' profiles is adequately reflected by the average squared Euclidean distance.

Certain technical details are important to remember in obtaining trustworthy results from a cluster analysis: (a) the choice of a sound clustering algorithm, (b) the inclusion of only variables with a reasonably high reliability, (c) the inclusion of only a limited number of variables in the profile if the analysis aims at finding homogenous clusters, and (d) a readiness, if necessary, to retreat from the demand of classifying everybody. Sometimes cluster analysis is criticized because different algorithms produce partly different classifications of the same data. This criticism appears to be misplaced for two reasons: (a) If proper attention is paid to the demands of a high-quality analysis and the specific aspects of the classification that is at focus, large differences in results are rare between different but trustworthy clustering algorithms (see also Morey et al., 1983); and (b) considering that different clustering algorithms focus on different aspects of a classification, a moderate difference in the resulting classification is no more surprising and alarming than the observation of a moderate difference between the arithmetic mean and the median computed on the same data. Nevertheless, as in other areas, it is extremely helpful to undertake cross-validation and replication studies, especially in cases when errors of measurement can be suspected to influence the results because the cluster analysis model does not take errors into account.

In the clustering method presentation given in this chapter, it is stressed that an important aim is to obtain homogenous clusters and to take both profile level and form into account. Homogenous clusters tend to be related to "natural" clusters, but they are in no way equivalent. Hence, in the specific situation, a researcher can have a definition of what is meant by a "natural" cluster, which puts less emphasis on homogenous clusters than we do here. Ward's method is then usually not the best method. Also, the use of the explained error sum of squares in deciding the number of clusters might be suboptimal in this case. For instance, it has been shown that cluster recovery in relation to an external criterion classification of "natural clusters" tends to increase when more dimensions are added to the description of each object (Milligan & Cooper, 1985). This is to be expected because a larger number of dimensions often contains more information as to the clustering in the data. Usually, however, a larger number of dimensions leads to more heterogeneous clusters as described by the error sum of squares within clusters. On the basis of cluster homogeneity, one might then erroneously judge a classification based on many dimensions as inferior to one based on fewer dimensions, which illustrates the danger of taking the two thirds rule of thumb too seriously. Note that the other LICUR-stopping rules might still work reasonably well in this case too.

The descriptive orientation of the methods suggested here is obvious, although certain possibilities exist for hypothesis testing also within this methodological framework. Without denying the obvious power of formulating and testing comprehensive statistical models, the usefulness of a more descriptive approach deserves to be defended. In the initial stages in a complex field, careful open-minded observation is paramount. Guidance in what to look for according to existing theories is, of course, important, but theories prematurely transformed into statistical models of data can turn into blinkers. If the model window opens at the wrong place, the interesting things may not be seen. This point has been made again and again by, among others, Cronbach (1975), Greenwald, Pratkanis, Lieppe, and Baumgardner (1986), and Magnusson (1992). When applying a pattern-oriented approach in a complex developmental setting, one is often at this initial stage. As such a field matures, a possible sequence of analyses could be (a) preliminary simple variable-oriented analyses to identify operating factors and to lay the foundation for the formulation of relevant patterns; (b) descriptive pattern-oriented analyses; (c) model-based pattern analyses for testing person-oriented theories; and (d) testing important results within a model-based, variable-oriented framework striving for a reconciliation of theories and results between these two approaches.

It was mentioned in the introduction that sometimes reality may not be continuous but rather operate to produce more or less discrete types. Or differently put: Only certain configurations of system states are in some way optimal and become stable and often observed. Arguments for this are given by, for instance, Kagan (1994) when discussing the emergence of temperamental types. It could be argued that, from this perspective and within a person-oriented framework, pattern-oriented methods like the ones presented here may be more natural than variable-oriented methods in certain settings. A typological approach, however, has been criticized by, for instance, Ekman (1951, 1952) as giving an over-simplified representation of the available information as compared with that given by what he called a *dimensional system of reference.* This can constitute a serious problem if the typological information is created directly, for instance, by a clinical observer as in the old typologies, but it does not constitute a serious problem in modern pattern-oriented analysis based on dimensional data. In this latter case, the truthfulness of a representation of the multivariate data by a classification can be measured, and other methods can also be applied for comparative purposes.

It is important that a person-oriented theoretical approach to the study of individual development is not mixed up with a pattern-oriented methodological approach (of which LICUR is one example). Although in many cases it is natural within a holistic orientation to use pattern-oriented methods, variable-oriented methods can be appropriate too, depending on the specific purpose. The variable is also a versatile tool: Out of pattern-oriented results, new variables can be constructed, building on these results (e.g., the presence or absence of a specific typical pattern is transformed into a dichotomous variable). Despite this, it is probably fair to say that there has been an overemphasis on using variable-oriented methods also for conducting person-oriented research in development, as exemplified by the attention given to this approach in a recent review concerning personality development in social context by Hartup and van Lieshout (1995). In addition, when they discuss pattern-oriented methods in this context, they have a very narrow perspective, concentrating on studies of *ipsative stability*—that is, the relative rank ordering among different behavioral characteristics occurring within a person across repeated measurements. The typology approach to personality development, wherein individuals are classified according to their patterns of relevant personality characteristics, is hardly mentioned. In my opinion, their article illustrates the overdominance of the variable-dimensional paradigm over the person-categorical paradigm in research on personality development, a dominance that made Carlsson (1971) lament, "Where is the person in personality research?" (p. 217)

The main conclusion of this chapter is that the pattern-oriented approach advocated here—using modern statistical methods and in proper balance with other approaches—brings back into developmental psychology a powerful set of tools for understanding the person as she or he really is and not just as correlations in a statistical model. I hope that the methods presented here contribute to some extent to this end.

∞⌇∞

COMMENTS ON CHAPTER 5

Lars Bergman describes his chapter as "a toolbox" for basic analysis of pattern-oriented approaches to studying individual development. However, the "box," if we accept his label, comes with a kit of perspectives, critique, and advice of an expert. On methods of investigating complex behavior, Lars Bergman is an advocate of a pattern-oriented approach, especially using cluster techniques, but at the same time he gives credits to both variable-oriented and pattern-oriented approaches.

He weighs the two approaches in relation to research purposes: When the structure of the individual is the information wanted, a pattern orientation is natural. In initial stages in a complex field, variable-oriented analyses can identify operating factors and lay the foundation for the formulation of relevant patterns, to be followed by descriptive-pattern-oriented analyses. In reverse, a pattern-oriented approach can provide new information, some of which can then be pursued in variable-oriented analyses. Certainly, we should not expect one approach to replace the other or expect to learn precisely the same information from each method. As Lars Bergman points out, the important message for research is to move back and forth between levels (types) of analysis strategies.

The empirical example of descriptive cluster analysis that Lars Bergman has chosen (the structure of intelligence) is didactically very effective. Would that all of the phenomena in behavioral research were so well classified and ordered as intelligence test data. But many are not—as examples, family stress as a risk for children, or a child's developing psychopathology. Cluster analysis is more challenged by these kinds of data.

Lars Bergman defends cross-sectional cluster analysis of longitudinal data, but he also expresses unrest regarding issues involved in "genuine" longitudinal analyses. He is undoubtedly the frontiersman for further development of longitudinal analytic methods. Where the ultimate goal is to understand the developing individual, these are necessary tools. We anticipate that Lars Bergman will add them to his toolbox.

Marian Radke-Yarrow

~ 6 ~

The Individual in Context

Joan Stevenson-Hinde

Sub-Department of Animal Behaviour
University of Cambridge

*W*hile pursuing various methods for considering the individual as the focus in developmental research, we must not lose sight of the fact that, in real life, an individual behaves within a social context—involving social relationships against a background of culture. Indeed, from a systems perspective, the individual is never a separate entity, but is always part of a whole. Such integration may be conceptualized as a continuous cycle of mutual influences operating through time:

This carries the implication that "the individual" is not fixed, but rather one who may take on different characteristics in different contexts (Hinde, 1987, 1997). Thus, to understand and predict the behavior of an individual over time and over different situations, identifying "context" is crucial.

123

On an *evolutionary time scale*, it is evident that behavior patterns must have evolved within particular contexts: fearful behavior—when in unfamiliar or challenging situations; fearful or aggressive behavior or both—when threatened; fearful, aggressive, or sexual behavior—when warding off rivals and attracting a potential mate. Therefore, if one is focusing on a particular individual characteristic—for example, fearfulness—there is no evolutionary reason why an individual's observed behavior should appear consistent across different motivational settings, such as those indicated. Even if a "tendency to withdraw" were postulated to be consistent across these situations, interactions with a "tendency to approach" in such different motivational contexts could produce inconsistent behavioral outcomes.

Nevertheless, within *an individual's lifetime*, learning may operate to make behavior *more* consistent across contexts, particularly if others expect one to behave in a consistent manner. That is, if an individual behaves fearfully, sees herself as behaving fearfully, perceives that others see her as fearful, and if others indeed treat her accordingly, she may become more apt to behave fearfully across contexts, thereby maintaining the integrity of the "self-system" (e.g., Backman, 1988; Hinde, 1997; Snyder, 1984). This is different from, but not incompatible with, a social learning theorist's view of effects of learning—to make individuals potentially *less* consistent across contexts. Both processes could be operating.

One aspect of fearfulness—the "concept of approach versus withdrawal when faced with novel and challenging events" (Kagan, 1989, p. 2)—has been recognized in all current major theories of childhood temperament (e.g., see Goldsmith et al., 1987; Kohnstamm, Bates, & Rothbart, 1989). In addition, initial approach/withdrawal has been studied directly, rather than solely by temperament questionnaires, at both the behavioral and physiological levels, from infancy through childhood (e.g., Kagan, 1994; Reznick, 1989; Rubin & Asendorpf, 1993). Various indexes of inhibition "are among the most stable and heritable in contemporary psychology" (Kagan, 1989, p. 3). The Harvard studies suggest that although not many people are either restrained or outgoing in every context, about 10% to 15% of the population lie consistently in one category or another across contexts (Kagan, 1989). Perhaps one reason—among others (see Kagan, 1994)—for the robustness of this characteristic is that context is incorporated into both its definition and subsequent assessments. With most individual characteristics—such as those within the temperament framework of Thomas and Chess (1977)—context is either unspecified (e.g., the "mood" dimension) or covers a huge range of situations (e.g., the "activity" dimension). Only "initial approach/withdrawal" and the related temperamental characteristic "adaptability" are context-specific, in that they are defined in terms of a "response to a new stimulus." Making other characteristics similarly context-specific would tighten one's concepts, as well as permit the following strategy, which is well suited to tracking individuals.

With inhibition, one may target context—to specify small groups within larger samples and to identify individuals with unique developmental profiles (Kagan et al., this volume, Chap. 4). The following examples from the Harvard group and our own group recommend a strategy involving (a) sample selection for extremes, based on behavior in more than one context; and (b) categorical analyses—to understand real, as opposed to statistical, individuals.

∞ THE INDIVIDUAL IN UNFAMILIAR CONTEXTS

A Dimensional Approach

Although an "unfamiliar" context is part of the definition of inhibition, variation may occur—in both "setting"—whether a "natural" or laboratory setting, whether mother present or absent, and so forth—and "stimuli"—characteristics of an unfamiliar person, animal, object, and so forth. With normative samples, consistency across these unfamiliar contexts is not high, even allowing for some measurement error.

For example, within the same laboratory setting with mother present, the correlation between fear of strange room and fear of stranger was .39; and between fear of stranger and fear of strange animals (two Mongolian gerbils), $r = .24$ (for our normative sample at 2.5 years: $N = 82$). When fear of stranger *within* the lab was compared with fear of stranger rated by mothers in settings *outside* the lab, the correlation was higher than any of the others at 2.5 years: $r = .44$ (Stevenson-Hinde, 1989), and this consistency decreased with age: $r = .35$ at 4.5 years ($N = 80$) and $r = .28$ at 7 years ($N = 70$; Stevenson-Hinde & Shouldice, 1995). Such a decrease from 2.5 to 4.5 to 7 years is consistent with Kagan's view that a female stranger becomes a less salient threat stimulus with age.

However, the high correlations across contexts obtained with our *selected* sample at 4.5 years (described below) suggests that a stranger does remain a salient stimulus for inhibited children. Here, consistency across settings was higher than for any of the age points in the normative sample (Table 6.1). Not only were different contexts involved—playgroup, laboratory, and situations described in parental temperament questionnaires—but different instruments and observers were involved as well.

In contrast, with *normative* samples over a very broad range of contexts, intercorrelations between indexes of inhibition may be nonsignificant, and sometimes even negative. For example, intercorrelations ranged from .45 to near zero (.04) to −.31 for indexes of peer play inhibition, laboratory inhibition, school inhibition, risk avoidance, and low frequency of looking at an examiner (Reznick et al., 1986). The low intercorrelations may be a result of at least two factors: (a) The different contexts may involve different degrees of "threat" for any particular child, and (b) they may also involve different degrees of positive, "nonthreatening" stimuli—as with peer play—eliciting approach as well as withdrawal. To the extent that contexts differ in nonthreatening ways, outcome measures of inhibition would be less consistent than if any tendency to approach were held constant.

Indeed, a behavior systems approach would predict that, in contexts such as the above, multiple systems *should* be involved: fear, affiliation, exploration, and even attachment. "Thus, there seem to be good theoretical reasons for distinguishing affiliative/ sociability constructs from those relating to fearfulness, though in practice interactions between behavioral systems mean that our behavioral measures are rarely pure reflections of one particular construct" (Stevenson-Hinde, 1989, p. 131; see also Kagan, 1989; Rothbart, 1989; Stevenson-Hinde & Shouldice, 1993). With this view, the consistency that is found across different unfamiliar contexts is remarkable. Lack of consistency may be understood in terms of different implications of context for different behavior systems.

A Categorical Approach

By dividing a dimension into categories, one may go on to identify those individuals who are consistently high or consistently low across contexts, mildly consistent, or inconsistent. This provides a more meaningful measure of individual differences

TABLE 6.1 Behavioral Inhibition Across Contexts, in the Selected Sample at 4.5 Years: A Dimensional Approach

	Mother	Father	Teacher
Natural contexts by Mother (TABC[1])	—		
Natural contexts by Father (TABC[1])	.86	—	
Playgroup by Teacher (EAS[2])	.73	.62	—
Lab—meeting stranger by observer (ratings from video)	.54	.50	.52

NOTE: Pearson coefficients: all at $p < .001$, two-tailed ($N = 119$–126).
1. Martin (1988).
2. Buss and Plomin (1984).
(Temperament questionnaires; for details, see Stevenson-Hinde & Glover, 1996).

than does averaging dimensional measures across contexts, when a highly inconsistent individual might misleadingly be assigned an "average" score.

To obtain our selected sample, children were selected as "shy" or "not shy" on meeting strangers in naturally occurring contexts. That is, they were initially screened into the sample according to cut-offs on a maternal questionnaire concerning initial approach/ withdrawal to unfamiliar people, which then had to be supported by an interviewer's observations and ratings made during her first home visit—both on initial arrival and after about 45 minutes, when the interviewer invited the child to come and sit by her for a story. This screening, by mother and then interviewer, was according to fixed criteria, rather than a cut-off based on a certain proportion of those sampled. This has the advantage of being less sample-dependent and less arbitrary: We know that the shy children were showing extreme withdrawal. Whereas the children screened as shy had to be extreme, the matched not shy children were allowed to be average-for-age or below to avoid getting children with problems in the other direction (see Stevenson-Hinde & Glover, 1996, for further details).

After the above screening, each child visited the laboratory where responses (both verbal and nonverbal) to another female stranger were rated on a behavioral inhibition scale, ranging from 1 (*extremely low*) to 4 (*norm for age*) to 9 (*extremely high*). When this scale was broken into categories—low (1-3), medium (4-6), and high (7-9)—individuals could be identified across contexts (see

Table 6.2). Nearly half the children (54 out of 126: 43%) were consistent—either low shy in both natural situations and the laboratory or high shy in both contexts. In contrast, only 9 (7%) were inconsistent across contexts—high shy in one but low shy in the other. These percentages indicated greater consistency than a dimensional approach with the same sample, in which correlations with the laboratory ratings ranged from .50 to .54 (Table 6.1). When the correlations listed in Table 6.1 were calculated separately for boys and girls, no gender differences emerged, with three correlations higher for girls and three for boys. A gender difference is suggested, however, by the categorical approach (Table 6.2). Whereas 58% of girls categorized as high in natural contexts remained high in the laboratory context, only 24% of boys did so, with 60% moving into the medium category—a possible reflection of social pressure on boys to not appear shy when tested.

Thus, a categorical approach provides a result that is more impressive, as well as more precise, in terms of suggesting gender differences obscured by correlations. In further analyses, the consistently high shy boys and girls differed significantly from the medium and low shy children on several variables, including negative mood, worries and fears, and behavior problems in preschool (Stevenson-Hinde & Glover, 1996).

An Individual Approach

The categorical approach highlighted an unsuspected handful of individuals: six "inconsistent" boys (Table 6.2). Unlike the three inconsistent girls, the boys were inconsistent in only one direction: high shy in natural settings but low shy in the laboratory. In comparison with the other three groups of boys—consistently low, medium shy (lab ratings of 4-6 and either low or high shy at home) and consistently high shy—the behavior of the inconsistent boys never differed significantly from, and indeed resembled, that of the consistently high shy boys—including negative mood, worries and fears, and the highest levels of problem behavior in playgroup. All six inconsistent boys had problems stemming from birth: three were cesarean births, surrounded with anxiety (e.g., previous miscarriages, slow to breathe); one was a traumatic delivery (facially presented) with subsequent speech problems (and a tendency to "bark" at strangers when greeted by them); and two had early-appearing neurological problems, including suspected cerebral palsy, which is not now apparent (Stevenson-Hinde & Glover,

TABLE 6.2 Behavioral Inhibition Across Contexts, in the Selected Sample at 4.5 Years: A Categorical Approach

	Laboratory Context					
	(Rating scale, with 4 as "norm" for age)					
	Girls *(n = 68)*			Boys *(n = 58)*		
Natural Contexts[1]	*Low (1-3)*	*Medium (4-6)*	*High (7-9)*	*Low (1-3)*	*Medium (4-6)*	*High (7-9)*
Low	**10** (40%)	13 (52%)	*2* (8%)	**10** (48%)	11 (52%)	*0*
High	*1* (2%)	17 (40%)	**25** (58%)	*6* (16%)	22 (60%)	**9** (24%)

NOTES: **Bold type:** Number of individuals who were consistent across contexts.
Italics: Number of individuals who were inconsistent across contexts.
(%): Percentage of girls (or boys) who were Low, Medium, or High in the laboratory context, relative to the total number of girls (or boys) who were either Low or High in natural contexts.
1. Temperament ratings by mother and interviewer assessments; see Stevenson-Hinde and Glover (1996; screening criteria).

1996). These findings suggest that these boys were qualitatively different from the other boys. Had their shyness ratings at home and in the lab been averaged, they would have received an average rating; had only laboratory observations been used, the boys would have received a low rating. In either case, their negative behavior would have clouded the clear differences found between the low, medium, and high groups when these inconsistent children were excluded.

THE INDIVIDUAL WITHIN THE CONTEXT OF CLOSE RELATIONSHIPS

If a child's shyness is seen as influencing and being influenced by close relationships, then one would expect associations to be found between shyness and mother-child interactions. Here again, however, interpretations depend crucially on whether the sample contains a sufficient number of highly shy children and whether shyness is treated dimensionally or categorically. Parallels between selected and normative samples occur if one considers that most high scorers in a normative sample would probably fall into the medium shy group of our selected sample (ratings of 4—the "norm" for age—up to 6, on a 9-point scale). Thus, previous studies that found positive associations with shyness in girls should not be taken to imply that this holds for the category of extreme shyness— assessed by meaningful scale cut-offs, rather than by reference to a proportion of a "normal" sample.

For example, in our normative sample, we had found that a dimension of shyness was correlated with more positive maternal interactions with girls, but with fewer positive or negative maternal interactions with boys (e.g., Stevenson-Hinde & Hinde, 1986; see also Radke-Yarrow et al., 1988). However, this result was reflected by the medium shy children of the selected sample; that is, the medium shy girls received the most positive interactions from mothers on a family drawing task, significantly higher than either the medium shy boys or the high shy girls. Indeed, on a summary index of sensitive/positive maternal style at home, mothers of high shy girls were lowest, and significantly lower than all other groups, except the six inconsistent boys (Stevenson-Hinde & Glover, 1996). Thus, extreme shyness in girls was not associated with positive maternal interactions.

Although boys in general and high shy boys in particular had the highest problem behavior scores in preschool (including acting-out behavior), their mothers were rated highest on the summary index of sensitive/positive maternal style at home, significantly more than for the high shy girls. Thus, extreme shyness in boys was associated with positive maternal interactions, something not apparent with the normative sample.

∞ THE INDIVIDUAL WITHIN THE CONTEXT OF CULTURE

"A lot of people say that she should have been the boy, and her brother the girl. He's the little shy one" (from an interview with a mother of two children). Across many cultures, being shy is viewed as a feminine trait rather than a masculine one, such as being aggressive (Williams & Best, 1982). This suggests that cultural influences may be operating to exacerbate any initial biological predispositions, as indicated in the initial diagram of circular influences among individual, relationship, and culture.

In two independent samples—one unselected and one selected for extreme shyness—we have seen that *moderate* degrees of shyness on meeting a stranger are accompanied by positive family interactions for girls but not for boys (Stevenson-Hinde & Glover, 1996; Stevenson-Hinde & Hinde, 1986). In the Harvard studies, although it was rare for a child to move from the uninhibited to the inhibited category of behavioral inhibition, those who did so were "typically girls from working-class families. . . . The interview with these mothers suggested they wanted a more cautious child and encouraged such a profile" (Kagan, Reznick, & Snidman, 1987, p. 1462). In a different selected sample, whereas 20% of low reactive girls at 14 months became temporarily timid and fearful at 21 months, only 6% of boys did so (Kagan et al., this volume, Chap. 4). Such results support our everyday experience that, in our culture at least, shyness—provided it is not too extreme—is more acceptable in girls than in boys. Because most of us carry out research in only one cultural context, it is easy to overlook the influence of the context of culture on the development of behavior patterns and individual characteristics.

Culture may also influence what children worry about. With our normative sample at 7 years ($N = 70$), a puppet interview revealed worries in 70% of the sample, with the rest not naming any worries even when pressed (Stevenson-Hinde & Shouldice, 1995). Whereas mostly girls (14 girls, 1 boy) expressed worries about family members (e.g., "When Mum's ill"; "Mum and Dad"), mostly boys (10 boys, 3 girls) expressed worries about performance (e.g., "Going to the fair"; "Football"). Interestingly, this brings us full circle, in that a postulated cultural influence is not incompatible with biological theorizing about sex roles and adaptations to the environment in which we evolved (reviewed in Hinde, 1997).

A dynamic view of culture and individuals, not unlike the dynamic view of a family systems theorist, is proposed by Rogoff (e.g., 1996). She pursues a sociocultural perspective on development, with changes residing neither exclusively in individuals nor exclusively in environments. Instead, the individual is part of a continuous process, with development being a product of individual involvement in sociocultural activity.

CONCLUSION

Using behavioral inhibition as an exemplifier, we have argued that identification of *context* is crucial for assessment of one's construct and for subsequent analyses. Samples selected to contain children who remain extreme over more than one context produce results that go beyond those of unselected, normative samples. Categorical analyses that place individuals into meaningful, context-related categories may highlight different types of individuals, including those who are exceptional. Finally, the individual must be seen not as an isolated entity, but as part of a dynamic whole, involving the broader context of social relationships and culture.

∞ひ∞

COMMENTS ON CHAPTER 6

Joan Stevenson-Hinde's chapter on behavior in context identifies several issues that are at the heart of measurement of complex behavior. They are matters regarding the choice of samples of behavior to represent a concept, and the decisions of how to represent the individual in measurement. Both have major consequences for the operation and findings of research.

Consider first the selection of measurement situations. How explicit are we as investigators about our behavior samples? How much attention is given to other behavior systems that may be operating in the situations that we have chosen to measure a particular behavior system?

Suppose we want to assess children's altruism. For present purposes, our concept is narrowed to overt helping of someone in pain or distress. This leaves a range of possible contexts, and we want a range in order to measure the generality of the child's altruism: A child falls off the climbing bars on the playground. A woman is knocked down by a purse-snatcher. Mother suffers a severe burn when coffee is spilled on her hand. Although each situation is relevant to the child's inclination to help, it is easy to speculate about other systems that may also be activated, and differently, in each of the three situations. Conclusions concerning the generality of children's altruism, about the relation of altruism to children's temperament characteristics or to developmental stage are all likely to be influenced in unknown ways by the contexts. Findings begin to sound fragile. Therefore, Joan Stevenson-Hinde's plea for careful, theory-based samples of behavior and for the referencing of research findings to behavior in context is very much in order.

The second issue in Joan Stevenson-Hinde's chapter has echoes in several other chapters in this volume: Extreme children provide important information, and often distinctly different information from the "average." Her example of research conclusions regarding parents' evaluations of shyness in girls and boys, based in one instance on data from dimensional scores and in another instance on categorical scores, is convincing evidence. We need a caution, of course: The winner-take-all classification of extremes discards much information about most of the children. We have no reason to give up one approach for the other. In fact, from the comparison of the findings from the dimensional and categorical measures of shyness, we learn most about parents' evaluation of shy behavior.

Joan Stevenson-Hinde's discussion raises awareness of procedural and analytic issues that affect findings. The nature of the phenomenon being studied becomes clearly evident through the depth of her probing of the research process.

Marian Radke-Yarrow

~ 7 ~

The Typological Approach to Studying Personality

Richard W. Robins
⌖

University of California at Davis

Oliver P. John
⌖

University of California
at Berkeley

Avshalom Caspi
⌖

University of Wisconsin
at Madison

*I*n the 4th century B.C., Theophrastus pondered, "Why is it that, while all Greece lies under the same sky and all the Greeks are educated alike, it has befallen us to have characters variously constituted?" (trans. 1960, p. 37). Theophrastus classified the people of Greek society into 30 "characters," or personality types, such as The Flatterer and The Unseasonable Man, according to the "kinds of conduct which characterize them and the mode in which they administer their affairs" (p. 37). At about the same time, Hippocrates described four temperament types—sanguine, melancholic, choleric, and phlegmatic—and posited that they reflect different balances among the four "humors." What unites these conceptions of human nature is an emphasis on *types* rather than *dimensions* of personality, and a corresponding view of the person as a system of interacting components. The fundamental question posed by the ancient Greeks continues to intrigue contemporary psychologists: What are the basic personality types, and where do they come from?

Psychologists have proposed a variety of personality typologies. Most of these are based on the theories of Freud, Jung,

135

Horney, Kretschmer, and others. For example, the Myers-Briggs Type Indicator (Myers & McCaulley, 1985) classifies individuals into 16 personality types inspired by Jungian theory. These theoretically derived typologies show few similarities to each other, however, and seldom hold up to the rigorous empirical standards of replicability, construct validity, and generalizability across diverse populations.

Thus, despite its long history, the study of personality types is still in its infancy. Just as researchers studying traits had difficulty reaching consensus on a taxonomy of their subject matter, little progress has been made toward a generally accepted taxonomy of people. As a result, researchers have developed their own typologies, and like a modern-day Babel, each speaks a different language: No overarching framework connects the various typologies and provides the basis for a common language. In part, the lack of an accepted typology reflects the paucity of empirically based attempts to generate a replicable typology.

Typological conceptions of temperament and personality, however, are currently enjoying a renaissance in psychology (Kagan, 1994), and the search for an empirically defensible typology has been reinvigorated. This new research adopts methodologically rigorous standards and aims to identify a basic set of replicable and generalizable personality types that would serve as a classification system for the field. This chapter provides an overview of these recent attempts to derive personality types through empirical methods. Specifically, we (a) discuss why the field of psychology needs a general personality typology, (b) describe the typological approach and contrast it with the traditional dimensional approach, (c) describe some ways psychologists have created typologies in previous research, (d) review several recent attempts to derive personality types by using empirical methods, and (e) outline a few unanswered questions and directions for future research.

∞ WHY DO WE NEED A PERSONALITY TYPOLOGY?

In the past, research on personality types has been plagued by methodological problems (Meehl, 1979; Mendelsohn, Weiss, & Feimer, 1982; Tellegen & Lubinski, 1983; Waller & Meehl, 1997). Why, then, is the search for a replicable and comprehensive personality typology worthwhile? A *typology* provides a system for classifying people into categories—categories composed of individuals who have similar configurations of personality attributes. Thus, a typology would serve the same function in psychology as taxonomic systems serve in other sciences. *Taxonomies* play a crucial role in the natural sciences. Each field has developed a framework for classifying its subject matter: Biologists study animals, so they developed a way to classify animals into categories such as mammals, birds, and fish; chemists study elements, so they developed the periodic table; and astronomers study stars, so they developed a classification system for stars. Psychologists study people, yet we do not have a standard way to classify people.

Figure 7.1 illustrates this point. At the top is a basic taxonomy of animals. When biologists encounter an animal, they can classify it into one of the categories of the taxonomy. For example, a horse would be classified as a mammal on the basis of its physical appearance and biological attributes. Then, everything the biologist knows about mammals becomes known (with great probability) about the horse (e.g., it is warm-blooded, has hair, bears live young). This is the power of a taxonomic system; by classifying something, we learn a great deal about it. Just as the animal taxonomy helps the biological sciences, a taxonomy of people would be useful for psychology. Individuals could be classified into groups, and then we would know something about them by virtue of their personality types. Such a typology would provide an effective descriptive system for conveying general information about a person and help us refine our predictions. And by delving into the etiology and psychological dynamics of each type, we could learn more about the mechanisms that drive behavior and about the role of individual differences in personality. Thus, taxonomies facilitate the basic goals of science: description, prediction, and explanation. Despite the obvious benefits, however, psychology lags behind other sciences because we still lack a basic taxonomy of our subject matter. As a result, when psychologists study an individual (e.g., the man shown in Figure 7.1), we have no general classification system to help us understand that individual's behavior; we do not even know what the essential types are.

Instead of classifying people, psychologists have developed ways to classify *variables*, such as traits, motives, and values. For example, the five-factor model (FFM) provides one way to classify personality traits. The FFM postulates that at the broadest level of description are five personality domains: (a) extraversion, (b) agreeableness, (c) conscientiousness, (d) neuroticism, and (e) openness to experience (e.g., John, 1990). Thus, when a psychologist proposes a new trait construct or develops a new individual-difference

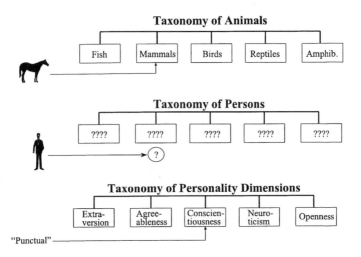

Figure 7.1. Examples of Taxonomies in Three Domains

measure, a psychological understanding of the new construct can be obtained by locating it within the overarching nomological network provided by the FFM. More generally, such dimensional taxonomies of personality are useful because they specify the interrelations among traits and thus help us understand the basic building blocks of personality. If the field of biology were in the same situation as psychology, biologists would be using a taxonomy to classify the attributes of animals, such as blood temperature or furriness (referred to as "R-clustering" by Sneath & Sokal, 1973), but they would have no way to classify the animals themselves (referred to as "Q-clustering"). Thus, a taxonomy of people—that is, a typology—would provide an important complement. By focusing on individual attributes in isolation, psychologists have neglected how these attributes combine within a person. But the overall combination and patterning of attributes defines a person's personality type, just as a combination of attributes determines whether an animal is a mammal.

∞ DIMENSIONAL VERSUS TYPOLOGICAL APPROACHES TO PERSONALITY

The distinction between a taxonomy of people and a taxonomy of dimensions reflects the distinction between the typological and

TABLE 7.1 The Dimensional and Typological Approaches

	Dimensional	Typological
Definition	Dimensions order people on a continuum from low to high.	Typologies classify people into groups.
Basic approach	Focuses on variables as the unit of analysis (variable-centered).	Focuses on the person as the unit of analysis (person-centered).
Taxonomic goal	Identify basic categories of personality dimensions.	Identify basic categories of people.
Current status	The five-factor model provides a replicable taxonomy of personality traits.	No generally accepted taxonomy of personality types.

dimensional approaches to personality research (see Table 7.1). The vast majority of researchers adopt a *dimensional approach.* They conceptualize personality in terms of trait dimensions, such as extraversion and conscientiousness, and attempt to order people on these continuous dimensions. The dimensional approach is variable-centered because it focuses on understanding similarities and differences among variables (e.g., is extraversion associated with need for achievement?).

In contrast, researchers adopting a *typological approach* focus on people, rather than variables. Just as laypeople often think about personality in terms of types (e.g., "He's a bully"; "She's a saint"), typological researchers try to identify groups of people with similar personalities, focusing on the unique patterning of attributes within the persons. The approach is person-centered because it focuses on understanding similarities and differences among people (e.g., which types of people increase in self-esteem during adolescence, and which types decrease?). Thus, whereas the dimensional approach asks what the most important dimensions of personality are, typological research asks whether groups of people share the same overall pattern of traits. Similarly, whereas the dimensional approach asks what the implications are of being high versus low on a particular dimension, the typological approach asks what the implications are of the total constellation of traits defining a person.

In short, the taxonomic goal of the dimensional approach is to identify the basic domains of personality and then to classify individual traits into these domains. The taxonomic goal of the typological approach is to identify the basic types into which people can be classified. Psychologists have described the typological approach as "carving nature at its joints" because, in some sense, it attempts to carve human nature into categories (Meehl, 1979, p. 566).

∞ IDENTIFYING PERSONALITY TYPES

The relative paucity of empirically derived personality typologies may reflect the lack of well-accepted procedures for identifying types. Figure 7.2 shows four ways that researchers have created typologies in previous research (see Waller & Meehl, 1997, for a more detailed and technical discussion of empirical methods for identifying types).[1]

Univariate typologies are typically created by using extreme cut-off points on a single dimension. In this case, individuals at the extremes of a distribution are considered qualitatively different from the rest of the population. For example, Kagan (1994; Kagan et al., this volume, Chap. 4) distinguishes between extremely inhibited and extremely uninhibited children and provides evidence that these two groups are distinct, both psychologically and biologically.

A second form of univariate typology derives from a bimodal distribution on a single dimension.[2] In this case, two relatively distinct groups can be meaningfully divided into two types. For example, Strube (1989), adopting Meehl and Golden's (1982) taxometric approach, provided evidence that most people tend to have either a Type A or a Type B personality, with relatively few people in between.

A third way to create a typology is by using a *bivariate,* or two-dimensional, system. Typically, two independent dimensions are divided at their medians and then are crossed to form four groups. For example, Covington (1992) crosses the motivational dimensions of approach and avoidance to form four types based on achievement orientations: (a) success-oriented (high approach, low avoidance), (b) overstrivers (high approach, high avoidance), (c) failure avoiders (low approach, high avoidance), and (d) failure acceptors (low approach, low avoidance). Each type is linked to a unique constellation of achievement behaviors, goals, attributional styles, and self-worth maintaining strategies. One problem with bivariate, as well as univariate, typologies is that the cut-off

1. Univariate: Extreme Groups (Kagan, 1994)

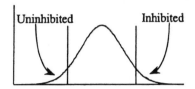

2. Univariate: Bimodal Distribution (Strube, 1989)

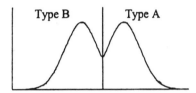

3. Bivariate: 2 x 2 Classification (Covington , 1992)

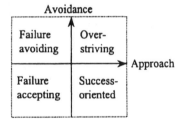

4. Multivariate: Factor or Cluster Analysis (Block, 1971; Caspi & Silva , 1995)

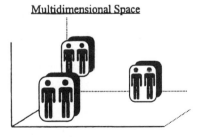

Figure 7.2. Four Ways to Classify People Into Types

points (e.g., the median) used to classify people are often arbitrary and thus are neither empirically nor theoretically defensible. A second problem arises if the dimensions composing a bivariate typology are highly correlated; if so, identifying types in the off-diagonal categories (high-low; low-high) will be difficult. A fourth way to derive types involves identifying groups of individuals who have similar personality profiles across multiple dimensions. This *multivariate* approach has the advantage of identifying general personality types—that is, types based on a person's overall configuration of attributes. In contrast, univariate and bivariate typologies are specific to a particular domain; for example, inhibition is only part of a person's personality (albeit an important part). The multivariate approach requires a method for determining the similarity between two individuals' personality profiles and for identifying distinct groupings of individuals. The most commonly used method is *inverse (or Q) factor analysis* (McKeown & Thomas, 1988; for examples and discussion of the strengths and weaknesses of this approach, see Bergman, this volume, Chap. 5; Block, 1971; Robins, John, Caspi, Moffitt, & Stouthamer-Loeber, 1996; Waller & Meehl, 1997; York & John, 1992). This method analyzes intercorrelations among people, rather than among variables. These interperson correlations indicate the similarity between two individuals' personality profiles. The factors generated by an inverse factor analysis can be interpreted as personality types because they represent groups of people with similar personality profiles.

To determine the number of type factors in a given sample, York and John (1992) recommend the use of a *factor replicability criterion* adapted from Everett (1983). This procedure determines the degree to which the same factors emerge in two random halves of the sample. Specifically, the sample is randomly divided into two nonoverlapping halves, an inverse factor analysis is conducted in each half, and then the convergence between type factors found in each half is examined. The number of replicable type factors is indicated by the solution with the highest number of factors before a clear drop in replicability occurs.

Inverse factor analysis does not classify individuals uniquely into a type, but rather determines how similar each individual is to each type. Specifically, factor loadings indicate the degree to which an individual's personality configuration resembles the personality configuration defining the type factor. Thus, factor-analytically-derived personality types should be considered proto-type categories with fuzzy boundaries, rather than classical categories with discrete boundaries. That is, inverse factor analysis should not be considered a way to identify natural taxons (Waller & Meehl, 1997). Nonetheless, the results of an inverse factor do provide a way to classify individuals into discrete typological categories. The simplest classification procedure is to classify individuals into the type on which they have the highest loading. This procedure is problematic, however, when an individual has relatively low loadings on all types or has relatively high loadings on more than one type. Thus, cut-off rules are needed to maximize within-type homogeneity and to minimize overlap among the types (see York & John, 1992, for possible cut-off rules and Robins et al., 1996, for an example of how to use discriminant function analysis to classify unclear cases).[3]

Another way to derive multivariate types is through *cluster analysis* (e.g., Caspi & Silva, 1995; Magnusson & Bergman, 1990), which classifies individuals into discrete categories. Cluster analysis yields a hierarchical structure, with one overall cluster broken down into as many clusters as there are individuals. The clusters are based on some measure of similarity between individuals, such as a *Euclidean distance function* (the distance between two individuals is the sum of the squared differences between the values of the clustering variables). Like factor analysis, however, there is no definitive way to determine the appropriate number of clusters. Again, replicability provides the best criterion. For example, Caspi and Silva (1995) conducted a replicated cluster analysis in which they split their large sample into two subsamples, extracted clusters in one subsample, and tested the replicability of the clusters in the other subsample.

Cluster analysis can also be conducted by using *neural network* and *fuzzy clustering* methods (Laudeman & John, 1995). Unlike traditional cluster analysis, individuals are not uniquely classified into clusters, but rather receive continuous membership values for each cluster. This newer approach computes similarity between individuals by using pattern recognition algorithms that can detect nonlinear patterns in the data. Such algorithms can more effectively categorize data in which the boundaries between objects are poorly delineated, a common situation in psychological data. It remains to be seen whether this new method is superior to other typological procedures, and direct comparisons are needed. Regardless of the particular method used, however, the multivariate approach is the most direct way to identify general personality types, and in the following section we review recent research that uses this approach.

∞ REVIEW OF RESEARCH ON MULTIVARIATE PERSONALITY TYPES

Given the various typologies that have been discussed in psychology, it seems surprising that the field has made such scant progress toward a generally accepted taxonomy. This is, in part, because most research on personality types has not been conducted in a systematic, methodologically rigorous manner. In contrast, research on dimensional taxonomies generally follows much stricter empirical standards, attending to issues of replicability, generalizability, and construct validity. It seems reasonable that the best way to develop an empirically defensible personality typology would be to adopt these same strict standards. Thus, research on personality typologies should (a) identify types *empirically* by using a multivariate approach; (b) focus only on *replicable* types; (c) interpret types through *construct validation* studies by using multiple independent data sources; (d) attend to issues of *generalizability*, particularly across gender, developmental period, ethnicity, and culture; and (e) work toward a *hierarchical* taxonomy that classifies people both at a general level of broad types and into more specific, narrower subtypes.

By advocating an empirically oriented approach, we are not adopting an anti-theory stance. Rather, we are suggesting that psychological theories should be invoked to help us understand types identified by using empirical methods (e.g., York & John, 1992, use Rankian theory to interpret empirically derived types). The history of both trait and type research suggests that theory-driven psychologists, when left to their own devices, do not reach the type of consensus needed to develop a standard taxonomy for the field. Below, we summarize the findings from several studies that meet most of the standards we have advocated.

Block's Pioneering Study

Perhaps the most prominent empirical work on personality types is Block's study *Lives Through Time* (1971). Block aimed to identify "the personality types manifested during adolescence as well as those discernible during adulthood" (p. 112) on the basis of an analysis of personality descriptions obtained at two time periods—early adolescence and early adulthood. He referred to these types as *developmental* types to emphasize that they capture patterns in both the organization and the development of personality over time (see also Ozer & Gjerde, 1989).

Block (1971) used the *Q-sort method* of personality description to analyze personality continuity and change in the Berkeley Guidance and Oakland Growth Studies at the Institute of Human Development (IHD). Several clinicians read the case materials of each participant in the IHD studies and then completed a Q-sort of the participant. In the Q-sort method, a sorter describes an individual's personality by sorting a set of cards containing personality attributes into piles ranging from attributes that are least characteristic to those that are most characteristic of the individual (Block, 1978). This produces a person-centered description because the sorter explicitly compares each attribute with the other attributes for the same individual. The resemblance between two individuals can then be indexed by the correlation between their respective Q-sorts, which reflects the degree to which the Q-sort items are ordered the same way within the two individuals.[4]

Block identified five personality types among the male subjects by using inverse factor analysis of the Q-sort descriptions. Three of these types represented groups of individuals with personality structures that remained stable from adolescence to early adulthood: (a) *Ego resilients* were well-adjusted and interpersonally effective; (b) *unsettled undercontrollers* were highly impulsive and antisocial; and (c) *vulnerable overcontrollers* were rigidly overcontrolled and maladapted. The remaining two types represented groups of individuals who showed particular patterns of personality change: (d) *Belated adjusters* appeared maladjusted during adolescence but seemed to function effectively by adulthood, whereas (e) *anomic extroverts* showed the opposite trend.

Block's personality types provide one way to categorize individuals and suggest that meaningful types can be identified empirically. These types may be specific to the IHD sample, however, which was composed of individuals who were almost exclusively Caucasian, were generally above average in intelligence, and grew up several generations ago. Moreover, somewhat different types were found among the females. In fact, the Block types have never been replicated, and it remains to be seen whether this particular cleavage of "nature at its joints" constitutes a generalizable typology. Evidence for a generalizable typology requires that the types replicate across a broader range of populations.

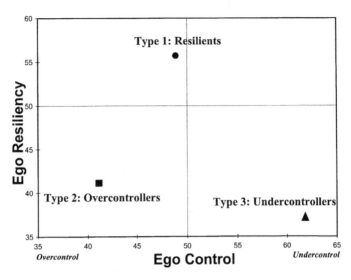

Figure 7.3. Personality Types as a Function of Ego Control and Ego Resiliency (in *T*-Score Metric)

Recent Research

In a recent study (Robins et al., 1996), we identified personality types in a large heterogeneous sample of adolescent boys selected to be representative of public school students in an urban environment.[5] Like Block, we derived types by using inverse factor analysis of Q-sort personality descriptions provided by primary caregivers when the boys were between 12 and 13 years old. Factor analyses in the two half-samples indicated a three-factor solution, suggesting that three personality types were replicable. We labeled these types "resilients," "overcontrollers," and "undercontrollers" on the basis of their similarity to three of the types identified by Block (1971): ego resilients, vulnerable overcontrollers, and unsettled undercontrollers.[6] The Q-sort profiles of the types indicated that resilient adolescents were characterized by self-confidence, independence, verbal fluency, and an ability to concentrate on tasks; overcontrolling adolescents were shy, quiet, anxious, and dependable; undercontrolling adolescents were impulsive, stubborn, and physically active.

Figure 7.3 shows how the types differ on Block and Block's (1980) dynamic dimensions of ego functioning—ego resiliency and ego control. The resilients scored high on ego resiliency but intermediate on ego control. The other two types were both low on ego resiliency, but one type showed excessive levels of overcontrol, whereas the other showed excessive levels of undercontrol. When coupled with low resiliency, ego control has important consequences for cognitive, emotional, and interpersonal functioning. More specifically, ego control channels the expression of maladjustment. For the undercontroller, it directs impulses outward and provokes the individual to act out against the world. For the overcontroller, it directs impulses inward, creating anxiety, introversion, and dependency. Thus, the overcontrolling and undercontrolling types represent two different manifestations of poor psychological adjustment.

The three types also differed on the Big Five dimensions of the FFM. Whereas ego resiliency and ego control reflect regulatory processes within the individual, the Big Five describe the individual differences in behavior that result from these different processes. Table 7.2 shows mean differences among the types on the Big Five. Resilients had positive characteristics in all five domains. Overcontrollers were the most agreeable of the three types but were also neurotic and highly introverted. Undercontrollers were distinguished by their very low levels of agreeableness and conscientiousness, reflecting antisocial tendencies; they were also high on neuroticism and relatively low on openness. In summary, resilients have a high level of adjustment and effective functioning in both interpersonal and task domains, suggesting that they are likely to respond adaptively and flexibly to situational demands. Resilient boys show neither the impulsive, antisocial pattern characterizing the undercontrolling type, nor the overly inhibited, anxious pattern characterizing the overcontrolling type.

On the basis of these findings, we made predictions about the real-world implications of the three types. Using self-reports, teacher ratings, and objective test data, we found that resilients, on average, were intelligent, successful in school, unlikely to be delinquents, and relatively free of psychopathology; overcontrollers enjoyed some of the same positive outcomes but were also prone to internalizing problems. Undercontrollers were most likely to show a general pattern of academic, behavioral, and emotional problems. In summary, the three types had coherent relations with the Big Five dimensions, ego resiliency, and ego control and showed a distinct, predictable pattern of correlates with a wide range of developmentally relevant variables (see Table 7.2).

TABLE 7.2 Summary of Findings for the Three Types:
Nomological Network of Personality and Real-World
Correlates

	Three Replicable Types		
	Resilients	Overcontrolled	Undercontrolled
Personality functioning			
Ego resiliency	High	Low	Low
Ego undercontrol	Medium	Low	High
Big Five dimensions			
Extraversion	High	Low	Medium
Agreeableness	High	High	Low
Conscientiousness	High	Medium	Low
Neuroticism	Low	High	High
Openness to experience	High	Medium	Low
Real-world variables			
IQ	High	Medium	Low
School performance	High	Medium	Low
School conduct	High	High	Low
Delinquency	Low	Low	High
Internalizing disorder	Low	High	Medium
Externalizing disorder	Low	Low	High

NOTE: Effect of type membership is significant ($p < .01$) for all variables. Adapted from Robins, John, Caspi, Moffitt, & Stouthamer-Loeber (1996).

We also found evidence that the types generalize across African Americans and Caucasians. First, the same three types emerged in both ethnic groups. Second, the psychological implications of type membership were similar for the two groups; that is, no interactions were found between personality type and race for ego resiliency and ego control, for any of the Big Five dimensions, or for IQ, academic performance, delinquency, and psychopathology. Finally, in terms of their overall personality, Caucasian boys were no more similar to each other than they were to African American boys; the average interperson correlation between the Q-sort profiles of Caucasian and African American boys was identical to the average interperson correlation between boys *within* either ethnic group. These findings show that the three types generalize across two ethnic groups represented in the present sample. Do the same types emerge in other samples?

Similar personality types have been identified in several recent studies using a diverse range of subject populations. Table 7.3 adopts our three replicated personality types (Robins et al., 1996) as a general framework and summarizes the findings of Block's (1971) study, as well as six additional empirical studies of personality types. The studies are described in terms of several *substantive* facets of generalizability (gender, age, birth cohort, and geographic region) and several *methodological* facets (source of personality information, assessment instrument, and the procedure used to derive types).

The three types have been identified in several countries. In a sample of 79 Dutch boys and girls ages 7, 10, and 12, van Lieshout, Haselager, Riksen-Walraven, and van Aken (1995) performed a typological analysis by using Q-sort descriptions provided by teachers; specifically, they conducted a cluster analysis of Big Five scales scored from the Q-sort items. They found three personality types that generalized across age and gender and that showed "remarkable similarity" (p. 13) with the groupings and external correlates reported by Robins et al. (1996). In the Dutch sample, however, the overcontrollers were the most prevalent type and seemed better adjusted than the overcontrollers from the American sample. This may reflect a true cultural difference between the two samples, a difference in the statistical procedure used to derive the types (factor analysis vs. cluster analysis), or simply a sampling effect.

Hart, Hofmann, Edelstein, and Keller (1997) examined personality types in a sample of 168 Icelandic boys and girls—half judged by their teachers to be well adjusted, and half judged to be poorly adjusted. Hart et al. performed an inverse factor analysis of Q-sort descriptions based on transcribed interviews and interviewers' comments. Again, the types they found resemble those found in previous research: "The findings reported by Robins et al. (1996) were clearly replicated. Like them, we found solid evidence for three (and only three) personality types" (p. 26). In addition, the types showed behavioral characteristics similar to those reported by Robins et al.; for example, Hart et al. found that resilients received higher grades in school than members of the other two types.

Another comparison can be made with the research of York and John (1992), who identified four replicable personality types in a sample of middle-aged women. Three of these types correspond with the three identified in previous research, despite the fact the York and John subjects were middle-aged, rather than adolescent, and the personality descriptions were based on archival materials, rather than obtained directly from knowledgeable

(text continued on p. 152)

TABLE 7.3 Across-Investigation Generalizability of Three Empirically Derived Personality Types

	Study			
	Robins, John, Caspi, Moffitt, & Stouthamer-Loeber (1996)	*Block (1971)*	*van Lieshout, Haselager, Riksen-Walraven, & van Aken (1995)*	*Hart, Hofman, Edelstein, & Keller (1997)*
Personality Types				
Type 1	Resilients	Ego resilients	Resilients	Resilients
Type 2	Overcontrollers	Vulnerable overcontrollers	Overcontroller	Overcontrollers
Type 3	Undercontrollers	Unsettled undercontrollers	Undercontrollers	Undercontrollers
Facets of Generalizability				
Participants	300 boys	84 boys/men	79 boys and girls	168 boys and girls
Age	12-13 years	Both 13 and 35 years	7, 10, 12 years	7 years
Birth cohort	Late 1970s	1920s	Early 1970s	1970
Geographical region	Pittsburgh	San Francisco Bay area	The Netherlands	Iceland
Data source	Caregivers' reports	Clinical judgments from data archives	Teacher reports	Interviewer's assessments
Instrument used	Child Q-set	Adult Q-set	Child Q-set	Child Q-set
Type derivation	Replicated Q-factors	Q-factors across two time periods	Cluster analysis	Replicated Q-factors

	York & John (1992)	Klohnen & Block (1996)	Caspi & Silva (1995)	Pulkkinen (1996)
Personality Types				
Type 1	Individuated	Resilients	Well adjusted	Resilients/Individuated
Type 2	Traditional	Overcontrollers	Inhibited	Introverts/Anxious
Type 3	Conflicted	Undercontrollers	Undercontrolled	Conflicted/Undercontrolled
Facets of Generalizability				
Participants	103 women	106 men and women	1,024 boys and girls	275 men and women
Age	43 years	23 years	3 years	26 years
Birth cohort	1937–1939	1960s	1972–1973	1960s
Geographical region	San Francisco area	San Francisco area	New Zealand	Finland
Data source	Clinical judgments from data archives	Interviewers' assessments	Examiners' observations during a testing session	Self-reports
Instrument used	Adult Q-set	Adult Q-set	Behavior ratings	Scale scores
Type derivation	Replicated Q-factors	Q-factors	Replicated clusters	Cluster analysis

informants. The first (and most prevalent) type, labeled "Individu-ated," was the most resilient and had a well-adjusted Big Five profile. Their second type ("Traditional" women) was overcon-trolled, highly agreeable and conscientious, and relatively intro-verted; this type was prone to feelings of guilt, consistent with the internalization of emotional problems we found for our adolescent overcontrollers. Their third type ("Conflicted" women) shared features with the maladjusted undercontrollers—specifically, low resiliency and undercontrolled expression of antagonism and hos-tility. Rather than engage in delinquency and have problems in school like the adolescent male undercontrollers in Robins et al. (1996), however, these middle-aged women externalized their problems in their relationships (e.g., marital instability) and at work (e.g., underachievement and dissatisfaction; see John & Os-trove, 1994; York & John, 1994).

Klohnen and Block (1996) performed a typological analysis of young adults by using Q-sort descriptions provided by inter-viewers on the basis of extensive individual assessments. Three replicable types were identified in both the male and female samples. These three types closely resemble the resilients, over-controllers, and undercontrollers.

The studies reviewed so far all relied on Q-sort personality descriptions. But other data sources reveal similar findings. Caspi and Silva (1995) used cluster analysis to identify five replicable types in a large birth cohort sample from New Zealand on the basis of behavior ratings by examiners when the subjects were 3 years old. Three of these types match the three types in Table 7.3. The "well-adjusted" type was the most prevalent and resembled the resilient type; this type was described as "capable of reserve and control when it was demanded of them; they appeared adequately self-confident and attempted to cope with difficult tasks, but they didn't become unduly upset if the task was too difficult" (p. 14). The second type, given the label "inhibited," paralleled the over-controlling type and was described as restrained, shy, fearful, and easily upset. The third type, labeled "undercontrolled," included children described as impulsive, restless, and distractible. The replication of the three types in this research is impressive, given that Caspi and Silva studied 3-year-old children from a country other than the United States, used examiners' observations as the data for the typology, and relied on behavior ratings and cluster analysis (rather than on Q-sorts and factor analysis).

Pulkkinen (1996) conducted a cluster analysis of extensive self-report data to identify personality types among young adults from Finland. The three male types identified in her study (labeled "resilients," "introverts," and "conflicted") clearly match the three types in Table 7.3. Although the female types were less clearly defined, they correspond to some extent with the types in Table 7.3. A large group of "adjusted" individuals included two groups of women ("feminine" and "individuated") who differed from each other primarily in their adherence to, or separation from, conventional female roles. A smaller group of "conflicted" individuals included women characterized by their "anxious" and "undercontrolled" behavior.

Together, these studies provide grounds for optimism concerning the generalizability of the three broad personality types. Across studies, the same set of types repeatedly emerges. This convergence is noteworthy because the studies differ in numerous ways, including age, gender, ethnicity, historical period and geographic location in which the subjects grew up, source of personality information used to derive the types, and even the way the types were derived. Still, the convergence across studies is not perfect, and more typological research needs to be done before anything close to a comprehensive, generalizable typology can be said to exist. In particular, more attention should be directed toward the generalizability of the types across gender and across other racial and ethnic groups. The studies reviewed provide a cross-national replication of the types, but all the studies were conducted in relatively industrialized countries, and none of the studies included significant proportions of Asians or Latinos of any nationality.

Despite these caveats, the findings in Table 7.3 show sufficient convergence across studies to suggest that the three replicable types constitute a minimally necessary set. That is, if broad personality types are studied in a large, heterogeneous sample, one should find one well-adjusted type, one maladjusted overcontrolling type, and one maladjusted undercontrolling type. At this point, these three types are good candidates to become an integral part of any generalizable personality typology. This does not mean that only three types exist, just as the FFM does not imply that only five personality dimensions exist. It simply means that, at the most general level, psychological theories must account for the development of these three types.

∞ UNANSWERED QUESTIONS AND FUTURE DIRECTIONS

A First Step in the Search for Subtypes: How Many Kinds of Personalities Are There?

Let's assume for a moment that there are three broad, generalizable personality types. What is the next step? The three types provide a fairly rough categorization system, somewhat like the general categories of bird, fish, mammal, and so on. Despite its breadth, a classification system at this level can still be useful. On the one hand, identifying an animal as a mammal, rather than as a fish, tells us a great deal about the animal because it presumably shares characteristics common to all mammals. On the other hand, important distinctions can be made among mammals: Orangutans clearly differ in important ways from mice. This is why the animal taxonomy is hierarchical and makes many more distinctions than the broad classes; for example, both apes and rodents are types of mammals. In fact, most systems in nature are organized hierarchically, and thus we would expect a taxonomy of persons to be hierarchical as well. Thus, a complete typology should provide a way to classify people into broad types, such as those described here, as well as into more specific subtypes that afford a richer and more detailed understanding of the person. Thus, the search for subtypes within each broad type is an important task for the future.

In our most recent work, we have begun to identify replicable subtypes in the sample of adolescent boys we examined (Robins et al., 1996). We performed a typological analysis to identify distinct subgroups within each of the three types. Again, our criterion for accepting a subtype was replicability. For example, we randomly divided the resilient boys into two subgroups, conducted an inverse factor analysis within each subgroup, and then examined the convergence between the type factors found in the two subgroups. We repeated this procedure for the overcontrollers and the undercontrollers. No replicable subtypes were found in the relatively small group of overcontrollers. Two subtypes replicated in the resilient group, however, and two replicated in the undercontrolling group.

Figure 7.4 shows the three broad types and the two sets of subtypes. To interpret these subtypes, we examined differences among them on the Big Five dimensions, ego resiliency and ego

Personality Types and Subtypes

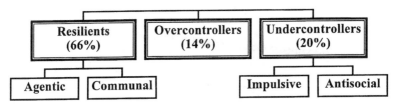

Figure 7.4. Toward a Hierarchical Taxonomy of Personality Types

control, and intelligence. The two resilient subtypes seem to reflect agentic and communal aspects of adjustment (Bakan, 1966):

> Agency refers to the individual's striving to separate from others, to master the environment, to assert, protect, and expand the self . . . Communion refers to the individual's striving to lose his or her own individuality by merging with others, participating in something that is larger than the self, and relating to other selves in warm, close, intimate, and loving ways. (McAdams, 1993, p. 71)

Agentic resilients were characterized by very high extraversion and low neuroticism, whereas communal resilients were characterized by very high agreeableness and high conscientiousness. As expected, both types were high in ego resiliency. Agentic resilients were somewhat undercontrolled, however, whereas communal resilients were somewhat overcontrolled; moreover, on the Big Five, communal resilients had a prosocial personality profile. Communal resilients were slightly lower than agentic resilients in intelligence, although were still above average.

The two subtypes of undercontrollers seemed to differ mostly in the degree to which they showed antisocial tendencies. One subtype seemed particularly prone toward antisocial behavior, whereas the other subtype seemed prone toward impulsivity but not necessarily in an antisocial way. Consistent with this interpretation, the antisocial undercontrollers were extremely low in agreeableness and conscientiousness, whereas the impulsive undercontrollers were about average on these two Big Five dimensions. Although both subtypes were low on ego resiliency and high on undercontrol, the antisocials were particularly nonresilient and particularly undercontrolled; correspondingly, their personality profile was highly consistent with that of the antisocial personality. Both subtypes had below normal levels of intelligence and did not differ from each other. Thus, each subtype has a distinctive personality profile. These findings need to be replicated, however, and the psychological nature of the subtypes needs to be explicated further. Nonetheless, it is already apparent that extending the typology to the subtype level provides a more fine-grained classification system than is afforded by the three broad types alone. The additional degree of descriptive precision provided by subtypes should improve our ability to predict important developmental outcomes.

Developmental Issues

The study of personality types provides a descriptive map of human nature that may help us refine our search for distinct developmental pathways. Members of a given type are assumed to share a common etiology and to follow a similar developmental path. The studies reviewed in this chapter provide the foundation for a psychological understanding of the three types and their developmental implications. Yet, questions remain about the nature, origin, and consequences of these types. Future research should explore when, why, and how these types emerge and trace their long-term consequences. Looking backward, we can ask questions about the developmental precursors of the types: Why do some individuals become agentic resilients, whereas others become impulsive undercontrollers? Can we trace the roots of these types to particular configurations of temperamental characteristics (e.g., Caspi & Silva, 1995) or to specific childhood experiences (e.g., York & John, 1994)? With regard to questions about nature and nurture, most behavioral genetic research on personality development has focused on dimensional models (e.g., Loehlin, 1992), and we know little about the heritability of personality types. One intriguing question concerns the relative heritability of broad types versus subtypes. Research on such questions will allow us to understand how nature and nurture combine to shape an individual's personality structure.

Looking forward, we can ask questions about the continuity of the types over time and across developmental transitions, and about their long-term consequences. For example, to what extent do individuals remain in the same type over the life course? Does the 3-year-old undercontroller become a 23-year-old undercontroller? In examining this issue, the possibility of heterotypic continuity should be considered. With regard to long-term consequences, what future does a person's personality structure portend? So far, our findings suggest that boys from different types vary in their risk for developmental problems, such as dropping out of school, delinquency, and psychopathology. More generally, a complete understanding of the types requires that they be embedded in a developmental framework that traces their etiology and charts their future course and consequences.

∞ CONCLUSIONS AND IMPLICATIONS

This chapter has provided a progress report on the search for a general personality typology. We see the three personality types as an initial step toward a more complete typological account of personality. Clearly, we have a long way to go before we have a typology that is anything like taxonomies in the other sciences or even one as advanced as existing taxonomies of personality traits. Several issues remain to be addressed. First, we need further evidence of the generalizability of the three types across a more diverse range of cultures, age-groups, and so on. Second, we need to search for additional broad types. Several studies that we reviewed found more than three types, but so far none of these additional types has proved as replicable as the three broad types discussed here; future research needs to explore whether any of them constitute independent broad types or whether they are subtypes that can be subsumed within the three replicable types. Third, we need to continue the search for subtypes. An interesting question is whether the subtypes described here show as much cross-cultural generality as the three broad types. Fourth, we need to develop a deeper psychological understanding of the types by linking them to personality processes and to basic cognitive and physiological processes. For example, the three types seem to have a clear link to Ainsworth's (Ainsworth, Blehar, Waters, & Wall, 1978) attachment styles (e.g., resilients should tend to be secure, overcontrollers should tend to be anxious/resistant, and undercontrollers should tend to be anxious/avoidant). More generally, we believe that the ultimate goal of typological work on personality should be an explanatory taxonomy (one rooted in psychological and physiological mechanisms), rather than a descriptive system.

Finally, we need to explore developmental issues further. Research on personality development has typically been oriented toward dimensional constructs such as personality traits. However, this variable-centered orientation does not fit well with a new perspective that seems to be gaining prominence in developmental psychology. This perspective conceptualizes development in terms of dynamic person-environment relations and views the person as an active agent transforming the environment and being transformed at multiple levels. Correspondingly, movement has been away from basic nomothetic laws of development and toward an emphasis on intraindividual processes involved in change and interindividual differences in developmental paths. The study of individual differences in personality can clearly play a larger role in this emerging paradigm. But we need to refine our conceptualization of individuals, not just of variables. The first step is to develop a replicable and generally accepted typology. If we continue working along the lines described in this chapter, we hope to eventually arrive at a taxonomic system for psychology that fulfills the same function as taxonomies in other sciences.

∞৻৵∞

COMMENTS ON CHAPTER 7

With roots dating back to the 4th century B.C., interest in personality types is certain to be current as well. Robins, John, and Caspi have given us a 20th-century version, stating the case for an "overarching framework for classifying individuals." These investigators describe a multidimensional approach for empirically identifying general personality types. Three broad types have emerged: resilient, overcontrolled, and undercontrolled. Their research continues toward identifying subtypes.

This chapter promotes many ideas, as well as questions, regarding this person-oriented approach. From a developmental perspective, it opens exciting questions: From whence cometh the individual's "type"? How early in development do these organizations of traits become apparent? How do they evolve in the contexts of developmental stage characteristics and in relation to experience? The kind of "permanence" generally ascribed to personality could thereby be subjected to empirical test.

A question that can be raised regarding the types presented here concerns their universality and timelessness. Because the personal-

ity descriptions from which the types are derived grow out of the perspectives of Western culture, are we not locked into that culture with whatever conceptualizations we reach? I cannot escape my culture sufficiently to describe human behavior from a totally different perspective, but I could imagine the possibility and, therefore, the chance that types might be different in cultures very different from our own. Whether culture-bound or culture-free, however, does not detract from the value of having a shared, generalizable system of classifying individuals.

Indeed, a personality classification could enrich findings in many areas of study. Taking again a developmental view, research on parental influences on offspring is one such area. In the long history of research on this topic, the person-characteristics of the parent have been given scarcely a glance. Yet, it seems highly probable that the personality type of the parent is a significant context for the parent's rearing behavior and its impact on the child.

Similarly presenting a challenge for personality types are the person classifications in psychopathology, and in personality disorders in particular. How are personality types from the distinctly different classification systems of psychopathology and normality interrelated? What do they have to offer to each other?

Research on personality types has many directions to pursue. Not only is there promise in the elaboration of subtypes, but this work can also introduce into a wide swath of studies a long-time neglected person-variable.

Marian Radke-Yarrow

∞ Notes

1. Obviously, there are more than four ways to create a typology. For example, other chapters in this volume discuss typologies based on common developmental pathways or outcomes (chaps. 1, 9, 11), latent variables (chap. 5), theory or problem-based criteria (chap. 2), and longitudinal data (chap. 5).

2. This form of typology assumes that the distribution of the *latent* variable is bimodal. The *observed* distribution, however, is unlikely to be bimodal because of measurement error, although it should be flatter than a normal distribution; that is, the distribution should show negative kurtosis (be platykurtic).

3. One issue that has yet to be fully resolved is whether to classify all individuals or to leave unclear cases unclassified (see Bergman, this volume, Chap. 5). At the most fundamental level, the issue reflects the trade-off between power and precision: Classifying all individuals increases power by boosting sample size, whereas classifying only clear cases increases within-type homogeneity and may sharpen differences among typological categories. In our own research (e.g., Robins et al.,

1996), we have run analyses in which only "pure" cases were classified to ensure that the findings and interpretations remained the same.

4. The Q-sort method is particularly useful for deriving types because the ipsatized format was specifically designed for person-centered descriptions of individuals. When non-ipsatized personality descriptions are used, the similarity between two individuals' profiles may be confounded by response style differences among judges (e.g., two individuals may appear to have different personalities simply because the people describing them differ in their rating style). In contrast, individual differences in profile level are eliminated in the Q-sort methodology, which assumes that people do not differ in the "amount" of personality they have.

5. The participants are from the Pittsburgh Youth Study, a longitudinal study of the antecedents and consequences of juvenile delinquency. All analyses reported in this chapter were conducted by using a reconstituted sample that does not over-represent boys at risk for delinquency.

6. There is a danger of reification when verbal labels (e.g., "resilient") are applied to the results of complex multivariate analyses, particularly when these labels apply to personality types. The only solution, which we have tried to adopt, is to provide extensive information about the psychological profile of each type so that the reader will rely less on the specific label assigned to the type.

~ 8 ~

Levels of Longitudinal Data Differing in Complexity and the Study of Continuity in Personality Characteristics

Lea Pulkkinen
∞✧∞
University of Jyväskylä

*T*he predictability of individual characteristics in adults from data collected in childhood has been a challenging problem for researchers who use longitudinal data. Many problems in these studies are related to conceptual constructs and measurement techniques used at different ages. One problem is caused by the lack of a theoretical framework for the analysis of continuity in behavioral characteristics, especially in the study of *heterotypic continuity* of them. This term refers to continuity of an inferred attribute presumed to underlie diverse behaviors, as distinguished from *homotypic continuity*, which refers to continuity of similar behaviors over time (Kagan, 1969).

As Caspi and Bem (1990) have pointed out, *continuity* itself has several meanings. In regard to homotypic continuity, these researchers differentiate among absolute, differential, structural, and ipsative stability, and additionally introduce the concept of coherence to enlarge the definition of *stability* to include heterotypic continuity. *Absolute stability* refers to "the constancy in the quantity or amount of an attribute over time," *differential stability* to "the consistency of individual differences within a sample of individuals over time," *structural stability* to "the persistence of correlational patterns among a set of variables across time," and *ipsative stability* to "continuity at the individual level" (pp. 550-552).

In the current study, the theoretical framework for the study of continuity in behavioral characteristics was a model of impulse control (Pulkkinen, 1982), recently adapted for emotional and behavioral regulation (Pulkkinen, 1995). The model consists of inhibitory and enhancing processes of emotion and behavior and defines four behavioral types (Ae-Di)[1] differentiated by self-control and activity (Figure 8.1). Here, *emotion* refers to a mostly negative emotional state subject to control, and *emotion regulation* to the redirection, control, and modification of this state, which enables an individual to function adaptively.

The inhibitory and enhancing processes included in the model are the neutralization and intensification of emotion and the suppression and activation of behavior (see Pulkkinen, 1995). The combinations of these inhibitory and enhancing processes define four behavioral types (Ae-Di), which are not categorical concepts per se, but rather are the corners of the two-dimensional map. *Type Ae behavior* is likely to emerge when both enhancing processes (intensification and activation) are active, and it may be manifested, for example, as impulsive and aggressive behavior. *Type Bsp behavior* is the result of simultaneous neutralization and activation, wherein an individual focuses her or his attention on situational factors that mollify an emotional state and thus help promote cooperative behavior. *Type Ccp behavior* contains both inhibitory processes; behavior is suppressed and emotion is neutralized. *Type Di behavior* is the result of the simultaneous suppression of behavior and the intensification of emotion, wherein an individual perceives the situation as emotionally exciting but does not exhibit overt behavior. Type Di behavior concerns the *internalizing* expression of dysfunction (denoted by the letters D*i*), and Type Ae behavior the *externalizing* expression of dysfunction (denoted by the letters A*e*; Achenbach & Edelbrock, 1983; Cicchetti & Toth, 1991), whereas Type Bsp behavior indicates *spontaneous* prosocial behavior (denoted by the letters B*sp*), and Type Ccp behavior indicates *compliant* prosocial behavior (denoted by the letters C*cp*; Eisenberg, Pasternack, Cameron, & Tryon, 1984). Empirical results have confirmed the validity of the model with 8-year-old children (Pulkkinen, 1995).

The predictive power of the model was investigated by using both variable-oriented and person-oriented approaches:

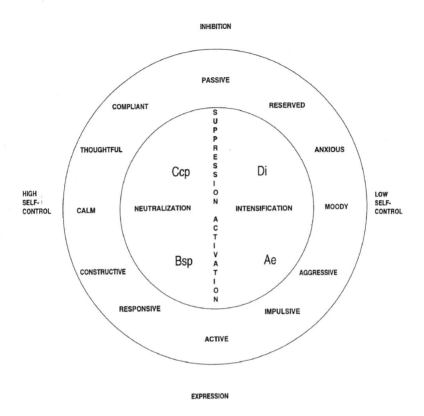

INHIBITION

PASSIVE

COMPLIANT   RESERVED

THOUGHTFUL   ANXIOUS

                    Ccp   S U P P R E S S I O N   Di

HIGH   LOW
SELF-   CALM   NEUTRALIZATION   INTENSIFICATION   MOODY   SELF-
CONTROL   CONTROL

                    Bsp   A C T I V A T I O N   Ae

CONSTRUCTIVE   AGGRESSIVE

RESPONSIVE   IMPULSIVE

ACTIVE

EXPRESSION

Figure 8.1. A Model of Emotional and Behavioral Regulation (Pulkkinen, 1995)

1. The homotypic continuity (differential stability) of individual characteristics over time was studied by using the correlation coefficients between corresponding variables measured at different ages. I expected that stability correlations would be lower as the interval between the measurement points was increased.

2. The heterotypic continuity (personality coherence) between child characteristics and adult behavior was studied by correlating childhood behaviors with select variables in adult behavior. I assumed that Types Ae and Di behaviors in childhood would predict maladjustment, such as criminality and heavy drinking in adulthood, and that Types Bsp and Ccp behaviors would predict adult adjustment, indicated by long education and

stable working careers. Attributes underlying the progression from Types Ae and Di behaviors to adult problem behaviors were assumed to be related to low self-control, whereas attributes underlying the progression from Type Bsps and Ccp behaviors to adult adjustment were assumed to be related to high self-control.

3. The stability of behavioral patterns (ipsative stability) was studied by investigating, first, whether children's characteristics exhibited the same patterns as the types in the model (Figure 8.1); second, which types of behavioral patterns were present in the adult data; and third, whether an individual's behavioral pattern in childhood predicted his or her behavioral pattern in adulthood. On the basis of recent analyses of adult personality styles (Pulkkinen, 1996), I expected that children's behavioral patterns identified as Type Bsp and Type Ccp would predict adult personality styles characterized by adjustment, whereas those patterns identified as Type Ae and Type Di would predict adult personality styles that involved conflicted behavior.

∞ METHOD

Subjects

The subjects consisted of 196 boys and 173 girls from an ongoing longitudinal study. The original sample included 12 school classes drawn randomly from downtown and suburban schools of a medium-sized town in central Finland. The subjects were first studied at age 8 in 1968. At age 14, 96% were reached for a follow-up study. At age 27, 137 women and 138 men (75% of the sample) were studied again.

Procedures and Variables

Teacher ratings on the subjects' social behavior were made at ages 8 and 14. The number of variables was 19 at age 8, but 8 at age 14 after combining indicators of behavioral patterns. At age 27, self-ratings on 8 corresponding variables were collected. These variables, grouped by the concepts of the model of emotional and behavioral regulation (Figure 8.1), and Cronbach's alphas for the age-8 data are presented in Table 8.1.

The class teacher was asked to rate each student at age 8 on a scale from 0 to 3, 3 given to those students in whom the charac-

(text continued on p. 167)

TABLE 8.1 Variables at Different Ages Grouped by the Concepts of the Model of Emotional and Behavioral Regulation

Age 8 (Teacher rating)	Age 14 (Teacher rating)	Age 27 (Self-rating)
Activity		
Always busy and plays eagerly with other children	Is energetic, always on the go, has often contacts with others	I am energetic, active, and social. I have many hobbies and friends.
Aggression (Type Ae)		
Hurts another child	Attacks without reason, teases others, says nasty things	I often become angry, and I easily get involved in quarrels or fights.
Attacks somebody		
Teases smaller peers		
Kicks objects		
$\alpha_b = 0.86$[1] $\alpha_g = 0.79$[2]		
Low self-control		
Lack of concentration	Is impulsive, lacks concentration, changes moods	It is difficult for me to concentrate on something. My moods change often, and I lose my temper easily.
Anxiety (Type Di)		
Starts crying if others treat rastily	Is fearful, helpless in others' company; target of teasing, unable to defend him- or herself	I am shy and nervous in the company of others. I try to avoid new situations.
Afraid of other children		
Cries at the dentist's		
$\alpha_b = 0.69$,[1] $\alpha_g = 0.69$[2]		
Passivity		
Always silent and does not care to be busy	Does not move much, stands alone, silent	I am quiet, withdrawn, and often alone.
Too withdrawn and timid		
$\alpha_b = 0.67$,[1] $\alpha_g = 0.67$[2]		

TABLE 8.1 Continued

Age 8 (Teacher rating)	Age 14 (Teacher rating)	Age 27 (Self-rating)
Compliance (Type Ccp) Calm and patient Dislikes squabbling company Never quarrels $\alpha_b = 0.89,^1 \alpha_g = 0.69^2$	Is calm, patient, and compliant	I give up easily. I try to avoid conflicts and behave according to expectations.
High self-control Reliable classmate Friendly to others $\alpha_b = 0.81,^1 \alpha_g = 0.75^2$	Is reliable, keeps promises, and does not get excited	I am dependable and stable. I keep my composure in all situations.
Constructiveness (Type Bsp) Acts reasonably Discusses problems Sides smaller and weaker peers $\alpha_b = 0.84,^1 \alpha_g = 0.83^2$	Tries to solve annoying situations reasonably, discusses problems, conciliates, and strives for fairness	I solve difficult problems reasonably. I discuss problems and consider other people.

NOTE: 1. α_b = Cronbach's alpha for boys.
2. α_g = Cronbach's alpha for girls.

teristic in question was very prominent and 0 to those students in whom the teacher had never observed the characteristic in question. Teacher ratings were made, at students' age 14, on a scale from 0 to 100. The teacher was asked to compare the subject in question with 100 same-sex students and to rank order each subject for each variable. Students recollected as being among the most aggressive were ranked between 1 and 10, and those among the least aggressive between 90 and 100. The rating scale was changed from the one used at age 8 because the teacher was asked to rate only the students in his or her class who belonged to the original sample; in many cases, this meant only one student in the class. Because of the move from elementary school to lower secondary school and family relocation, the subjects had spread from 12 school classes to 78. Peer nominations were also available at age 8 in the same variables as teacher ratings for the study of concurrent validity. The validity of teacher ratings was satisfactory.

At age 27, *self-ratings* were made on a scale from 1 to 4: 4 = characteristic in question fits me very well, 3 = fits me well, 2 = fits me sometimes, and 1 = doesn't fit me at all. For *criminal arrests,* two registers were examined: (a) the government register that contains information about offenses for which the sentence was imprisonment and (b) the local, more informal register held by the police containing information about misdemeanors such as arrests for public drunkenness.

Problem drinking was assessed on the basis of arrests for public drunkenness and an alcoholism screening test, the CAGE Questionnaire. Subjects were assigned to numerical categories: 1 = no problems; 2 = some problems; and 3 = severe problems based on defined criteria; for instance, a subject was assigned to Category 3 if she or he gave at least three affirmative answers to the four questions in the CAGE Questionnaire or if she or he had been arrested at least three times for alcohol abuse (see Pulkkinen & Pitkänen, 1994).

Length of education was coded on a 5-point scale: 1 = basic compulsory education (BCE) at most; 2 = BCE and an employment course; 3 = BCE and vocational school; 4 = higher secondary school (HS) and vocational training; 5 = HS and university studies.

Working career was dichotomized on the basis of data collected in the interview: 1 = unstable working career (several changes of workplace, periods of unemployment, and work not corresponding to training) and 2 = stable working career.

To analyze possible patterns of attributes in adulthood, numerous other variables measuring the three components of personality style (personality characteristics, life orientation, and behavioral activities) were additionally examined. Data were collected from a mailed questionnaire, an interview, and personality inventories. Data were then reduced to 12 composite scores based on a factor analysis for each component of personality style (Pulkkinen, 1996). The composites measured the following: (a) for personality characteristics: nonconscientiousness, extraversion versus introversion, neuroticism, and agreeableness versus aggressiveness; (b) for life orientation: reflectiveness, positive versus negative life attitudes, and resignation versus exploration; and (c) for behavioral activities: family versus single-life orientation, social integration versus disintegration, alcoholism, intellectual interests, and party culture.

∞ RESULTS

Homotypic Continuity

Figure 8.2 shows the correlation coefficients between the corresponding teacher ratings over 6 years, from age 8 to 14, and their correlations with the age-27 self-ratings. The correlations between the age-8 and -14 teacher ratings (Figure 8.2, inner circle) were significant except for anxiety in boys and high self-control in girls. A significant gender difference was found in the stability of low self-control from age 8 to 14: It was higher for boys than for girls.

The age-8 teacher ratings on boys' behavior also correlated significantly with the age-27 self-ratings (Figure 8.2, outer circle) except for aggression and weak self-control, but for females, these correlations were only significant for passive behavior (anxiety, passivity, and compliance). A significant difference between the sexes was evident in the stability of constructiveness, it being lower for females than for males. The length of time did not affect the size of the stability correlations when self-ratings in adulthood were used as criteria. The age-14 teacher ratings correlated with the age-27 self-ratings (middle circle) as highly as the age-8 teacher ratings.

In general, the homotypic continuity of personality characteristics was higher at school age than from school age to adult-

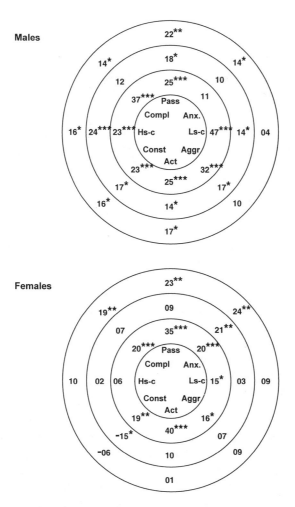

Figure 8.2. Correlations (Decimal Points Omitted) Between Teacher Ratings at Age 8 and 14 (Inner Circle), Between Teacher Ratings at Age 14 and Self-Ratings at Age 27 (Middle Circle), and Between Teacher Ratings at Age 8 and Self-Ratings at Age 27 (Outer Circle); Corresponding Variables at Each Age (cf. Table 8.1 and Figure 8.1).

hood, especially for males. This difference may be partly a result of differences in methods; at school age, teachers made the ratings, whereas in adulthood, only self-ratings were available. The long-term continuity of personality characteristics was most significant for passive types of behavior in females. In males, no clear differences between the characteristics existed in their long-term continuity.

Heterotypic Continuity

Variable Approach

To study how personality attributes in childhood predicted expected outcomes in adulthood, correlation coefficients between the age-8 teacher ratings and adult criminality, problem drinking, length of education, and stability of working career were calculated. Figure 8.3 shows that aggression and low self-control at age 8 correlated positively with male problem drinking (inner circle) and criminality (outer circle), whereas male compliance and high self-control correlated negatively with them. For females, no characteristic predicted criminality, but negative correlations were found between active prosocial behavior (constructiveness) and criminality. Heavy drinking in women was predicted by low self-control, aggressiveness, and anxiety.

A reverse pattern of correlations was obtained for length of education and stability of working career (Figure 8.3, correlations in parentheses). Both constructiveness and compliance predicted length of education (inner circle) and stable working careers (outer circle) in males, whereas low self-control, aggression, and anxiety correlated negatively with them. For females, a longer education and stable working careers were predicted by behavioral activity, constructiveness, and high self-control, whereas passivity, anxiety, and low self-control correlated negatively with them. Consequently, a gender difference was found in the predictive power of personality characteristics; early behavioral activity in girls was a stronger indicator of positive outcomes in adulthood than in boys in whom early passive behavior (compliance) predicted a longer education.

Gender differences were further confirmed by stepwise multiple regression analyses. These were computed by treating adult outcomes (problem drinking, criminality, length of education, and stable working career) as dependent variables and the age-8 teacher ratings as predictors. For males, significant predictors were aggression and low self-control. Aggression predicted problem drinking ($r = .24$, $p < .01$), and with low self-control, criminality ($r = .34$, $p < .001$). Low self-control predicted short education ($r = .20$, $p < .01$) and an unstable working career ($r = .30$, $p <$

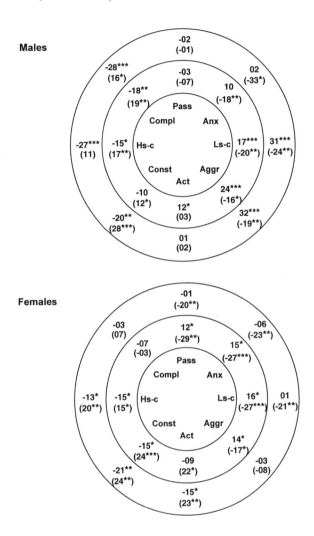

Figure 8.3. Correlations (Decimal Points Omitted) of Teacher Ratings at Age 8 With Problem Drinking (Inner Circle) and Number of Arrests (Outer Circle) When Alcohol-Related Offenses Were Excluded (Outer Circle). In Parentheses, Correlations of Teacher Ratings at Age 8 With Length of Education (Inner Circle) and Stability of Working Career (Outer Circle).

.001). For females, aggression did not appear as a significant predictor, but low self-control predicted problem drinking $(r = .16, p < .05)$, and with low constructiveness, an unstable working career ($r = .30$, $p < .001$). In particular, low self-control with passivity predicted a short education in women ($r = .41$, $p < .001$).

Person Approach

Patterns of Child Behavior. To study whether individuals with a specific pattern of behavior in childhood exhibited given characteristics in adulthood more or less frequently than expected, patterns of child behavior were examined by using a clustering technique based on squared Euclidean distances (WARD; SPSS-x package). The age-8 teacher rating variables were first recoded on a "quasi-absolute" scale (Bergman & Magnusson, 1991, 1996) with the following definitions: 0 = no characteristic in question; 1 = characteristic not strongly evident; 2 = characteristic clearly evident; 3 = pronounced characteristic. The number of clusters was gradually increased from two to eight. The best number of clusters was six for boys and girls. A higher number of clusters with the current sample size resulted in specific clusters with a small number of subjects.

For the interpretation of the clusters, they were compared in the age-8 clustering variables. One-way ANOVAs showed that the effect of grouping was very significant ($p < .001$) on each variable for men and women (Table 8.2). Sheffe's test on group differences (on the $p < .05$ significance level) confirmed that the cluster labeled as aggressive had higher means than the clusters labeled as anxious, compliant, and stable in aggression, as well as in activity, whereas the cluster labeled as anxious had the highest means in anxiety and passivity. The cluster labeled as compliant had high means in compliance and passivity, compared with its means in other characteristics, whereas the cluster labeled as constructive had high means in constructiveness, high control, and activity. In addition to these clusters that delineated Type Ae to Type Di behaviors (cf. Figure 8.1), two other clusters were extracted. One of them suggested low self-control and was labeled as labile; another suggested high self-control and was labeled as stable. Some differences between the sexes existed in the coverage of the clusters. The cluster labile covered more characteristics for boys than for girls (the boys' cluster received high means in activity, aggression, low self-control, and anxiety, but the girls' cluster only in activity and low self-control). In contrast, the coverage of the cluster anxious was broader for girls than for boys.

TABLE 8.2 Age 8 Cluster Means in the Clustering Variables, Teacher Ratings Recoded on a "Quasi-Absolute" Scale From 0 to 3

Clusters	Sex	N	Activity	Aggression	Low control	Anxiety	Passivity	Compliance	High control	Constructiveness
1. Aggressive	M	31	2.06	1.52	.90	.10	.19	.23	.00	.45
	F	27	2.26	1.48	.67	.52	.15	.07	.15	.78
2. Labile	M	39	1.82	1.72	2.21	1.13	.46	.08	.10	.28
	F	38	1.18	.45	1.00	.45	.95	.34	.16	.18
3. Anxious	M	27	.93	.85	1.33	2.22	2.19	.96	.30	.59
	F	21	.95	71.00	.62	2.57	2.19	1.33	1.14	.33
4. Compliant	M	32	.84	.13	.41	.47	1.58	1.41	.84	.78
	F	16	.88	.00	.38	.44	1.63	1.88	1.06	.13
5. Stable	M	47	1.57	.26	.28	.72	1.06	2.02	2.15	2.26
	F	34	1.59	.03	.24	.56	1.15	1.29	1.94	1.47
6. Constructive	M	20	2.25	.90	.45	.10	.15	.80	1.45	1.85
	F	37	2.57	.43	.11	.24	.38	1.62	2.16	2.08
Total (mean)	M	196	1.56	.87	.94	.81	.95	.98	.86	1.06
Scheffe			1,2,5, 6 > 3,4 1,6 > 5	1,2 > 3,4,5 2 > 6 3,6 > 4,5	2,3 > 4,5,6 1 > 5 2 > 1,3	2,3 > 1,4,6 3 > 2,5 5 > 1,6	3,4,5 > 1,2,6 3,4 > 5 3 > 4	4,5 > 1,2,3,6 5 > 4 3,6 > 1,2	4,5,6 > 1,2,3 5,6 > 4 5 > 6	5,6 > 1,2,3,4 4 > 2
Total (mean)	F	173	1.67	.51	.50	.69	.95	1.02	1.14	.95
Scheffe			1,6 > 2,3,4,5 5 > 3,4	1 > 2,3 4,5,6 3 > 5	2 > 6,5 1 > 6	3 > 1,2 4,5,6	2,3,4,5 > 1,6 3 > 2,5	3,4,5,6 > 1,2	5,6 > 1,2,3,4 3,4 > 1,2	5,6 > 1,2,3,4 6 > 5 1 > 2

173

The concurrent validity of the clusters was studied by comparing the means of the clusters in peer nominations made at the same time as the teacher ratings on identical variables. For boys, the concurrent validity of all clusters was high. For instance, the aggressive boys were distinct (Scheffe's test, $p < .05$) from the other clusters in aggressiveness; the anxious boys differed from their constructive, stable, and aggressive counterparts in anxiety; and the constructive boys differed from the other clusters in constructiveness. The concurrent validity of the clusters was also good for girls except for the cluster compliant: The teacher-rated compliant girls did not differ from the other clusters in compliance rated by peers.

Adult Outcomes of Childhood Behavior Patterns. The clusters were cross-tabulated with dichotomized variables for criminality (arrested once or more vs. no arrests), problem drinking (Category 3 vs. the rest for men; Categories 2 and 3 vs. the rest for women), education (Categories 4 and 5 for high education vs. the rest), and stability of working career (stable working career vs. the rest). The cross-tabulations (Table 8.3) showed that the prediction was most accurate for the stable boys; they were to have high education and a stable working career more often than expected from the independence model (called type) and were to be arrested and become a problem drinker less often than expected (called antitype). The labile boys were not likely to maintain a stable working career, and the anxious boys were not likely to have a long education. It is to be noted that 20% also of the stable and constructive boys had been arrested at least once, compared with about 40% of the labile, anxious, and aggressive boys. A much smaller proportion of the stable, constructive, and compliant boys were to be arrested at least twice (only 6%), whereas about 30% of the aggressive, labile, and anxious boys were to be arrested at least twice.

Belonging to the constructive group predicted high education and a stable working career in women. As mentioned above, the cluster compliant did not differ from other clusters in compliance when peer nominations were used as criteria. A questionable validity of the cluster may explain the fact that, unexpectedly, the compliant girls had ended up committing a disproportionate number of criminal offenses as adults. None of the anxious girls had committed offenses, but they were likely to have had a shorter education.

TABLE 8.3 Patterns of Behavior in Childhood and Their
Appearance in Some Categories for Adult Outcomes
(Percentages)

		Percentages that appear in categories for			
Cluster at age 8	*N*	*Arrested*	*Problem drinker*	*High education*	*Stable working career*
Males					
Aggressive	31	35.5	33.5	27.16	74.1
Labile	39	41.0	33.3	16.7	51.5^{at}
Anxious	27	40.7	40.7	4.2^{at}	65.0
Compliant	32	28.1	15.6	20.0	72.4
Stable	47	19.1^{at}	12.8^{at}	33.3^{t}	85.0^{t}
Constructive	20	20.0	25.0	27.8	83.3
Females					
Aggressive	27	7.4	22.2	40.0	76.0
Labile	38	15.8	18.4	45.7	60.0
Anxious	21	0.0	19.0	25.0^{at}	57.9
Compliant	16	25.0^{t}	18.8	26.7	69.2
Stable	34	5.9	8.8	48.3	82.1
Constructive	37	5.4	10.8	67.6^{t}	85.7^{t}

NOTE: t = Type; the percentage is higher than expected from an independence model; at =
Antitype; the percentage is lower than expected.

The results concerning the adult outcomes of childhood patterns differed from the correlative results. For instance, the aggressive boys were not to be arrested more often than predicted from the independence model, nor were they to become problem drinkers. Nevertheless, aggressiveness at age 8 correlated significantly with criminal arrests and problem drinking (Figure 8.3).

In an attempt to explain the conflicting results, the most aggressive individuals (above the 75th percentile) and individuals with the lowest self-control, respectively, were excluded from correlative analyses. About half of the excluded individuals were the same in both cases (they belonged to the highest quartile in both variables). After the exclusion, the correlations turned out to be insignificant, male aggressiveness correlating with criminality by .03 and with problem drinking by .12 (cf. Figure 8.3: .32 and .24, respectively). Correspondingly, low self-control correlated with criminality by .03 and with problem drinking by .08 (cf.

Figure 8.3: .31 and .17, respectively), indicating that when the most aggressive individuals or individuals with the lowest self-control were not included in the analysis, these variables did not predict criminality or problem drinking. Although boys belonging to the highest quartiles in the current study appeared significantly more often than expected in the aggressive and labile clusters, they made up only half of the size of the clusters. Boys with less prominent aggressiveness or low self-control in these clusters were not to be arrested or were not to become heavy drinkers more often than other boys, and therefore criminality and problem drinking were not predicted by these clusters.

The findings on the insignificant correlations between child and adult maladjustment when the boys belonging to the highest quartiles for aggressiveness and low self-control were removed are in accordance with the results of Bergman and Magnusson (1996). They found that adult maladjustment (criminality and alcohol abuse) is predicted by aggressiveness in childhood only when it is an indicator of a multiple-problem syndrome in childhood, but not when aggressiveness is a single problem. Because the clustering variables in the current study did not include school motivation, poor peer relations, and school achievement as in the Bergman and Magnusson study, the cluster analysis did not produce comparable multiproblem clusters. Previous analyses with the current data (Pulkkinen, 1992a, 1992b), however, have shown that the patterns (including the multiproblem clusters) extracted by Magnusson and Bergman (1988) were replicated with the Jyväskylä longitudinal data. The most predictive of adult criminality was a severe multiproblem cluster in childhood. As pointed out elsewhere (Pulkkinen & Hämäläinen, 1995), low self-control is a characteristic that easily causes problems in peer relations and school adjustment, and it is itself at least partly a consequence of adverse child experiences and home conditions. In very extreme cases wherein disadvantageous factors are most accumulated, the risk of crime is highest.

Pattern Stability

Patterns of Adult Behavior

To study whether an individual remains in his or her pattern of social characteristics from childhood to adulthood, a clustering technique (WARD) was also applied to the age-27 self-ratings. Different numbers of clusters were cross-tabulated with the clusters extracted from the age-8 teacher ratings. The cross-tabulations did not show significant stability in these clusters.

The age-27 self-ratings concerned personality characteristics that form only one of the three components of personality style. Two other components, life orientation and behavioral activities, were added to the analysis of the patterns of adult behavior. As mentioned in the methods section of this chapter, 12 composite scores were extracted to represent these components. Separate cluster analyses for men and women were computed by using these scores. Altogether, seven clusters were extracted for males and females (Pulkkinen, 1996), but only the first three were included for analysis in the current study.

Males. Figure 8.4 shows that the first two clusters divided the men into two groups, adjusted (n = 103; 75% of the men) and conflicted (n = 35; 25% of the men). When three clusters were extracted, adjusted men divided into two subclusters, resilient (n = 59; 43% of the men) and introvert (n = 44; 32% of the men). The conflicted men remained unaffected.

Men and women differed significantly in all composites for behavioral activities: women were more family-oriented, had more intellectual interests, and were socially more integrated than men (Pulkkinen, 1996). Men, in contrast, had higher means in alcoholism and party culture. In personality variables, men and women differed only in nonconscientiousness (women were more conscientious), and in life orientation they differed only in resignation (women scored higher in it).

The comparison of each cluster with the complement (including all other same-sex participants) revealed that the conflicted men had more negative life attitudes, drank more heavily, and were less integrated into society, more neurotic, less agreeable, less conscientious, and less family-oriented than the adjusted men, but they were more entertainment-oriented (Pulkkinen, 1996). Attributes that distinguished resilients from the other men were high extraversion and low neuroticism, positive life attitudes, reflectiveness, and high social integration in terms of a stable working career. The resilients were also more oriented to family and intellectual matters but less oriented to entertainment and alcohol abuse than other men. Introverts, in contrast, were lower in extraversion and nonconscientiousness but higher in social integration, especially in terms of their very low number of criminal arrests, than the other men. Introverts were also more agreeable and less reflective than the other men.

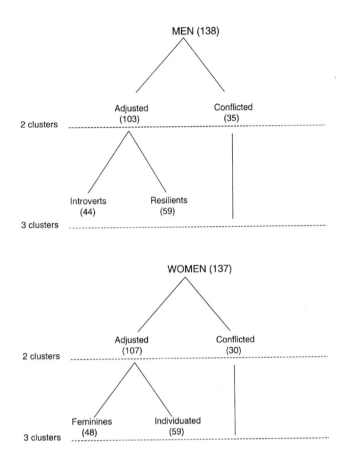

Figure 8.4. Personality Styles

Females. As seen in Figure 8.4, the first two clusters also divided the women into two groups, adjusted ($n = 107$; 78% of the women) and conflicted ($n = 30$; 22% of the women). When three clusters were extracted, the adjusted women divided into two subgroups, feminine ($n = 48$; 35% of the women) and individuated ($n = 59$; 43% of the women). The conflicted women remained unaffected.

The personality characteristics that were typical of the conflicted women were neuroticism and introversion, whereas those typical of the conflicted men were neuroticism, aggressiveness, and nonconsciousness (Pulkkinen, 1996). Both the conflicted women and men drank more heavily, were less integrated into society, and had more negative life attitudes than the adjusted women and men. The conflicted women also scored lower than the adjusted women in reflectiveness and intellectual interests. Attributes more characteristic of feminines than of all other women included high conscientiousness, extraversion, and agreeableness, and high family orientation, resignation, and social integration. The feminines scored lower than the other women in alcoholism and intellectual interests. The individuated women, in contrast, scored higher than the other women in intellectual interests and reflectiveness; they had also a longer education (Pulkkinen, 1996). The individuated women were more often single at age 27 than the other women. Compared with the other women, they were also characterized by higher exploration and nonconscientiousness and lower neuroticism.

Roots of Personality Styles in Child Characteristics. The mean of each age-27 cluster was compared (*t* test) with the mean of the complement (including all other same-sex participants) in the age-8 teacher ratings. As Table 8.4 shows for males, the conflicted men had been characterized by aggressiveness, low self-control, low compliance, and low constructiveness as children. Introverts had been more passive and more anxious in childhood than other men, and resilients had been less passive and less anxious than other men. In terms of the model of emotional and behavioral regulation (Figure 8.1), the two adjusted male groups had differed from the conflicted men in self-control, whereas the two adjusted male groups had differed from each other in passivity. The low self-control among the conflicted men had been characterized by Type Ae behavior: The conflicted men had been more aggressive than the other boys. The introverts had been more passive than the other boys, passivity being characterized by Type Di behavior (anxiety). The resilients had been nonanxious and nonpassive boys but otherwise not distinct from other boys. It means that, in addition to the boys who had been characterized by high self-control, many boys who had been characterized by low self-control in childhood had also become resilient men.

In contrast with men, the low self-control among the conflicted women had been characterized by Type Di behavior in childhood; the conflicted women had been more anxious and passive than other girls (Table 8.4). The individuated women had been nonanxious girls. Feminines had not differed from other women in any studied characteristics in childhood.

TABLE 8.4 Male and Female Personality Styles; the Means of the Age-27 Clusters in the Age-8 Teacher Ratings Compared With the Means of the Complement (All Other Men or Women)

Teacher ratings		Men	
Age 8	Resilient	Introvert	Conflicted
Activity	0.17	−0.28*	0.01
Aggressiveness	−0.03	−0.18	0.41**
Low Control	−0.11	−0.18	0.35**
Anxiety	−0.23**	0.34*	0.17
Passivity	−0.28***	0.49**	0.01
Compliance	0.09	0.18	−0.38**
High Control	0.05	0.19	−0.44**
Constructiveness	0.12	−0.01	−0.37**

Teacher ratings		Women	
Age 8	Individuated	Feminine	Conflicted
Activity	0.05	0.22	−0.25
Aggressiveness	0.00	0.04	0.14
Low Control	−0.08	−0.08	0.39*
Anxiety	−0.30*	−0.11	0.47**
Passivity	−0.14	−0.13	0.33*
Compliance	−0.11	0.07	−0.14
High Control	−0.08	0.15	−0.17
Constructiveness	0.10	0.12	−0.20

NOTE: * $p < .05$; ** $p < .01$; *** $p < .001$.

Cross-tabulations of the six age-8 clusters and the three adult personality styles revealed that no pattern in childhood strongly predicted a given adult lifestyle. The stability was higher if the prediction only concerned the two major clusters, adjusted and conflicted. A slight continuity from the six age-8 clusters to the two age-27 clusters was obtained ($\chi^2 = 10.36$, $df = 5$, $p = .07$ for males; $\chi^2 = 10.15$, $df = 5$, $p = .07$ for females). Compared with the independence model, (a) the compliant boys had more often than expected become adjusted men, (b) the anxious girls had become conflicted women, and (c) the constructive girls had become adjusted women.

The results suggested that low self-control in childhood precipitated a high incidence of being conflicted as an adult, whereas high self-control tended toward one's becoming adjusted. To confirm this general finding, 2 × 2 cross-tabulations were made after combining the clusters for low self-control (aggressive, labile, and anxious) and the clusters for high self-control (constructive, stable, and compliant). There was a significant dependency between the age-8 and -27 groupings ($\chi^2 = 9.79$, $df = 1$, $p < .01$ for males; $\chi^2 = 5.08$, $df = 1$, $p < .05$ for females). High self-control in childhood predicted adjustment in adulthood, whereas low self-control predicted problems in adjustment.

It is to be noted, however, that two thirds of the boys and girls who had been characterized by low self-control in childhood were well adjusted in adulthood, and only one third became conflicted individuals. Among the conflicted individuals, those individuals were overrepresented who scored in the highest quartiles for aggressiveness and low self-control (and an anxiety for females) in childhood. Of the children who were characterized by high self-control, 13% became conflicted adults.

∞ CONCLUSIONS

The hypothesis that the homotypic continuity (differential stability) between behavioral characteristics decreases when the interval between the measurement points increases was not uniformly supported. Continuity was greater during the school years, between age 8 and age 14, than between school age and adulthood, but this might be a result of methodological factors. At ages 8 and 14, teacher ratings were used as measures, whereas in adulthood, self-ratings were used. Correlations between the age-14 teacher ratings and the age-27 self-ratings were not higher than the correlations between the age-8 teacher ratings and the age-27 self-ratings, as the hypothesis suggested.

The hypothesis on heterotypic continuity (coherence of personality) was supported. Children's behavioral characteristics that depicted Type Rsp and Ccp behaviors predicted long education and a stable working career, whereas Type Ae and Di behaviors predicted criminal arrests and problem drinking. The latter prediction, however, was valid only for children with the most prominent problem behaviors. The highest quartile did not only determine the size of correlations for low behavioral control; also, the exclusion of individuals who had been most prominent in high behavioral control mollified correlations, except for constructiveness in women, which remained a significant predictor of long education and a stable career, as well as of low drinking and criminality despite the exclusion of the highest quartile of constructive girls. This analysis demonstrates that significant predictive correlations may be explained by the continuity of behavior in a few extreme cases. In these cases, a person-environment interaction may accumulate to facilitate a given outcome. For instance, the child's aggressiveness may lead to a negative teacher-student relationship, reduce school motivation, cause a dropout, and increase the likelihood of having antisocial peers and committing criminal offenses. To understand the stability and changes of behavior, a more person-oriented approach is needed.

The hypothesis on pattern stability (ipsative stability) was confirmed only after all three components of personality style (personality characteristics, life orientation, and behavioral activities) were included in the adult behavioral pattern analysis and the basic division into adjusted and conflicted individuals was taken into consideration. When adult personality styles were scrutinized in more detail, the pattern stability became weaker.

In general, the results showed some continuity between childhood and adult behavior. This demonstrates what Caspi, Elder, and Herbener (1990, p. 14) described as follows: There is a "coherence of interactional styles across social transformations in the age-graded life course." It is to be noted, however, that conflicted behavior in adulthood was less common than problem behavior in childhood; only one fourth of adults were identified as conflicted, whereas one half of subjects belonged to the clusters aggressive, labile, and anxious in childhood. Two thirds of the children with low self-control became well-adjusted adults. The risk of exhibiting conflicted behavior for adulthood was highest in individuals who had very prominent problem behavior in childhood.

The identification of children with prominent problem behavior and the development of an intervention program for them is one recommendation that can be made on the basis of the current findings. Most children with milder problems appear to develop positively in any case. The current findings also showed, however, that about 10% of children who had a good prognosis (who belonged to the clusters constructive, stable, and compliant) became conflicted adults. A detailed life history analysis would be needed for the study of possible risk factors in their lives.

Results were, on the whole, similar for men and women. Notable differences included the fact that social activity, especially the constructiveness versus anxiety dimension, was more strongly related to adult outcomes in women than in men. In contrast, self-control, especially the aggressiveness versus compliance dimension, was a more potent predictor of adult outcomes in males than in females. The results also suggested that externalizing behavioral problems in boys predict maladjustment in adulthood, whereas both externalizing and internalizing problems in girls predict maladjustment.

∞∾∞

COMMENTS ON CHAPTER 8

Lea Pulkkinen began her longitudinal study more than 25 years ago. It has weathered well through the many changes that have taken place within the disciplines during this time. It asks the question that continues to be asked: What is the predictability of adult characteristics from childhood behavior? The question has many answers, depending on the particular continuities being investigated, the ages being compared, and the characteristics of the sample.

In this study, continuities in personality characteristics and lifestyle patterns are investigated over a substantial span of years (8-year-olds to 27-year-olds) in a culturally homogeneous sample. This is a rare body of information; it undoubtedly avoids many confounding influences that would be present in a more heterogeneous sample. This study is rare and valuable in following individuals across major developmental transitions—middle childhood to adolescence to established adulthood. Life course has been examined for homotypic stability and heterotypic coherence, with variable and cluster analyses.

Measured in these various ways, connections between the qualities of the 8-year-old and the 27-year-old adult are visible, but the links are not strong. The strongest association is between high self-control in childhood (measured broadly) and adjustment in adulthood –a not unimportant finding. It is consistent with data from other studies covering earlier stages in development. In following children of well and psychiatrically ill mothers, from 3 years to 15 years of age, we found that failure to develop age-appropriate self-control in the early years was predictive of a child's disruptive behavior problems at 15 years.

As Lea Pulkkinen indicates, her study did not intend to focus on children with extreme patterns of behavior, but the significance of the extremes was "thrust upon it." The association between childhood aggression and lack of self-control and adult drinking and criminality was accounted for solely by the children at the extremes. It would be interesting to examine other early extremes in this sample for predictions to adulthood.

Another kind of subgroup appears in the sample: children whose early qualities are much out of line with adult outcomes. As Lea Pulkkinen suggests, the life histories of these individuals will provide insights into development counter to prediction.

This continuing study holds many potential clues that can bring fuller understanding of when and how continuity and discontinuity along the life course occur.

Marian Radke-Yarrow

∞ Note

1. The four behavioral types were called from A to D in Pulkkinen (1995, 1996). Renaming them Ae to Di was suggested to avoid a confusion with the Type A behavior that is a predictor of coronary heart disease.

~ *9* ~

A Prospective Replication of Developmental Pathways in Disruptive and Delinquent Behavior

Rolf Loeber

University of Pittsburgh

Mary S. DeLamatre

University of Pittsburgh

Kate Keenan

University of Chicago

Quanwu Zhang

Rutgers University

*W*hen a child presents to a mental health clinic for services, the clinician will want to know the history of past problems and the nature of the presenting problems and will assess various risk factors in the child's environment. The clinician will then determine the child's prognosis and, when appropriate, formulate a treatment plan. It is likely that some clinicians draw on research findings on disruptive child behavior during the process of assessment and may experience that some research findings better address their needs for knowledge than others. In our experience, although mental health workers are often aware of correlational data, they rarely use them in clinical practice. Instead, they often are keenly interested in *individual-based* information that can help in answering prognostic questions; whether a child is likely to outgrow disruptive behavior or instead become worse over time.

A diagnostic system such as the *Diagnostic and Statistical Manual of Mental Disorders* (*DSM-IV*; American Psychiatric Association [APA], 1994) usually provides little help in this regard because the symptoms of diagnoses such as oppositional defiant disorder and conduct disorder are relatively static. Again, in our experience, mental health workers often want a more developmentally relevant classification scheme that takes into account developmental transitions from age-normative to serious disruptive behaviors as these unfold over time. This chapter presents a set of findings, based on prospective data, that replicates our earlier work on developmental pathways to serious disruptive behavior in boys (Loeber, Keenan, & Zhang, 1997; Loeber et al., 1993). We show that a dynamic classification of disruptive behavior can be based on both a variable- and an individual-based set of analyses. Specifically, we propose that meta-analyses of disruptive behavior help in identifying major dimensions of disruptive behavior. Such information can then be used to generate developmental models on within-individual changes on each dimension of disruptive behavior in a dynamic, developmental fashion. We use the term *disruptive behavior* in a broad sense that includes behaviors that are bothersome to adult caregivers (e.g., highly stubborn behavior, lying, truancy, running away from home) or that inflict harm or property loss on others (e.g., physical aggression, vandalism, theft, violent acts), whereas the term *delinquency* refers to that category of disruptive behaviors that can lead to referral to a juvenile court (e.g., robbery, fraud).

VARIABLE-BASED APPROACHES

Many studies on disruptive child behavior are correlational and have demonstrated that one type of disruptive behavior (e.g., aggression) often is associated with another disruptive behavior (e.g., theft; Jessor & Jessor, 1977). The central focus in this variable-based approach is the strength of association between *variables* representing different behaviors. Recently, the correlational approach has been used to develop structural models, in which networks of variables are linked to "latent" constructs, representing "antisocial behavior" (e.g., Patterson, DeBaryshe, & Ramsey, 1989). The practical application of this information, however, is limited. We argue that the correlational approach lacks important information for mental health workers who engage in assessments and interventions. For example, correlational approaches do not usually provide information about (a) the risk status of individual children, (b) their history of earlier disruptive behavior, (c) sequences in the development of disruptive behaviors, and (d) changes in the level of severity of disruptive behavior over time.

∞ INDIVIDUAL-BASED APPROACHES

Another set of studies has focused on identifying *categories of individuals*. In cross-sectional studies, the criteria for distinctions between categories of disruptive individuals have either been based on preconceived notions, as in *DSM-IV* (APA, 1994; e.g., those youths with conduct disorder or oppositional defiant disorder), or on some variant of cluster analytic methods (e.g., Edelbrock & Achenbach, 1980; Frick et al., 1993). A major problem, however, has been that techniques such as cluster analyses have difficulties dealing with behavior patterns that change with development (e.g., Huizinga, 1995). The reason is that a clustering method at Time 1 may produce different clusters than at Time 2 or Time *n*. The linking of these clusters often is difficult to accomplish, especially when there are many assessments over time (Huizinga, 1995).

Dynamic Classification Schemes

Longitudinal analyses have attempted to better capture *individual change* by incorporating changes in the *pattern* of disruptive behaviors of *individuals* over time (e.g., Baicker-McKee, 1990; Block, 1971; Le Blanc & Kaspy, 1995; Loeber, 1991; Magnusson, 1988; Pulkkinen & Hurme, 1984). These studies all focus on within-subject changes on dimensions of disruptive behavior. The within-subject approach to disruptive and delinquent behavior has the advantage of identifying different developmental progressions for different youths. After the onset of minor disruptive behaviors, some children's behaviors may escalate over time to serious acts. Others may experience an onset but level off at moderately serious disruptive behaviors. Key questions are whether such different developmental changes over time take place in an orderly rather than in a random fashion, and whether individuals progress along one or more dimensions of disruptive behavior.

One advantage of the study of within-subject changes of behavior over time is that disruptive behavior can be placed in the context of an individual's developmental history. Such information is most useful for individually formulated prognosis and interventions. As to prognosis, future behavior often is better predicted by a history of earlier behavior than by current behavior alone (Loeber & Dishion, 1983). Concerning interventions, these should be optimally informed not only about the current and past disruptive behavior but also about possible future disruptive behaviors that are "developmentally in line" and may constitute target behaviors for prevention.

We are of the opinion that the conceptualization of past, current, and future disruptive behavior can be best captured by means of developmental pathways (Loeber et al., 1993). A *developmental pathway* is defined by the stages of behavior that unfold over time in a predictable order. Similar to Bowlby's (1973) description of personality development, we hypothesize that individuals may proceed along single or multiple developmental pathways toward serious antisocial behavior, each pathway representing major dimensions of disruptive behavior.

Basic Dimensions
of Disruptive Child Behavior

A major question is what dimension(s) of disruptive behavior can be best used to formulate developmental pathways. Researchers face a plethora of choices, such as impulsive behavior, sensation seeking, underarousal, and other known aspects of disruptive behaviors (e.g., Loeber, 1990). Inevitably, there is some arbitrariness in the choice of one or more dimensions. We argue that one way to minimize such arbitrariness is by using information from factor analyses of disruptive child behavior. Factor analyses based on parents' and teachers' ratings have provided a powerful tool with which to extract basic dimensions of disruptive behavior. Thus, before addressing pathways, we first need to examine the major behavioral dimensions of child disruptive behavior, which can then constitute the "paving stones" for the pathways.

Loeber and Schmaling (1985) executed a meta-analysis on 28 factor analyses based on either parent or teacher ratings of disruptive child behaviors. A multidimensional scaling demonstrated one major dimension of disruptive behavior with overt disruptive behavior on one pole (e.g., temper tantrums, attacks people), covert problem behavior on the other pole (e.g., theft, setting fires), and disobedience situated in the middle of this dimension. More recently, Frick et al. (1993) repeated the meta-analysis on an expanded number of studies involving more than 28,000 children. The results basically replicated those reported by Loeber and Schmaling, with one difference: A destructive-nondestructive dimension of problem behavior was also extracted.

The two studies had in common, however, the overt-covert dimension of disruptive child behavior. It should be noted that meta-analyses have not specifically focused on disobedience. Disobedience, defiance, truancy, and running away differ from most other disruptive behaviors in that they usually do not inflict the same degree of harm on others. We see these problems as different manifestations of conflict with authority that are germane for the development of overt and covert disruptive behavior (this has been postulated by Patterson, 1980, 1982). Also, Fergusson, Horwood, and Lynskey (1994), in a confirmatory factor analysis, found that the structure of disruptive behavior best fitted a model consisting of three disruptive factors: (a) oppositional defiant behavior, (b) overt conduct problems, and (c) covert conduct problems. That disruptive child behavior has more than one dimension is a point not shared by all researchers, with some holding that a single dimension can best represent that behavior (e.g., Patterson, 1992).

Developmental Sequences and Pathways

The next question is whether there are orderly sequences in the onset of different disruptive behaviors. Earlier work on sequences in the development of delinquency has been undertaken by Huizinga (1995) and Elliott (1994) in their analyses of longitudinal data from the National Youth Survey and by Le Blanc, Côté, and Loeber (1991) in the analysis of Quebec longitudinal data. A common finding of the studies was that less serious forms of delinquency over time preceded the onset of more serious delinquent acts. No attempts were made to identify and integrate sequences across dimensions of delinquent acts (e.g., property vs. person offenses). Also, the studies did not aim to elucidate developmental sequences between nondelinquent disruptive behaviors and various forms of delinquency.

In our approach, we wanted to combine knowledge of dimensions of disruptive behavior with knowledge of developmental sequences involving early and later manifestations of delinquency (e.g., Loeber, Stouthamer-Loeber, & Green, 1991). In our previous work (Loeber et al., 1993; Loeber, Green, Keenan, & Lahey, 1995), we used the information from the above-mentioned meta-analyses to formulate and test three developmental pathways (see Figure 9.1). The first pathway is the *authority conflict pathway*, which starts with stubborn behavior and has defiance (doing things own way, refusing to do things, disobedience) as Stage 1 and authority avoidance (staying out late, truancy, running away) as Stage 2 and Stage 3, respectively. This pathway fits best for boys engaging in these behaviors before age 12. The second pathway is the *covert pathway*, which has minor covert behavior as Stage 1 (lying, shoplifting), property damage (setting fires, damaging property) as Stage 2, and moderate to very serious forms of delinquency as Stage 3 (joyriding, picking pockets, stealing from a car, fencing, writing illegal checks, using illegal credit cards, stealing a car, selling drugs, breaking and entering). The third pathway is called the *overt pathway* and has aggression (annoying others, bullying) as Stage 1, physical fighting (fighting, gang fighting) as Stage 2, and violence (attacking someone, strong-arming, forcing sex) as Stage 3.

The pathways represent developmentally formulated stages that are sensitive both to age-appropriate manifestations of problem behavior and to increases in severity, with each stage of a pathway serving as a stepping stone toward more serious behaviors. Each of the three hypothesized pathways can be thought of as representing different developmental tasks: (a) The overt pathway represents aggression, as opposed to positive social problem solving; (b) the covert pathway represents lying, vandalism, and theft versus honesty and respect for property; and (c) the authority conflict pathway represents conflict with, and avoidance of, authority figures versus respect for authority figures. This conceptualization implies that juveniles who meet one developmental task (e.g., honesty) will not necessarily meet another developmental task. Thus, some youths may fail several developmental tasks. This implies that pathways in disruptive behavior can be conceptualized as different lines of development, with some multiproblem boys occupying several pathways at the same time.

A key to the identification of stages within a pathways model is documenting the age of onset curves for disruptive behaviors. In our earlier work on the middle and oldest samples (Loeber et al., 1993), we found that the onset of behaviors in Stage 1 of a pathway (e.g., minor theft) tended to be earlier than the onset of behaviors in Stage 2 of a pathway (e.g., property damage), which in turn took

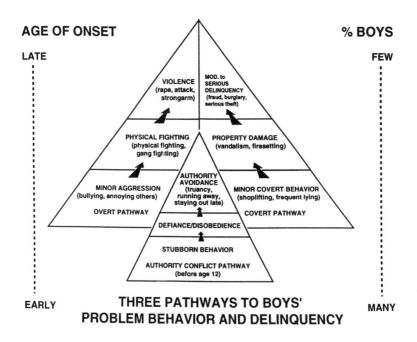

Figure 9.1. Three Pathways to Boys' Problem Behavior and Delinquency
SOURCES: Loeber et al. (1995); Loeber et al. (1993).

place earlier than the behaviors in Stage 3 of a pathway (e.g., moderate to serious forms of delinquency). The findings applied to each of the stages in the three pathways (Figure 9.1), with the exception that, by age 12, the onset of Stages 2 and 3 of the authority conflict pathway coincided, which restricted that pathway to those younger than age 12.

The cumulative onset curves then provided the basis for the pathway model, in which individuals' progression in disruptive and delinquent behavior is thought to go through an orderly sequence of disruptive behaviors (Loeber et al., 1993). For that purpose, we examined how many boys entered a pathway at its Stage 1 and how many entered a pathway at later stages. For the middle and oldest samples, we found that the majority of boys fitted on one or more pathways; that is, most boys entered a pathway at Stage 1, rather than at a later stage, and most boys who had engaged in serious antisocial behavior were shown to have engaged first in behaviors constituting the earlier stages of a given pathway.

A proportion of boys could be located on several pathways. Multiplicity of pathways was found to be related to the frequency of self-reported and official reports of offending. The rate of offending was highest among those boys in all three pathways (authority conflict, overt, and covert). Among the dual pathways, however, the rate was highest among the boys in the overt-covert and the authority conflict-covert pathways than among boys in the authority conflict-overt pathways.

∞ EXPERIMENTERS AND PERSISTERS

Our prior work was hampered by an overinclusion of individuals in pathways (Loeber et al., 1995) because it included all youths engaging in disruptive behavior, irrespective of the duration of the behavior, such that classification along the three stages of each developmental pathway were based on the occurrence but not on the persistence of disruptive behavior. Thus, any notions about the possible temporary nature of the disruptive behavior were not taken into account. This was remedied in a second paper (Loeber et al., 1995), in which we made a distinction between experimenters and persisters in disruptive behavior. Childhood and adolescence are periods in which many youths "experiment" with various behaviors, such as shoplifting or skipping school (Richters & Cicchetti, 1993). We assume that, for most youths, this experimentation is common and temporary in nature during that period of life. We also assume that experimentation allows youths to find out the negative consequences of their behavior and to learn from it. This is not the case for some youths, who after experimentation continue to "persist" in the disruptive behavior and whose behavior is more orderly than that of experimenters. For example, we found that a higher proportion of persisters, as compared with experimenters, entered a pathway on Stage 1 rather than on Stage 2 or Stage 3 of the pathway.

The question may be asked whether the distinction between experimenters and persisters is important for boys' escalation in severity of disruptive behavior. Because our definition of persistence is not confounded with escalation in severity, we were able to address this question (Loeber et al., 1995). We found that persisters, as compared with experimenters, were much more likely to follow the progressive stages in the pathways from less to more serious stages. In other words, the development of different manifestations of disruptive behavior in persisters was more predictable than that of experimenters. Also, we found that the rate of offending was highest for persisters who progressed to the later stages of one or more pathways (Loeber et al., 1993; Loeber et al., 1995).

Several authors have argued that conduct problems (including many problems in disruptive pathways) are associated with a diagnosis of attention-deficit hyperactivity disorder (ADHD; APA, 1994). Specifically, ADHD has been linked to boys' transition from oppositional defiant disorder (ODD) to conduct disorder (CD) and to a worsening of CD over time (e.g., Farrington et al., 1990; Lambert, 1988; Loeber et al., 1995; Moffitt & Silva, 1988; Satterfield, Hoppe, & Schell, 1982). In our earlier work on the middle and oldest samples in the Pittsburgh Youth Study (Loeber et al., 1995), we found that few experimenters received the diagnosis of ADHD, whereas proportionally more persisters qualified for that diagnosis in each of the three pathways. The rate of ADHD did not differ, however, on the basis of severity of the behaviors.

Finally, an important test for any classification system is the extent to which it is comprehensive and accounts for the majority of the most serious cases. Our previous work showed that 78.7% and 72.9% of the high-rate self-reported, nonviolent offenders in the middle and the oldest samples, respectively, were persisters who had progressed to Stages 2 and 3 in a pathway.

There is a need to cross-validate the results from the middle and the oldest samples against findings on pathways in the youngest sample in the Pittsburgh Youth Study. First, the availability of nine half-yearly data waves from Grade 1 onward makes it possible to cross-validate the findings prospectively. Second, the influence of ADHD on disruptive pathways can be assessed much better in a younger sample because symptom scores for ADHD tend to decrease later (Hart, Lahey, Loeber, Applegate, & Frick, 1995).

This chapter focuses on the above issues and addresses the following questions:

Do the onset curves of disruptive behavior show the same developmental sequence of disruptive behaviors that had been observed in the previous analyses with the middle and oldest samples?

Can a majority of individuals in the youngest sample who display disruptive behaviors be categorized as "fitters" in the pathway model?

Do a majority of individuals who persist in one or more pathways follow a predictable progression along the stages of the pathway?

Are persisters more likely than experimenters to enter the pathways at earlier phases, as had been found previously?

Is a diagnosis of ADHD associated with persistence in, and progression into, pathways for individuals in the youngest sample?

Is the rate of offending related to experimentation, persistence, and progression in single and multiple pathways?

Do demographic differences exist between experimenters and persisters in each pathway?

Does the pathways model account for the majority of high-rate offenders in the youngest sample?

∞ METHOD

Subjects

Subjects were participants in the Pittsburgh Youth Study, a longitudinal survey of the causes and correlates of delinquency, substance use, and mental health. The study consists of three samples of boys who were in Grades 1, 4, and 7 when the study began. Potential subjects were randomly selected from a list of all boys in these grades in the Pittsburgh Public Schools. At the time of the sample selection, 72% of all schoolchildren in Pittsburgh attended public schools. Of those selected for this study, 84.6% of the boys and their parents consented to participate in the study, resulting in a sample of about 850 boys in each of the grades. There were no significant differences in achievement test scores or the proportion of African American students between study participants and the districtwide male student population.

During the initial screening assessments, each boy, his primary caregiver, and a teacher were administered the appropriate form of the Child Behavior Checklist (Achenbach & Edelbrock, 1983), supplemented by additional items drawn from a delinquency inventory (Elliott, Huizinga, & Ageton, 1985) to identify boys at risk for delinquency and criminal behavior. The information provided by the three informants was combined into an overall risk index by counting a delinquent behavior present if the boy, his caregiver, or his teacher reported the problem as having occurred. Boys ranking in the top 33% were retained in the study, together with an additional 30% randomly selected from the remaining 67%. This report concerns the youngest cohort (503), who subsequent to the initial screening (S), were followed up eight times at 6-month intervals over 4 years (Phases A-H). Boys were, on average, 6.9 years old at Phase S and 10.9 at Phase H.

About half of the boys in the youngest sample were African American and half were Caucasian; this is comparable with the racial composition of the Pittsburgh Public Schools. Approximately 40% of the boys lived with single parents, and about 40% of the caregivers received public assistance (for additional details about the sample, see Van Kammen, Loeber, & Stouthamer-Loeber, 1991). Cooperation rates remained high during the follow-ups. At Phase H, 94% of the subjects were successfully reassessed. The cooperation rates for Phases A through G varied from 93.6% to 99.6%.

Measures

At the first phase following the screening (Phase A), the primary caregiver was administered the Diagnostic Schedule for Children (DISC; Costello, Edelbrock, Dulcan, Kalas, & Klaric, 1984), a structured interview covering lifetime *DSM-III-R* (APA, 1987) symptomatology. The primary caregiver was administered an extended version of the Child Behavior Checklist (CBCL; Achenbach & Edelbrock, 1983; Loeber, Stouthamer-Loeber, Van Kammen, & Farrington, 1991) at each of the Phases S through H. Boys at Phases S through F were administered the 33-item Self-Reported Antisocial Behavior Scale (SRA), which included six items on substance use (Loeber, Stouthamer-Loeber, Van Kammen, & Farrington, 1989) because the more widely applied Self-Reported Delinquency Scale was judged to be too difficult for young children to understand. For the final two phases (G and H), the boys completed the Self-Reported Delinquency Scale (SRD, the adolescent version of the SRA) and the Youth Self-Report (YSR, the child version of the CBCL; Achenbach & Edelbrock, 1983), which covered occurrence of disruptive behavior over the past half year since the previous assessment.

When possible, information about disruptive behavior was pooled across informants so that a behavior was considered positive if it was endorsed by either the child or the caregiver. In the case of defiant behavior, information was gathered from the caregiver only because children often are not good informants about defiant behavior (Loeber, Green, & Lahey, 1990; Loeber, Green, Lahey, & Stouthamer-Loeber, 1989). Information regarding serious covert acts was gathered from the child only because many parents are often unaware about such acts (see Loeber et al., 1993, for details of informants used for certain behaviors).

Retrospective age of onset data were gathered at Phase A from the caregivers' adapted CBCL and DISC, and at Phase G from the boys' report on the SRD (this measure, unlike the SRA, provided an indication of the frequency of self-reported offenses). Overall, however, the majority of onset of behaviors that constitute stages in the pathway model took place during the assessments and were thus measured prospectively.

Analyses

The goal of the current study is to determine the extent to which developmental pathways, which were established by using the middle and oldest samples, can be validated in the youngest sample. Data reduction and analyses conducted for the establishment of the developmental pathways have been described elsewhere and are not repeated here (Loeber et al., 1993; Loeber et al., 1995).

The first step in validating the pathways was to plot the cumulative onset for behaviors in each stage of each pathway to determine whether the stages of the authority conflict, covert, and overt pathways occurred in the order specified by the pathways model. Subsequently, for subjects entering each of the pathways, we calculated the percentage of subjects who fit the sequences of behaviors for each pathway model (fitters). As in previous studies (Loeber et al., 1993; Loeber et al., 1995), *fitters* were defined as those boys who exhibited disruptive behaviors in the developmental sequence that was postulated in the pathways model. Those boys whose developmental sequence was inverse from what was postulated were categorized as *nonfitters*.[1] Within the fitter category, we distinguished between normative and nonnormative sequences. *Normative sequences* were those sequences that fully conformed to the pathway model (e.g., minor covert behavior followed by property damage, followed by moderate/serious delinquency). *Nonnormative sequences* were those in which a subject skipped one or more stages within such sequences (e.g., no minor covert behavior, but property damage followed by moderate/serious delinquency).

Next, following the methodology specified in Loeber et al. (1995), those fitting the sequence of behaviors specified in one or more of the pathways (fitters) were divided into experimenters and persisters. We defined *experimenters* as boys whose disruptive behavior within a given stage did not persist at follow-up assessments. Conversely, *persisters* were defined as those boys who were reported at more than one of the eight follow-up assessments to have engaged in a specific disruptive or delinquent behavior. To reduce the chances of false positive classification of the experimenters, boys who reported initiation of problem behavior at Phase H or who reported only one incident of problem behavior at one of the phases but had subsequent missing data were not classified and thus not included in the analyses. Also, for a small proportion of boys, we did not have full data on each of the nine phases, with *N* limited to 436 for analyses in the authority conflict pathway, 429 in the covert pathway, and 423 in the overt pathway.

Within the persister group, we further made distinctions between those who persisted in minor disruptive behaviors (Stage 1) and those who persisted in more serious behaviors (Stages 2 and 3). Moreover, those persisting in more serious behaviors were divided into boys who persisted in a single pathway and those who persisted in multiple pathways. Finally, we tested whether the pathways equally applied to African American and Caucasian boys.

✆ RESULTS

Developmental Sequences

The onset curve for stubborn behavior increased steadily from birth until it gradually flattened out by age 10. The curve for defiant behavior also increased steadily from birth, but the number of individuals experiencing an onset before age 4 was lower than for stubborn behavior. Then, starting at around age 4, the curve steepened and the onset curve approached that of stubborn behavior by age 10. For authority avoidance, the curve was flat until age 5; at age 6, the curve increased steeply until age 10, when it flattened out. By age 12, 28.6% of the subjects had engaged in authority avoidance, and 39.5% were reported to have engaged in defiance and stubborn behavior.

Few children experienced an onset of minor covert behavior until age 3 or 4, when the curve rose relatively steeply until age 11, at which time it flattened out. The curve for property damage increased only slightly until age 6 or 7, when it accelerated; then it leveled off at age 10 or 11. The curve for moderate to serious delinquency was flat until age 6, when it began a gradual increase until age 11 or 12. By age 12, only 15.8% of individuals had an onset of moderate to serious delinquency, in comparison with 42.4% and 46.5% for property damage and minor covert behaviors, respectively.

As to the onset of overt problems (Figure 9.2), the curve for minor aggression began to increase around age 3 or 4 and then increased sharply until age 10, at which point it leveled off at 44.1%. The onset curve for fighting is not as steep but gradually accelerated around age 9 or 10; by age 12, 24.2% of the boys had onset for fighting. The number of individuals who experienced an onset of violent behaviors increased very gradually, starting around age 8. By age 12, only 7.4% of the boys had an onset of violent behavior.

To summarize, in each of the three dimensions—overt problem behavior, covert problem behavior, and authority conflict—the number of individuals exhibiting disruptive behaviors increased with age, and the onset of minor disruptive behaviors usually took place at an earlier age than the onset of more serious disruptive behaviors. In this respect, results for the youngest sample replicate results for the middle and oldest samples reported earlier (Loeber et al., 1993). Some differences should be noted, however: The cumulative onset curves for the youngest sample, as compared with the other samples, *for most of the stages tended to be steeper with a larger proportion of boys reaching each level of disruptive behavior at a younger age.*

Developmental Pathways

In our prior work, we developed a pathway conceptualization based on developmental sequences in the middle and oldest samples (Loeber et al., 1995). According to this conceptualization, boys could progress along one or more of three developmental pathways in disruptive behavior: (a) an authority conflict pathway, prior to the age of 12, that starts with stubborn behavior and has defiance as Stage 2 and authority avoidance as Stage 3; (b) a covert pathway that starts with minor covert acts and has property damage as Stage 2 and moderate to serious delinquency as Stage 3; and (c) an overt pathway that starts with minor aggression and has physical fighting as Stage 2 and violence as Stage 3.

The cumulative onset data that are represented do not prove that boys with the most serious behavior first experienced the

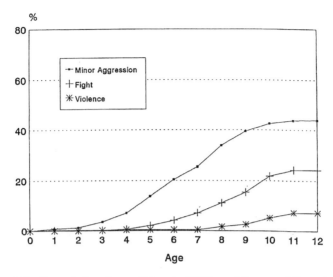

Figure 9.2. Cumulative Ages of Onset of Different Forms of Covert Behavior Problems

onset of less serious behaviors. Therefore, the next step in the analyses was to determine the percentage of individuals for whom the developmental sequence of different types of disruptive behaviors fit the sequences of behaviors specified by the authority conflict, covert, and overt pathway models and indicated by the onset curves. *Nonfitters* (those who did not fit the sequences specified) were defined as those who exhibited disruptive behaviors in a sequence inverse to what was specified by the pathway model. Results (Tables 9.1, 9.2, and 9.3) show that the percentage of nonfitters was 8.9% for the authority conflict pathway, 9.6% for the covert pathway, and 3.8% for the overt pathway.[2] Chi-square analyses comparing the percentage of nonfitters by ethnicity found no significant differences between African Americans and Caucasians (authority conflict: $\chi^2 = .52$, $df = 1$, n.s.; covert: $\chi^2 = .77$, $df = 1$, n.s.; overt: $\chi^2 = 46.4$, $df = 1$, n.s.). Thus, most of the boys who engaged in disruptive or delinquent behavior followed the developmental progression specified in the pathway model.

Progression Into Pathways

The next step was to examine more closely persisters' progression through each pathway and to compare the percentage of

TABLE 9.1 Authority Conflict Pathway: Persisters Only

	Total		African American		Caucasian	
	N	%	N	%	N	%
Persisters						
Normative Sequences						
Stubborn—defiance—avoidance	21	(4.8)	15	(5.9)	6	(3.3)
Stubborn—defiance	27	(6.2)	13	(5.1)	14	(7.7)
Stubborn	6	(1.4)	2	(0.8)	4	(2.2)
Total Normative	54	(12.4)	30	(11.9)	24	(13.2)
Nonnormative Sequences						
Stubborn —avoidance	10	(2.3)	4	(1.6)	6	(3.3)
—defiance—avoidance	12	(2.8)	9	(3.6)	3	(1.6)
—defiance	10	(2.3)	6	(2.4)	4	(2.2)
—avoidance	14	(3.2)	12	(4.8)	2	(1.1)
Total Nonnormative	46	(10.6)	31	(12.3)	15	(8.2)
Total persisters	100	(22.9)	61	(24.1)	39	(21.4)
Experimenters	120	(27.5)	68	(26.9)	52	(28.6)
Nonfitters	39	(8.9)	20	(7.9)	19	(10.4)
No authority conflict of any type	152	(34.9)	86	(34.0)	65	(35.7)
Onset of authority conflict						
after age 11	25	(5.7)	18	(7.1)	7	(3.8)
TOTAL	436		253		182	

NOTE: The ethnic background of one case was not identified.

individuals who exhibited normative developmental progressions with those who exhibited nonnormative developmental progressions. Based on the initial pathway model, seven pathway sequences are possible. The first three sequences in Table 9.1 represent the *normative developmental progressions,* defined as those individuals who exhibit disruptive behaviors in the order specified by the pathways model without skipping stages. The first normative sequence is progressing through all three sequences in the specified order; the second sequence is the first two stages in the specified order; and the third sequence is the first stage only. The remaining sequences are more atypical because they consist of boys who have skipped one or two stages of the pathway. Tables 9.1, 9.2, and 9.3 show the percentage of individuals who follow each of the seven sequences for the authority conflict, covert, and overt pathways.

Results show that the majority of those who persist in disruptive behavior followed one of the first three sequences that repre-

TABLE 9.2 Covert Pathway: Persisters Only

	Total		African American		Caucasian	
	N	%	N	%	N	%
Persisters						
Normative Sequences						
Minor Covert—Property Damage—Moderate/Serious Delinquency	33	(7.7)	24	(9.8)	8	(4.4)
Minor Covert—Property Damage	56	(13.1)	30	(12.3)	26	(14.2)
Minor Covert	22	(5.1)	12	(4.9)	10	(5.5)
Total Normative	111	(25.9)	66	(27.0)	44	(24.0)
Nonnormative Sequences						
Minor Covert —Moderate/Serious Delinquency	7	(1.6)	5	(2.0)	2	(1.1)
—Property Damage —Moderate/Serious Delinquency	2	(0.5)	2	(0.8)	0	(0)
—Property Damage	16	(3.7)	10	(4.1)	6	(3.3)
—Moderate/Serious Delinquency	1	(0.2)	0	(0)	1	(0.5)
Total Nonnormative	26	(6.1)	17	(7.0)	9	(4.2)
Total persisters	137	(31.9)	83	(34.0)	53	(29.0)
Experimenters	90	(21.0)	53	(21.7)	37	(20.2)
Nonfitters	41	(9.6)	28	(11.5)	13	(7.1)
No covert behavior of any type	161	(37.5)	80	(32.8)	80	(43.7)
Grand Total	429		244		183	

NOTE: The ethic backgrounds of two cases were not identified.

TABLE 9.3 Overt Pathway: Persisters Only

	Total		African American		Caucasian	
	N	%	N	%	N	%
Persisters						
Normative Sequences						
Aggression—fight—violence	14	(3.3)	8	(3.4)	6	(3.3)
Aggression—fight	38	(9.0)	25	(10.5)	13	(7.1)
Aggression	42	(9.9)	14	(5.9)	28	(15.2)
Total Normative	94	(22.2)	47	(19.8)	47	(25.5)
Nonnormative Sequences						
Aggression —violence	2	(0.5)	1	(0)	1	(0.5)
—fight—violence	3	(0.7)	2	(0.8)	1	(0.5)
—fight	3	(0.7)	3	(1.3)	0	(0)
—violence	0	(0)	0	(0)	0	(0)
Total Nonnormative	8	(1.9)	6	(2.5)	2	(1.0)
Total persisters	102	(24.1)	53	(22.4)	49	(26.6)
Experimenters	97	(22.9)	52	(21.9)	44	(23.9)
Nonfitters	16	(3.8)	12	(5.1)	3	(1.6)
No overt behavior of any type	208	(49.2)	120	(50.6)	88	(47.8)
TOTAL	423		237		184	

sent normative developmental progressions. Of the 100 persisters in the authority conflict pathway, 54 boys (54% of persisters) followed normative progressions, and 46 boys (46% of persisters) followed nonnormative progressions. For persisters in the covert pathway ($n = 137$), 111 boys (81% of persisters) followed normative progressions, and 26 boys (19% of persisters) followed nonnormative progressions. In the case of the 102 persisters in the overt pathway, 94 boys (92% of persisters) followed normative progressions, and 8 boys (8%) followed nonnormative progressions. These results show that persistence is more associated with normative sequences in the overt and covert pathways but less in the authority conflict pathway.

The percentages of boys who follow normative and nonnormative progressions were calculated separately for African Americans and Caucasians. For the authority conflict pathway, 49% of African American persisters followed normative progressions, as compared with 62% of Caucasian persisters. For the covert pathway, 80% of African American persisters followed normative progressions versus 83% of Caucasian persisters. Finally, for the overt pathway, 89% of African American persisters followed normative progressions versus 96% of Caucasian persisters. Chi-square analyses comparing the percentages of African Americans and Caucasians who follow normative and nonnormative progressions found significant differences for the overt pathway in the percentage of persisters following normative progressions (authority conflict: $\chi^2 = .09$, $df = 1$, n.s.; covert: $\chi^2 = .37$, $df = 1$, n.s.; overt: $\chi^2 = 5.94$, $df = 1$, $p < .05$).

Point of Entry Into Pathways

The next step was to examine differences between persisters and experimenters in their likelihood of entering at an early rather than a later stage of a given pathway. Chi-square analyses were used to detect significant differences between boys entering at Stages 1, 2, and 3 of a given pathway (Table 9.4). Persisters in the covert and overt pathways were more likely to enter in Stage 1 than in later stages. More specifically, persisters in the covert pathway were more likely to enter at Stage 1 than at Stage 2 ($\chi^2 = 19.8$, $df = 1$, $p < .0001$) or Stage 3 ($\chi^2 = 7.9$, $df = 1$, $p < .01$). Persisters in the overt pathway were more likely to enter the pathway at Stage 1 than at Stage 2 ($\chi^2 = 10.1$, $df = 1$, $p < .01$).

Chi-square analyses comparing the entry point of persisters and experimenters were performed separately for African Americans and Caucasians. Two significant differences were found. African American, as compared with Caucasian, persisters were significantly more likely to enter the covert pathway at Stage 1 than at Stage 2 ($\chi^2 = 15.1$, $df = 1$, $p < .0001$) or Stage 3 ($\chi^2 = 12.4$, $df = 1$, $p < .001$). Caucasian, as compared with African American, persisters were significantly more likely to enter the overt pathway at Stage 1 than at Stage 2 ($\chi^2 = 8.2$, $df = 1$, $p < .01$).

Rates of ADHD Among
Persisters and Experimenters

DSM-III-R (APA, 1987) diagnoses of ADHD were generated by the mother reports of current behavior problems at Phase A; 17.1% of boys in the youngest sample met the criteria for ADHD. To examine the relation between ADHD and persistence and progression of disruptive behavior, we systematically cross-tabulated the diagnosis of ADHD with each of the three developmental path-

(text continued on p. 206)

TABLE 9.4. Comparison of Entry Points for Boys With and Without Persistent Problem Behaviors

	Total Sample N	%		Total Sample N	%		Total Sample N	%	
Authority Conflict Pathway									
Enter Stage 1 (Stubborn)									
Persisters	64	(64.0)		39	(57.4)		30	(76.9)	1 vs. 2**
Experimenters	70	(58.3)					31	(59.6)	
Enter Stage 2 (Defiance)									
Persisters	22	(22.0)		15	(24.6)		7	(17.9)	
Experimenters	33	(27.5)		21	(30.1)		12	(23.1)	
Enter Stage 3 (Avoidance)									
Persisters	14	(14.0)		8	(11.8)		2	(5.1)	
Experimenters	17	(14.2)		12	(19.7)		9	(17.3)	
Covert Pathway									
Enter Stage 1 (Minor Covert)									
Persisters	118	(86.1)	1 vs. 2***	71	(85.5)	1 vs. 2****	46	(86.8)	
Experimenters	49	(57.1)	1 vs. 3**	25	(49.0)	1 vs. 3***	24	(68.6)	
Enter Stage 2 (Property Damage)									
Persisters	18	(13.1)		12	(14.5)		6	(11.3)	
Experimenters	32	(37.2)		21	(41.2)		11	(31.4)	
Enter Stage 3 (Moderate to Serious Delinquent)									
Persisters	1	(0.7)		0	(0)		1	(1.9)	
Experimenters	5	(5.8)		5	(9.8)		0	(0)	

TABLE 9.4 Continued

	Total Sample			Total Sample			Total Sample		
	N	%		N	%		N	%	
Overt Pathway									
Enter Stage 1 (Minor Aggression)			1 vs. 2***						1 vs. 2**
Persisters	96	(94.1)		48	(79.2)		48	(98.0)	
Experimenters	74	(76.3)		38	(73.1)		35	(79.5)	
Enter Stage 2 (Fighting)									
Persisters	6	(5.9)		5	(9.4)		1	(2.0)	
Experimenters	20	(20.6)		11	(21.2)		9	(20.5)	
Enter Stage 3 (Violence)									
Persisters	0	(0)		0	(0)		0	(0)	
Experimenters	3	(3.1)		3	(5.8)		0	(0)	

NOTE: Starred numbers indicate significant comparisons among the pathway entry points, by chi-squares.
* $p < .05$; ** $p < .01$; *** $p < .001$; **** $p < .0001$.

205

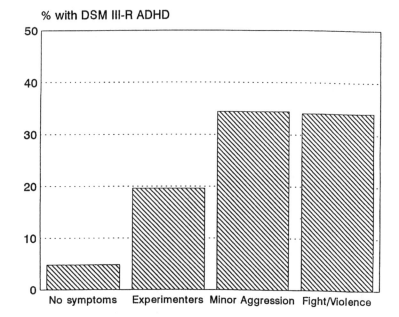

Figure 9.3. Percentage of Boys Diagnosed with ADHD in the Overt
Pathway

ways. Because of the small sample size, we combined the persisters
at Stages 2 and 3. All comparisons were tested by chi-square
analysis. Results for the overt pathway are presented in Figure 9.3.

For all three pathways, the rates of ADHD increased across the
four groups; rates were lowest for those who had not engaged in
any stages of the pathways and highest for those who persisted in
Stages 2 or 3 of the three pathways. Chi-square analyses showed
significant differences between groups for all three pathways
(authority conflict: $\chi^2 = 40.1$, $df = 3$, $p < .0001$; covert: $\chi^2 = 33.9$,
$df = 3$, $p < .0001$; overt: $\chi^2 = 46.4$, $df = 3$, $p < .0001$).

Subsequent 2×2 chi-square analyses were performed to show
the precise location of effects. Results showed no significant differences in the likelihood of ADHD diagnosis between persisters
in Stage 1 and persisters in Stage 2 or 3 (authority conflict: $\chi^2 = .6$,
$df = 1$, n.s.; covert: $\chi^2 = .9$, $df = 1$, n.s.; overt: $\chi^2 = 1.0$, $df = 1$, n.s.);
therefore, these two groups were combined for 2×2 analyses. With
the exception of boys experimenting in the authority conflict
pathway, experimenters were more likely to have a diagnosis of
ADHD than those with no symptoms (authority conflict: $\chi^2 = 3.5$,

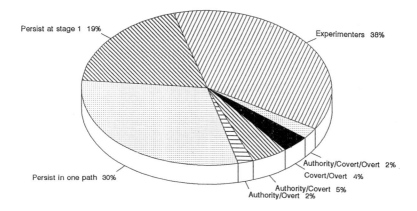

Figure 9.4. Distribution of Experimenters and Persisters in Single and Multiple Pathways

$df = 1$, n.s.; covert: $\chi^2 = 9.4$, $df = 1$, $p < .01$; overt: $\chi^2 = 16.8$, $df = 1$, $p < .0001$).

For each of the pathways, persisters were more likely to have a diagnosis of ADHD than those with no pathways symptoms (authority conflict: $\chi^2 = 35.0$, $df = 1$, $p < .0001$; covert: $\chi^2 = 33.8$, $df = 1$, $p < .0001$; overt: $\chi^2 = 48.0$, $df = 1$, $p < .0001$) or those classified as experimenters (authority conflict: $\chi^2 = 15.0$, $df = 1$, $p < .0001$; covert: $\chi^2 = 5.4$, $df = 1$, $p < .05$; overt: $\chi^2 = 5.4$, $df = 1$, $p < .05$).

In conclusion, a diagnosis of ADHD was related to each of the three disruptive pathways. The percentage of ADHD boys was higher for those who experimented, as compared with those with no disruptive symptoms. ADHD was also more common among persisters, as compared with experimenters, in each pathway. However, persisters' progression within a pathway was not related to ADHD.

Boys in Single and Multiple Pathways

So far, we have considered each of the three pathways separately. However, some boys had progressed in more than one pathway. The distribution of experimenters and persisters in single and multiple pathways is shown in Figure 9.4. This indicates that the largest group of boys with disruptive behaviors were experimenters (38%), followed by those who persisted at Stage 2 or 3 of only a single pathway (30%), and those who persisted at Stage 1 of any pathway (19%). A few subjects (13%) persisted at Stage 2 or 3 in multiple pathways, 2% in the dual authority conflict and overt pathways, 5% in the dual authority conflict and covert pathways, 4% in the dual covert and overt pathways, and 2% persisted at Stage 2 or 3 in all three pathways. We come back to these figures in the discussion section, where, on the basis of data from the youngest, middle, and oldest samples, we illustrate the degree that boys in multiple pathways increases with age.

Rates of Offending Among Persisters and Experimenters in One or More Pathways

The next goal was to replicate our previous finding (Loeber et al., 1995) that the rate of offending was related to the persistence, severity (e.g., progression within a pathway), and variety of disruptive behavior (number of pathways). The first step was to use the pathways model to categorize subjects on these three dimensions of persistence, severity, and variety (excluded were boys who did not fit any pathway and those who did not exhibit disruptive behaviors in any pathway). For that purpose, experimenters and persisters were classified by the level of progression in a given pathway (Stage 1 or Stage 2 or 3) and then by the number of pathways in which they progressed (one, two, or three pathways; see Figure 9.4). Seven categories were generated on the basis of the above classification process: (a) experimenters, and two main groups of persisters: (b) those who had reached Stage 1 of any one pathway, and (c) those who had reached Stage 2 or 3 of any one pathway. In the latter category, we distinguished persisters who were in more than one pathway: (d) those in the dual overt and authority conflict pathways, (e) those in the dual covert and authority conflict pathways, (f) those in the dual overt and covert pathways, and (g) those in all three pathways.

We next calculated the self-reported rate of offending for boys in the youngest sample. In our previous research that focused on the middle and oldest samples, we also calculated the rate of offending as measured by official records of court petitions. Given that most boys were 12 years old or younger at the final phase of analyses, it is understandable that only five subjects had juvenile court records. Therefore, the analyses for the current study focus on self-reported offending only.

Self-reported offending was calculated for violent and nonviolent offenses separately. As in our previous research (Loeber et al., 1993), to avoid a possible confound, we adjusted the total frequencies by subtracting from them a number equal to the total number of offenses necessary for an individual to qualify for the relevant pathway or pathways, identified as the 25% of subjects with the highest rate of offending. Because of the relatively small number of self-reported offenses in the youngest sample (recall that the SRD with its frequency estimates of offending could only be used at Phases G and H), dichotomous groups were formed by assigning a value of 1 to those who had reported an offense (other than those leading to pathway classifications) and a value of 0 to those who did not report an offense. This resulted in a distribution of 4.1% self-reported violent offenders and 25% self-reported nonviolent offenders.

Because the base rate of offending was low, the binomial distribution matched a Poisson distribution. For that reason, we used Poisson regression analyses to test the relation between the seven categories and the two categories of offending. The seven-category variable measuring persistence, severity, and variety was recoded into six dummy variables for the regression models. In this way, each regression model represented a contrast between one or more reference groups and all other persistence categories. The contrasts were designed to isolate systematically the dimensions of interest: persistence, severity, and variety of disruptive behaviors. Thus, each regression model represents a comparison between these dimensions. For example, the first model identifies experimenters as the reference group and examines the likelihood of offending for all other groups in comparison with the experimenters. Results are presented in Table 9.5.

Regarding differences in self-reported nonviolent offenders (Table 9.5a), Model 1 indicates that those persisting in two or more pathways, as compared with experimenters, were significantly more likely to self-report offending (with the exception of those persisting in the overt and authority conflict pathways that approached significance). Model 2 indicates that when the four groups of individuals in multiple pathways were combined, this group was significantly more likely to be self-report offenders, as compared with experimenters, those who persisted in Stage 1 of any one pathway, or those who persisted in Stage 2 or 3 in a single pathway. Finally, Table 9.5a shows that the overall chi-square of the log likelihood values for Models 1 and 2 were both significant at $p < .05$.

TABLE 9.5 Poisson Regression of Rate of Offending for
Experimenters and Persisters in Multiple Pathways

a). Self-reported nonviolent offenses

Comparison Groups	Model 1 (1 vs. remainder)		Model 2 (4, 5, 6, 7 vs. 1, 2, 3)	
	β	OR	β	OR
1. Experimenting	—	—	−.27***	.37
2. Stage 1	.04	1.22	−.17*	.45
3. Persist in any pathway	.10	1.50	−.15*	.56
4. Persist/overt & authority conflict	.08[a]	2.84	—	—
5. Persist/covert & authority conflict	.11*	2.62	—	—
6. Persist/covert & overt	.09*	2.47	—	—
7. Persist in all three	.09*	3.12	—	—
Chi-square of −2 LOG (L)	13.1*			12.9**

b). Self-reported violent offenses

Comparison Groups	Model 3 (1 vs. remainder)		Model 4 (4, 5, 6, 7 vs. 1, 2, 3)	
	β	OR	β	OR
1. Experimenting	—	—	−.56**	.13
2. Stage 1	−.10	.64	−.55*	.08
3. Persist in any pathway	.18	2.10	−.34*	.26
4. Persist/overt & authority conflict	.20**	12.70	—	—
5. Persist/covert & authority conflict	.11	2.58	—	—
6. Persist/covert & overt	.24**	11.09	—	—
7. Persist in all three	.20**	11.09	—	—
Chi-square of −2 LOG (L)	18.1**			14.8**

NOTE: *$p < .05$; **$p < .01$; ***$p < .001$.
a. $p = 0.55$.

The results of Poisson regression were similar for self-reported violent offenders (Table 9.5b). The comparison in Model 1 indicates that those who persisted in two or more pathways (with the exception of the combined covert and authority conflict pathways) were more likely to be self-reported violent offenders than those boys who experimented in disruptive behavior. In addition, Model 2 shows that individuals in multiple pathways were significantly more likely to be self-reported violent offenders, as compared with experimenters, those who persisted in Stage 1 of any one pathway, and those who persisted in Stage 2 or 3 in any one pathway. Finally, Table 9.5b shows that the overall chi-square of

TABLE 9.6 Demographic Characteristics of Experimenters and
Persisters in Each Pathway

	Experimenters		Persisters	
Authority Conflict Pathway	Mean	SD	Mean	SD
Age	6.5	.6	6.4	.5
SES	34.5	13.3	33.6	12.4
	N	%	N	%
African American	68	56.7	61	61.0
Single parent	36	30.5	46	46.0*
Family on welfare	58	51.3	53	57.0
Covert Pathway	Mean	SD	Mean	SD
Age	6.4	.6	6.5	.6
SES	35.0	13.4	33.1	13.0
	N	%	N	%
African American	53	58.9	84	61.3
Single parent	29	32.6	56	41.2*
Family on welfare	45	54.9	76	57.6
Overt Pathway	Mean	SD	Mean	SD
Age	6.5	.6	6.5	.6
SES	32.9	13.9	36.1	10.3
	N	%	N	%
African American	52	54.2	53	52.0
Single parent	61	64.2	56	55.4*
Family on welfare	52	57.1	55	55.5

NOTE: Comparisons between experimenters and persisters: *$p < .05$.

the log likelihood values for Models 1 and 2 were both significant
at $p < .001$.

Demographic Characteristics
of Experimenters and Persisters

Because the distinction between experimenters and persisters
proved important, we questioned whether experimenters and persisters in each of the pathways differed on demographic characteristics, including age of the child, family socioeconomic status,
ethnicity, family structure (one- or two-parent household), and
welfare status. Results of these analyses are presented in Table 9.6.
Differences between continuous and dichotomous data were tested
by ANOVA and by chi-square analyses, respectively.

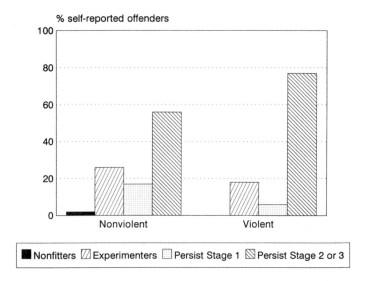

Figure 9.5. Percentage of Self-Reported Offenders Included Among the Nonfitters, Experimenters, and the Boys Who Persisted in Stage 1 and Those Who Persisted in Stages 2 or 3 in Any of the Three Pathways

Overall, the demographic characteristics of experimenters and persisters in each of the three pathways did not significantly differ, with the exception of persisters in the authority conflict pathway, who were more likely to come from single-parent households.

Comprehensiveness of the Classification of Boys

The final question addresses to what extent our classification of experimenters and persisters in single and multiple pathways identified the majority of self-reported offenders. For these analyses, we included all fitters and nonfitters. The previously discussed binomial variable was used as the index of self-reported offenders. The persistence variable was divided into four groups: nonfitters, experimenters, persisting at Stage 1, and persisting at Stage 2 or 3. Chi-square analyses (2 × 4) were performed to determine any significant differences for individuals at different levels of the persistence variable in the likelihood of being a high-rate offender. Results are presented in Figure 9.5.

Results showed significant differences among the four groups in their likelihood of being self-reported violent offenders (χ^2 =

9.24, $df = 3$, $p < .05$) and nonviolent offenders ($\chi^2 = 11.3$, $df = 3$, $p < .01$). Pathways analyses capture 100% of the violent offenders and 98% of the nonviolent offenders. Because of small sample size, 2×2 chi-square analyses to pinpoint the location of effects could not be performed.

∾ DISCUSSION

The main aim of this chapter was to approach disruptive behavior from both a variable and an individual-based point of view in a sample of first graders (the youngest sample) in the Pittsburgh Youth Study, who were assessed nine times at half-yearly intervals from age 6.9 to 10.9. The second aim was to cross-validate, in this younger sample, earlier findings on developmental sequences and pathways in disruptive behavior reported in two samples that were studied from ages 10 to 13 (the middle sample) and from ages 13 to 15 (the oldest sample). Before discussing the results, we address several caveats: The study included boys from metropolitan public schools. We do not assume that results of the study would apply to developmental pathways in disruptive behavior of boys in other types of schools or in girls. For such populations, the study of pathways is much warranted.

Perhaps the most distinct limitation in the current study is that we examined developmental pathways in isolation of risk factors that might explain boys' progression in one or more of the pathways. Our empirical approach was first to investigate developmental pathways with an eye on elucidating individual differences among boys in their entry and progression in the pathways. The second step was to examine risk and protective factors to explain why some youths progress along pathways, why some youths progress along more than one pathway, and why others not. For example, we have examined the role of neighborhood quality on boys' progression in the pathways (Loeber & Wikström, 1993), as well the role of deviant peers (Keenan, Loeber, Zhang, Stouthamer-Loeber, & Van Kammen, 1995). Also, we have examined the development of internalizing problems against the backdrop of boys' developmental pathways in disruptive behavior (Loeber, Russo, Stouthamer-Loeber, & Lahey, 1994). Undoubtedly, many other risk and protective factors need to be included in such analyses.

We briefly summarize current results for the youngest sample. Findings on cumulative onset curves of disruptive behaviors replicate previous results, indicating that the onset of less serious disruptive behavior tended to occur first, whereas the onset of moderately serious disruptive behavior emerged slightly later, with the onset of serious disruptive behavior occurring last. However, more boys in the youngest sample, as compared with those in the other samples, tended to experience the onset of disruptive behavior, including serious disruptive behavior, at an earlier age.

Even though the pathways model was developed by using the middle and oldest samples, the percentage of fitters in the covert and overt pathways in the youngest sample was much higher than for the middle and oldest samples (Loeber et al., 1995).[3] This may mean that either prospective data collection produced results more conforming to the pathway model or that boys' progression in pathways is more orderly at a younger, as compared with an older, age. There is a distinct need to explore this further in the current data and to relate the current findings to the two distinct types postulated by Moffitt (1993) of lifetime-persistent and adolescent-limited antisocial behavior to our developmental pathways.

As in previous analyses on the boys in the middle and oldest samples (Loeber et al., 1995), we found that persisters, as compared with experimenters, were more likely to enter a pathway at Stage 1 than at a later stage. This finding further reinforces the earlier conclusion that persisters tend to advance through a developmental pathway in disruptive behavior in a more orderly fashion than experimenters, and this applied especially to the overt and covert pathways. It should be noted, however, that boys differ enormously in the extent to which they progress through a pathway, with some advancing just to Stage 1, others to Stage 2, and the smallest proportion advancing to Stage 3, the most serious stage.

Results for the youngest sample also confirmed earlier findings that the percentage of boys who qualified for a diagnosis of ADHD was higher among experimenters than among boys with no symptoms, and higher among persisters than among experimenters. Differences between the persisters in Stage 1 and those in Stages 2 to 3 were negligible. Thus, ADHD was more related to persistence than to the severity of disruptive behavior as expressed by boys' progression in a pathway.

According to the pathway model we espouse, boys can progress on more than one pathway. We also expect that as boys develop, more of them may become engaged in behaviors of several pathways. To demonstrate this, we summarized the distributions of the youngest, middle, and oldest samples across the seven

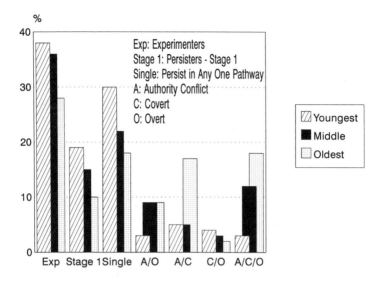

Figure 9.6. Comparison of the Distribution of Experimenters and Persisters in Single and Multiple Pathways in the Youngest, Middle, and Oldest Sample

SOURCE: Based on Loeber, Green, Keenan, and Lahey (1995) for the middle and oldest samples.

categories, as shown in Figure 9.6 (ages 7-11 for the youngest sample, ages 10-12 for the middle sample, and ages 13-14 for the oldest sample). A comparison of the distribution of the youngest sample with those of the two older samples shows that a higher percentage of boys in the middle and oldest samples (28% and 45%, respectively) persisted in multiple pathways than in the youngest sample (12.8%), thus doubling with each 3- to 4-year age interval. These differences are likely a result of the boys' worsening disruptive behavior with age. The sample differences, we assume, reflect the gradual process by which the severity of disruptive behavior increases in some boys and their increased variety into several dimensions of disruptive/delinquent behavior. Results agree with findings reported from the National Youth Survey, showing an increase with age of those engaging in both theft and aggression (Huizinga, 1995).

That some boys are at risk for entering into more than one pathway is of clinical importance because mental health workers often need to decide which boys are at great risk and which boys are at lesser risk. The emergence of a multiproblem group of youths should be seen against the backdrop of a larger body of youths growing out of disruptive behaviors, such as aggression (Cairns, Cairns, Neckerman, Ferguson, & Gariépy, 1989).

We stress that the pathway model presented here, consisting of three separate pathways representing authority conflict, covert, and overt behavior, contains more clarity in developmental progressions than we could achieve in our earlier research in which we explored a single pathway for all disruptive behaviors (Loeber et al., 1993). We argue that the pathway model that we espouse represents three developmental tasks of respect for authority figures (the authority conflict pathway), positive social problem solving (the overt pathway), and honesty and respect for property (the covert pathway). Children's deficits in one or more of these tasks are relevant for clinicians because, with this knowledge, they can better tailor interventions to these deficits than is possible with a single disruptive or antisocial construct.

In summary, we pose that the concept of developmental pathways is an advance of the traditional classification method, such as oppositional defiant disorder and conduct disorder in *DSM-IV* (APA, 1994), which focuses more on behavior from a cross-sectional perspective. That approach is logical for problem syndromes and disorders that are mostly constant over time (e.g., mental retardation, autism). There are limitations, however, when such a classification is applied to problem behaviors that gradually unfold with time, that border on normal development, and for which there are large individual differences in the course of the problem behavior. Disruptive behavior fits these three aspects. The approach to a dynamic, pathway classification of boys that we propose here derives strength from being based on both knowledge about relationships between behaviors or variables and knowledge based on changes within individuals over time. Moreover, the pathway classification summarizes knowledge about the history and current disruptive behavior and is likely to inform about potential next stages of development in disruptive behavior that children may experience some time in the future.

∞〰∞

COMMENTS ON CHAPTER 9

What does the clinician need to know about a child's problem behavior to determine treatment plans? What is the continuity of behavior over the course of development? What are the risks and protective factors in the development of disruptive behavior? For each of these questions, the pathways model developed by Rolf Loeber, Mary DeLamatre, Kate Keenan, and Quanwu Zhang furnishes information that sharpens the issues. The model provides a developmentally oriented scheme and a perspective of intraindividual progression in problem behavior.

In their developmental orientation, the authors map specific types of disruptive behavior onto specific failed developmental tasks (a very helpful, organizing framework): With overt disruptive behavior, the child has failed to overcome aggressive problem solving. With covert behavior, the child has not learned respect for property or honesty. In the third disruptive pattern, the child has not developed positive relationships with authority figures. Also, in their sensitivity to the evolution or progression of maladaptive patterns of behavior, Loeber et al. bring a finer grading to assessments of the child's development.

How does Loeber et al.'s approach bear on the questions of the clinic and research? Consider the implications of the model for issues of continuity in development. The research literature supports a generalization of high continuity in conduct disorders. Loeber et al.'s approach allows us to see this continuity (and discontinuity) at several levels of description, tuned to degree of severity and direction of behavior.

Loeber et al.'s approach brings yet another refinement to assessment by describing children's multiple-problem paths (e.g., both overt and covert disruptive patterns). Because children's repertoires of developmental difficulties often consist of multiple problems, a search for multiple paths and current or sequential progression of paths is needed. Thus, disruptive problems do not always exist alone; anxiety and depression are often accompaniments. Loeber et al.'s model, if applied also to these areas, offers a promising approach for investigating comorbidity in process terms. This important aspect of developmental psychopathology has not been extensively examined. The model would provide evidence on how diverse problems emerge and progress in relation to each other.

Loeber et al. mention as research-to-come, investigation of the contexts of problem patterns. In identifying links between children's disorders and conditions of risk, Loeber et al.'s specification of patterns and progression in problem behavior can be a significant aid.

Research is never finished business, and the research that Loeber and his colleagues are conducting is no exception. It has added much to current understanding of boys' disruptive behavior and has inspired ideas for much more to be explored.

Marian Radke-Yarrow

∞ Notes

1. If the onset of two different behaviors was reported or recorded to have taken place in the same half year, this was counted as a fit because it did not prove an inverse sequence of onsets.

2. The algorithm used in the Loeber et al. (1993) report was slightly different, but results did not vary much when this algorithm was used with the current sample: 9.1% for the authority conflict pathway, 9.3% for the covert pathway, and 3.6% for the overt pathway.

3. 86.8% and 92.0% for the authority conflict pathway in the middle and oldest samples, respectively, as compared with 91.9% in the youngest sample; 83.1% and 68.7% in the covert pathway in the middle and oldest sample, respectively, as compared with 90.4% in the youngest sample; 89.5% and 80.9% for the overt pathway in the middle and oldest samples, respectively, as compared with 96.2% in the youngest sample.

~ *10* ~

Retrospective Recall Recalled

Sir Michael Rutter
Barbara Maughan
Andrew Pickles
Emily Simonoff

MRC Child Psychiatry Unit and Social,
Genetic, and Developmental Psychiatry Research Centre
Institute of Psychiatry, University of London

A quarter of a century ago, Marian Radke-Yarrow and colleagues (Radke-Yarrow, Campbell, & Burton, 1970) published a highly influential monograph on the biases and distortions that occur with retrospective recall of childhood behavior and experiences. Its importance is clearly indicated by the fact that it continues to be cited in contemporary reviews on the topic (e.g., Brewin, Andrews, & Gotlib, 1993). The reason for its impact lies not only in the fact that empirical findings were presented on the differences between contemporaneous and retrospective accounts but also in its demonstration that the nature of the biases in retrospective recall were such as to lead to an artifactual confirmation of prevailing views regarding child development and influences on it. It was concluded that consumers of the outcome of research based on the retrospective method should respond to its findings with an awareness of *caveat emptor.*

Of course, the monograph also emphasized the limitations of the data used in the study. Thus, many measures were based on rather general questions (e.g., "Were there any changes for *X* or for his family . . . which you feel had an effect on him?" to assess early traumata), and usually there was only one question for each domain. It was argued that multiple indicators were to be preferred, that cause and effect should not be entwined in the same question, and that better craftsmanship in the design of interviews might help. Nevertheless, it was also suggested that much of the bias in retrospective recall derived from the ways memories functioned, rather than from imperfections in measurement as such. Further research to resolve the issues was called for. Our purpose in this chapter is to review the extent to which both the understanding of retrospective recall and the development of more accurate and less biased methods of obtaining recall have been achieved since that seminal report in 1970. We refer to our own research on this topic when relevant.

It is clear that the issues raised a quarter of a century ago continue in the forefront of those that preoccupy present-day researchers. Interestingly, however, this Festschrift appears at a time of very major resurgence of interest in the topic of retrospective recall (Maughan & Rutter, 1997). This has arisen for several rather different reasons. To begin with, researchers using either interview or questionnaire methods have become aware that all of these involve retrospective recall even when they are employed during the course of a prospective longitudinal study. Thus, if parents and children are seen every year over the course of development, it will still be necessary for them to remember things that have happened during the course of the previous 12 months—quite a long time. Longitudinal researchers certainly cannot afford to ignore the issues involved in retrospective recall. That is especially so in view of the growing interest in lifespan development and in the developmental pathways extending from childhood into adult life (e.g., see Cairns & Cairns, 1994; Rutter & Rutter, 1993). The need for data to cover long time periods also applies to psychopathological studies concerned with either psychosocial risk factors (Rutter, 1994b) or genetic influences (Rutter, 1994a). That is because both sets of risk factors need to be examined in relation to the overall liability to whatever psychiatric disorder is being studied. Most psychiatric conditions tend to be recurrent, and this means that lifetime estimates of disorder have to be obtained. Researchers have become concerned with the possible errors and biases that may be involved in retrospective assessments of episodes of disorder that occurred many years ago (Bromet, Dunn, Connell, Dew, & Schulberg, 1986; Fendrich, Weissman, Warner, & Mufson, 1990; Rogler, Malgady, & Tyron, 1992).

The second reason for the renewed interest in retrospective recall derives from the fact that cognitive psychology has come to be the most influential and pervasive of all branches of psychology.

The study of memory (e.g., Baddeley, 1990; Tulving, 1983) and the cognitive processing of experiences (e.g., see Teasdale, 1993; Teasdale & Barnard, 1993) constitute two major growth areas in cognitive research. As Marian Radke-Yarrow and her colleagues adumbrated in their monograph, considerations of retrospective recall have to be linked to studies of memory processes. Not only does the investigation of retrospective recall have to pay attention to what is known about the ways memories are recorded and retrieved, but so too the study of retrospective recall may be most informative in elucidating the answers to key questions about the functioning of memory. This is perhaps most obvious in relation to the explosion of research in the fields of infantile amnesia (Howe & Courage, 1993), false memories (Schooler, 1994), children's testimony in legal court hearings (Flin & Spencer, 1995; Goodman & Bottoms, 1993; Wells & Loftus, 1984), and the use of people's styles of dealing with memories about the past as a reflection of their personalities and interpersonal functioning (Main, Kaplan, & Cassidy, 1985; van IJzendoorn, 1995). With respect to the last topic, the key lay in Radke-Yarrow et al.'s (1970) finding that errors in retrospective recall were not just random, but rather reflected people's current views and attitudes. Although this is undoubtedly a major problem in gathering valid retrospective data, it also provides the opportunity to use styles of remembering as an index of characteristics of the person.

In this chapter, we briefly review developments in these and related topics, starting with the development of interview methods, together with investigations of their qualities.

∞ INVESTIGATOR-BASED INTERVIEWS

Researchers' concerns to maximize the reliability and validity of interview data have given rise to two rather different interviewing approaches. First there are the highly structured, questionnaire-style, *respondent-based interviews,* such as the DISC (Breton et al., 1995; Fallon & Schwab-Stone, 1994; Fisher et al., 1993; Schwab-Stone et al., 1993; Shaffer et al., 1993). The method relies on the very careful wording of closed questions that give rise to yes/no answers. Interviewers are required to ask the questions with the precise wording specified in the interview schedule, thus eliminating interviewer biases in the ways questions are put. Similarly, the coding of yes/no answers eliminates errors and biases in the interpretation of informants' accounts and descriptions. In recent times, the approach has included various modifications designed to motivate long-term recall and to reduce nay-saying (see Kessler et al., 1994). The method works well when the questions have been skillfully designed to make quite explicit what information is required and when the respondents' understanding of concepts can safely be assumed to match those of the researcher. More difficulties arise, however, when that is not the case, as for example with phenomena that may not be a part of the informants' experience, such as obsessional phenomena (Breslow, Kocsis, & Belkin, 1980). The approach may also not be so suitable with younger children (Fallon & Schwab-Stone, 1994; Fisher et al., 1993; Schwab-Stone, Fallon, Briggs, & Crowther, 1994).

The second interviewing approach is provided by the quite different form of structuring exemplified in *investigator-based interviews*. In this approach, the aim is to obtain detailed and accurate descriptions of behavior or happenings, rather than yes/no answers. The method has as its rationale Hoffman's (1960) argument that the memory processes involved in reliving an experience are rather different from those involved in providing a yes/no answer to a question on whether some specified behavior or experience had occurred. This approach has two main advantages. First, it facilitates the separation of attitudes from behavior. For example, Rutter and Brown (1966) gave the example of a woman who, when asked whether her husband helped much with the housework, replied that he did nothing. When the interview went on to ask more systematically about a series of different activities during the previous week, it became apparent that, in fact, the husband was much involved. The informant spontaneously said at the end of this portion of the interview, "He really does quite a lot, doesn't he?" The initial answer provided an accurate reflection of her negative attitude to her partner but gave a quite biased factual account of his behavior. The second advantage of getting the informant to relive the experience is that it should be possible to obtain much more detail.

A further feature of this interview approach is the use of *personalized timing* (Bradburn, Rips, & Shevell, 1987; Loftus & Marburger, 1983). On the whole, people do not remember that something occurred in 1989, nor do they tend to encode memories in terms of the fact that they were, say, age 10 at the time. Rather, people are more likely to remember something as an event or experience that occurred when they were on a particular family holiday, or just after they moved house, or at the time of a school transition, or just after the informant's partner changed her job or got a promotion. The task of the interviewer is to find a series of landmarks that help fix the time that things occurred during the period for which retrospective recall is required. In order that the informant is helped to relive the experience in his or her memory, the interviewer seeks to reconstruct the environmental and personal contexts that existed at the time. In addition, it may be helpful to tackle the recall by approaching it from a variety of perspectives or by using a range of cues. For example, when asking someone about antisocial behavior when he or she was younger, the interviewer might approach the issue in terms of an inquiry about specific types of behavior (e.g., stealing, truanting) or the responses of other people (e.g., getting into trouble at school, being involved with the police). The personalized time approach has been developed most systematically in Caspi et al.'s (1996) *life history calendar method*, which appears to have promising validity.

Sometimes the interviewer's task is to obtain information regarding some specific experience (an episode of depression in the past, or the experience of hospital admission, or the occurrence of family discord). In other cases, to obtain an understanding of developmental course, it is necessary to obtain data on a range of potentially relevant experiences of a major kind. Our naturalistic and experimental studies of diagnostic interviews in the clinical situation (Rutter & Cox, 1981; Rutter, Cox, Egert, Holbrook, & Everitt, 1981) have shown that most people have major experiences of a quite varied kind that would not be readily tapped by a series of inquiries on predetermined events (Cox, 1994). Findings showed that the fullest accounts are obtained through a mixture of more open questioning about domains of importance and systematic questioning on details to obtain a comprehensive behavioral description of the behavior or experiences in question. Neither highly structured closed questions nor a very open style leaving the informant to tell things her or his own way was as effective.

Our research group has developed a range of standardized investigator-based interviews to evaluate child and adolescent psychopathology (Angold & Costello, 1995; Angold et al., 1995), adult recall of childhood behavior and experiences (Holmshaw & Simonoff, 1996), acute life events and chronic psychosocial adversities (Glen, Simpson, Drinnan, McGuinness, & Sandberg, 1993; Sandberg et al., 1993), personality functioning during adolescence and adult life (Hill, Fudge, Harrington, Pickles, & Rutter, 1995; Hill, Harrington, Fudge, Rutter, & Pickles, 1989; Naughton, Oppenheim, & Hill, 1996), assessments of autistic features based particularly on the recall of children's behavior during the preschool period (Le Couteur et al., 1989; Lord, Rutter, & Le Couteur, 1994; Lord et al., 1989), and family functioning and relationships (Brown & Rutter, 1966; Quinton, Rutter, & Rowlands, 1976; Rutter & Brown, 1966). In each case, good reliability and discriminative validity have been obtained.

In recent times, some of these approaches to interviewing have been extended and elaborated in what has come to be called the *cognitive interview procedure* (Geiselman, Saywitz, & Bornstein, 1993). The *stepwise interview* for interviewing children about possible episodes of sexual abuse is also in the same tradition (Yuille, Hunter, Joffe, & Zaparniuk, 1993). Research has shown that cognitive retrieval methods tend to result in improved recall without an accompanying increase in incorrect details, provided that appropriate care is taken not to introduce bias through the use of suggestions or leading questions. In parallel, psychologists have developed *statement assessment (SA)* procedures designed to differentiate between true and fabricated accounts (Bekerian & Dennett, 1985, 1992). The technique is far from foolproof, but the data suggest that fabricated accounts tend to lack such features as logical consistency, perceptual details, embedding, complications, unusual details, superfluous details, misunderstood details, associations, and self-deprecation.

∞ ACCURACY OF RETROSPECTIVE RECALL

Before considering recent research on the accuracy of retrospective recall, it is necessary to note some important advances that have taken place in the understanding of memory processes (for details, see Baddeley, 1990; Fivush & Hudson, 1990; Neisser & Winograd, 1988; Tulving, 1983). Several distinctions are relevant to the issue of retrospective recall. To begin with, there are important differences between what Tulving (1983) called semantic and episodic memory. *Semantic memory* is concerned with generic knowledge, rather than specific events. Thus, people remember how to read, rather than a specific English lesson in a particular class at school. Similarly, there is an implicit knowledge of what holidays are like, as well as discrete memories of particular holiday trips. By contrast, *episodic,* or *event,* or *autobiographical memory* deals with specific personal events and experiences. The two function in rather different sorts of ways, and for the most part, autobiographical memories are the focus of retrospective recall. Since Bartlett's classic book in 1932, there has been a widespread acceptance that autobiographical memories are at least partly reconstructive. Our recall of particular events in the past is influenced by numerous later discussions with other people of these events, by our own concepts and attitudes (we develop memory schemata that seek to make sense of our memories), and by our mental state and circumstances at the time of the recall. Short-term memory works in somewhat different ways from long-term memory, as indicated by the differential impact of both disease processes and normal aging on the two. In extreme old age, short-term memory tends to be markedly impaired, whereas long-term memory is considerably preserved. In addition, the recall of past events involves processes that are separate from those involved in the original laying down of such memories.

With respect to the accuracy of retrospective recall, probably the most crucial issue concerns the extent to which reconstruction introduces systematic biases (Simon & VonKorff, 1995). No doubt, to some extent people use implicit theories to reconstruct their personal histories (e.g., see Neisser, 1982; Ross, 1989), and well-documented evidence provides examples of the ways accounts of the past may be distorted to coincide with current feelings and attitudes, with stereotypes of behavior, or with prevailing views on child rearing (Chess, Thomas, & Birch, 1966; Radke-Yarrow et al., 1970; Robbins, 1963). Crucial questions concern the extent and seriousness of such biases and the degree to which they can be overcome by skillful interviewing. In their review of empirical findings on the effects of current psychopathology on retrospective recall, Brewin et al. (1993) concluded that, on the whole, the recall of significant past events that occurred a long time ago do not appear to be much affected by current mood state and that the recall of psychiatric patients is as good as that of nonpatients. Similarly, Richters (1992) pointed to the poor quality of many studies that claimed evidence reporting to show that depressed mothers distorted their accounts of their children. Nevertheless, empirical findings do suggest that biases can sometimes arise from the psychiatric history of informants (see below).

Another key issue with respect to long-term memories is whether the original memories are retained unaltered (in addition to the reconstructed memories) so that, given the right approach and the right circumstances, it should be possible to revive the original accurate memory. In their theory that memories are made up of a kind of filing system of individual, unconnected records to each of which is attached a heading, Morton, Hammersley, and Bekerian (1985) argued that although original memories may be overlain by reconstructed and therefore different memories, the original memories can be neither deleted nor modified. That view has been questioned by other researchers, who have suggested that original memories may actually be changed by later reconstruction and therefore may not be open to recall, but the matter remains unresolved (Hall, Loftus, & Tousignant, 1984; Hammersley, 1994).

Robins et al. (1985) used two methods to examine the possibility of biases, as well as inaccuracies, in retrospective recall. First, they reanalyzed data from Robins's (1966) long-term follow-up of child guidance patients, comparing retrospective recall with information available in the contemporaneous records. They found that agreement was good in terms of whether the home had been broken, and fairly good with respect to such items as whether the child had ever been in a foster home or whether the mother went out to work. Agreement was poor, however, on whether the family had been on welfare and whether teenage supervision had been inadequate. They concluded that agreement was poor either when information may not have been available to the child (e.g., the child may not have been told that the family was on welfare) or when variables involved a judgment rather than a simple factual description. With respect to bias, they determined whether the retrospective recall was more accurate for those who are currently well when interviewed in adult life than for those with an antisocial personality disorder. It was found that healthier adults were more likely to deny adverse information about early home life. In other words, the main bias came from an underreporting by currently healthy adults, rather than from an overreporting by those with current psychopathology.

The second method used to examine the possibility of biases involved examination of agreements between psychiatric patients and their siblings, as compared with control subjects and their siblings in terms of retrospective reports of the home environment that they have experienced between ages 6 and 12. No evidence of bias associated with current patient status was found. It was found that, in both groups, factual data were reported better than variables requiring either inference or value judgements.

Bifulco, Brown, Lillie, and Jarvis (1997) similarly used sister pairs to assess the agreement between self-reports of physical or sexual abuse and reports on the same individual by the sister. Corroboration was moderately good, with kappa values (for 4-point scales) ranging from .37 (for sexual abuse by someone outside the household) to .70 (for parental neglect). Nevertheless, women's reports of their own adverse experiences was *not* corroborated in 18% (neglect) to 50% (sexual abuse) of cases. It is noteworthy that corroboration was most frequent (.74) when both sisters had had the same experiences.

Kendler et al. (1991) used twin comparisons similarly to assess the reporting of a history of psychiatric disorders in the parents. Twins who had themselves experienced major depression or a generalized anxiety disorder were more likely to report the same disorder in their parents than their co-twins who had not suffered from an episode of depression or anxiety. However, differences in both directions were found. Data could not differentiate between an effect of experiencing disorder oneself on the *recognition* of disorder in others and an effect on *recall* or *reporting*.

A somewhat similar approach, but comparing mothers' and teachers' accounts, was used by Chilcont and Breslau (1997) to investigate possible bias in the reporting of psychopathology in the children resulting from a maternal history of anxiety or depression. Findings suggested that mothers with both anxiety and depression tended to overstate and overgeneralize their children's emotional and behavioral difficulties, but teacher reports confirmed that the children of depressed or anxious mothers did also show a truly increased level of psychopathology. That is, maternal depression does not usually result in false reports, but as the result of hypersensitivity or misperception it may lead to an exaggeration (sometimes a substantial exaggeration) of effects.

Henry, Moffitt, Caspi, Langley, and Silva (1994) used data from the Dunedin longitudinal study to compare recall in adolescents with contemporaneous data obtained earlier in childhood. On the one hand, recall was quite good for certain factual data not requiring inferences (e.g., residence changes, height, weight, reading ability, police contacts). On the other hand, recall of both emotional symptomatology and family relationships were quite poor. Widom (Widom & Morris, 1997; Widom & Shepard, 1996) used data from a prospective study of abused/neglected and nonabused/neglected children to assess their retrospective recall of both physical and sexual abuse. Interview reports of major abuse in childhood showed generally good discriminative validity, but substantial underreporting occurred in relation to the contemporane ous official records. Also, the underreporting of sexual abuse was very marked for men, perhaps because they conceptualized their childhood sexual experiences as nonabusive. With respect to pos-

sible biasing effects on putative causal associations, it was particularly troubling that whereas self-reported childhood abuse was
associated with self-reported violence in adults, and official records of physical abuse predicted arrests for violent offenses, no
association was found across informants. That is, self-reported
child abuse did not predict violent arrests. That is perhaps reas-
suring insofar as it suggests that retrospective recall is not being
shaped by adult experiences of engaging in violence, but there has
to be concern over the effects of shared method variance. The
authors' recommendation on the need for measures from multiple
informants is apposite.

Raphael and Cloitre (1994) used a longitudinal study involving
the assessment of stressful life events to determine whether biases
in retrospective recall arose either from the mood of the informant
at the time of recall or from causal search processes (the groups
followed over time comprised a sample of those suffering from
chronic facial pain and a parallel sample of acquaintance controls).
Results showed no effect of either mood congruence or causal
search on the recall of event occurrence, but current mood did
influence the subjective appraisal of the events recalled, and
current depressed mood had a general tendency to impair recall,
though not to bias it.

A rather different sort of bias concerns the possibility that a
general tendency to forget events in the distant past may give rise
to spurious and artifactual cohort effects. Thus, several large-scale
epidemiological studies have reported higher rates of lifetime
psychopathology among recently born cohorts than among older
ones (Rutter & Smith, 1995). This applies in many different sorts
of psychopathologies but has perhaps been most evident in the
case of depression occurring in young adults (Fombonne, 1995). A
simulation study by Giuffra and Risch (1994) showed how easily
a relatively small tendency to forget could mimic true cohort
effects. A consideration of a broader range of data, in contrast,
suggests that the increase in psychopathology among adolescents
and young adults during the last few decades probably is real to
an important extent (Rutter & Smith, 1995).

In our own work, we have placed most reliance on comparisons between retrospective recall and contemporaneous records in
childhood. Although on the face of it, comparisons of the recall of
two siblings would seem a reasonable approach, it is open to the
objection that, even with experiences that involve all the children,
they tend to be experienced in different ways (Plomin & Daniels,
1987). In part, that is because familywide experiences may affect

children in different ways and to varying degrees (e.g., in the presence of general family discord and hostility, often only one child is scapegoated) and, in part, because children cognitively and affectively process their experiences in somewhat different ways (what is challenging to one child may be threatening to another), and because individuals vary in their susceptibility to adverse experiences (and therefore differ in the extent to which the experiences are memorable to them).

In addition, however, it cannot necessarily be assumed that contemporaneous records provide the best data. They may not for several rather different reasons. Thus, the original recording of information may have been judgmental or incomplete or biased in some way. Also, the contemporaneous data will have had to be recorded at some particular time, and necessarily this means the contemporaneous records will miss behavior or happenings after the time when they were recorded. By contrast, retrospective data can cover the whole time period. We found that that may well be a relevant consideration in some circumstances (Zoccolillo, Pickles, Quinton, & Rutter, 1992). In a follow-up into adult life of children experiencing an institutional upbringing when younger, three contemporaneous measures were available—a parental questionnaire (completed by the caregiver in the group foster home), a teacher questionnaire, and official records of delinquency. It was found that 27% of the sample showed deviance on the parental scale. For those who did not show deviance on either the teacher scale or the delinquency records but who were positive on the retrospective account, 40% were positive on the parental scale. In other words, the *positive* retrospective account agreed better with the contemporaneous parental account than did either the *negative* teacher report or the *negative* court record. The implication is that the retrospective measure here provided more valid data than either the teacher questionnaire or the official crime records.

Maughan, Pickles, and Quinton (1995) assessed retrospective recall by using data from a general population sample of 10-year-olds and from an epidemiological sample of families including a parent with mental disorder for whom systematic parental interviews had been undertaken in childhood, and who were reinterviewed in their late 20s. The possibility of bias and retrospective recall was determined by assessing agreement between the contemporaneous parental account (when the children were age 10) and the subjects' retrospective reports of parental hostility. A specific comparison was made according to whether the subjects showed good or poor psychosocial functioning in adult life. The level of association between retrospective and prospective accounts was only moderate, reflecting the fact that the variable required a degree of inference, but an important difference was found with respect to the effects of psychosocial functioning in adult life. Subjects with poor current functioning had very little tendency to overreport childhood problems, but substantial evidence indicated that those with good adult outcomes underreported childhood difficulties.

Holmshaw and Simonoff (1996) studied retrospective recall in a sample of 32 twins who had attended a psychiatric clinic in childhood. The agreement between contemporaneous records and retrospective recall was assessed in relation to the presence or absence of a range of different types of childhood psychopathologies. It was found that the recall of both conduct and anxiety symptoms was generally good and that the recall of depression and hyperactivity was fair, but not as good. The researchers concluded that with appropriate systematic interviewing, retrospective recall for major psychopathology in childhood can be quite high but that the accuracy (and the completeness) of recall is likely to be influenced both by the salience of the phenomena for the children at the time they were experienced and by the interview methods used in obtaining recall. Probably, recall is best when the phenomena can be assessed in terms of clearly definable events (e.g., stealing, avoidance of school), rather than of mood states or behaviors that rely on judgments about severity in relation to other people's behavior.

Menard and Elliott (1990) used the U.S. National Youth Survey to compare the findings from prospective data and retrospective recall of delinquent activities. They found that retrospective accounts tended to underreport substantially, as compared with contemporaneous accounts. This has not been evident in all studies, however, and the quality and style of interviewing about past behavior may be critical. More crucially, however, Menard and Elliott found that retrospective accounts differed from contemporaneous reports in the *time-ordering* of events and behavior. Both *telescoping* (bringing features forward in time) and *reverse telescoping* (reporting that a particular behavior had occurred but only before the specified time period) occurred. Telescoping was three times as common as reverse telescoping. In some circumstances, however, it may be that people would be willing to admit to discreditable behaviors if they could distance them from the present by reporting them only as occurring a long time ago.

∽ TELESCOPING OF EVENTS IN
RETROSPECTIVE RECALL

Nevertheless, one consistent finding in the literature concerns the tendency for events in the distant past to be telescoped in such a way that they are brought forward nearer to the time at which retrospective recall takes place. This tendency can be reduced through the use of personalized timing landmarks, provided that the reference points are meaningfully associated with whatever events are to be recalled. Skilful questioning based on knowledge of how memory processes work can help interviewers obtain more accurate timing of past events. People's tendency to use schemata and to make inferences about what is likely to have been the case, however, constitute potential sources of significant bias. Although the phenomenon of telescoping is well demonstrated, the same level of agreement is not shown on why this occurs. It could come about through several quite different mechanisms. Thus, it could come about because of a true time distortion, such that time tends to shrink to the present; because retention of memories is greater for recent events; because errors in dating increase linearly with the time since the dated event; and because intrusions often occur from events outside the period being asked about, but such intrusions cannot come from events that have not yet occurred (Friedman, 1993; Huttenlocher, Hedges, & Prohaska, 1988; Rubin & Baddeley, 1989; Squire, 1989; Thompson, Skowronski, & Lee, 1988).

∽ OPERATIONALIZING MODELS OF RECALL
FOR EMPIRICAL DATA ANALYSIS

Although the research described has made considerable progress in characterizing the kinds and scale of recall errors and the conditions under which they may be made, the value of this work for the analysis of recall data has often been limited by a failure to pursue the work to the stage of a statistical model. The widespread use and success of latent variable models as a means of combining information from several sources, each subject to error, suggests that such a step would be worthwhile with recall data. Standard latent variable models, however, typically embody very simple structures of measurement error that would not adequately reflect the complexity that has been found with recall data. For example, de Leon (1995) used a *latent variable model* to study contemporaneous and retrospective reports of parenting behavior and negative expressed emotion (EE). A path was required to reflect an association between childhood exposure to low (high) levels of maternal EE and a tendency to report retrospectively lower (higher) levels of exposure to all negative parenting behaviors. This represents a more complicated decomposition of measurement variance than the independent trait and method factors have usually assumed.

Measurement models for the dating of events have been particularly poorly developed. Pickles, Pickering, and Taylor (1996) have begun to develop such models and have applied them to compare the contrasting, but not mutually exclusive, hypotheses of time compression and heteroscedastic random measurement error as explanations for telescoping. Random error can give rise to telescoping as the result of greater error in the reported timing of events in the distant past. This can lead to more of the distant events being substantially brought forward than recent events are pushed back. Within simulated data, the statistical models could correctly identify the telescoping mechanisms and correct for their impact. In data from the Virginia Twin Study of Adolescent Behavioral Development on mothers' reports of the timing of puberty in girls, evidence of substantial telescoping was found, being larger for the typically less "salient" onset of breast development measure than for the more salient menarche measure. The paper also examined "current status errors" of the sort likely to be more common where what constitutes onset is not clearly defined. As expected, these were also found to be substantially greater in the case of breast development than of menarche.

∞ CHILDREN'S MEMORIES

Particularly stimulated by the need to evaluate the accuracy of children's reports when they appear as witnesses in legal courts, a tremendous upsurge of empirical research into children's memories has occurred (see Ceci & Bruck, 1993; Ceci, Ross, & Toglia, 1987; Fivush, 1993; Goodman & Bottoms, 1993). Attention has focused on three main issues: (a) the extent to which young children have memories that are as detailed and accurate as adults'; (b) the techniques needed to obtain good recall by children; and (c) the question of whether children are more suggestible and susceptible to distortions of memory as a result of leads provided by other people. A variety of experimental and naturalistic research strategies have been used to examine these issues.

The main findings can be summarized as follows: The general tendency is for memories to fade with time, and this applies to children in much the same way as to adults. Nevertheless, even young children are remarkably accurate in their autobiographical recall and retain information about personally experienced events over quite long periods of time. Their memories are inevitably influenced by what makes events memorable or significant or meaningful to them at the time these occurred. For obvious reasons, this is different in early childhood from the situation in adult life or even in later childhood. Although young children's memories are surprisingly good, preschoolers' recall is not as detailed or as exhaustive as is that of older children. Most especially, preschool children do not recall as much information spontaneously as do older children and adults.

Young children need many questions and cues if they are to recall in detail even recently experienced events. This means that the style of interviewing needs to provide much external support in the form of contextualization, questions, and cues if memory retrieval is to be at all full. Younger children are also less consistent in their recall than are older children or adults. This is not a matter of their being inaccurate, and it is clear that it would be a mistake to infer inaccuracy from the presence of inconsistency in the case of young children. Age differences are also found in how children tend to remember things as a consequence of their age at the time. Young children tend to focus on routine and general information and therefore are less good at recalling what is distinctive and different about specific events. As children grow older, they begin to build up a better general knowledge about events and hence become more able to focus on what makes a specific event different and unusual. Taken together, these findings suggest that young children encode a great deal of information about events but that sometimes they have difficulty retrieving the information in an interview situation (Fivush, 1993).

Although contradictory claims have been made about the suggestibility of children, Ceci and Bruck's (1993) systematic review of the evidence, especially from their own studies (Ceci & Huffman, 1997), indicates that the weight of evidence points to several conclusions. First, even very young children are capable of providing accurate recall of significant events in the past. Second, in ordinary circumstances, they are not particularly suggestible.

Nevertheless, people of all ages are subject to distortions of memory, particularly when suggestions are made by people perceived as in positions of power.

Younger children (3- to 4-year-olds) have a significant tendency to be more susceptible than older ones. This seems to come about through several rather different mechanisms. First, social factors are important; for example, when children are given erroneous post-event suggestions by an adult, this is more likely to result in distortion than when similar suggestions are made by another child. Second, unlike adults, children rarely challenge the credibility of adult questioners; accordingly, they show an increased tendency to incorporate the content of questions into their answers. Third, suggestibility effects are influenced by the dynamics of the interview itself; children tend to attempt to be good conversational partners by complying with what they perceive to be the belief of their questioner.

Fourth, it may well be, too, that when memory traces are weak, children may be more compliant and willing to accept suggestions because there is no competing memory trace to challenge the suggestion. Findings on the role of stress are contradictory and inconclusive. It is possible that stress at the time of encoding might aid the storage of information, whereas stress at the time of retrieval could impair access, but further research is needed to test this suggestion. It has sometimes been thought that preschool children cannot lie because the decentration is beyond their cognitive capacity. It is now clear, however, that young children are able to engage in some sorts of deception (Ceci & Bruck, 1993). In some circumstances, young children will consciously distort reports of something they have witnessed or experienced. They are more likely to do so, however, in response to a fear of reprisal or an avoidance of embarrassment than they are in order to gain rewards, although they will sometimes lie for personal gain.

∞ INFANTILE AMNESIA

It has long been known that most adults can recall few, if any, specific events from the early years of life (Pillemer & White, 1989). The amnesia specifically involves personal memories of particular episodes from an individual's past (Brewer, 1986; Tulving, 1983) and not to general knowledge about the world acquired early in life. Young children have no difficulty carrying forward such semantic knowledge. Although the phenomenon of *infantile am-*

nesia has been generally accepted for many years, only during the 1980s was it subjected to much systematic research. The impetus came both from a resurgence of interest in developmental aspects of memory processes (as part of the broader growth of cognitive psychology) and through the stimulus provided by the need to establish whether preschool children can recall specific episodes relevant to legal testimony in cases of sexual abuse or witnessing of other crimes (see Ceci et al., 1987).

Three very different theoretical explanations for infantile amnesia have been proposed. First, in the early part of this century, Freud (see vol. 7 and vols. 15-16 of his collected papers, 1905/1953 & 1916-1917/1963) argued both that the phenomenon extended up to the age of 6 or 7 years and that it resulted from active repression or blockade, rather than from either a failure to encode the original experiences or a cognitive limitation to their retrieval. Second, Schachtel (1947), by contrast, suggested that the phenomenon derived from socially induced changes in reconstruction and interpretation of past events. Because the meaning of experiences is so different in infancy from later childhood, because the memory cues vary so much across age periods, and because later memories are so much influenced by language-related cognitive processing, adult memory provides an inadequate set of schemata for the recall of experiences in early childhood. Third, cognitive-developmental explanations postulate that neurophysiological immaturity means that young children cannot process information in a way that facilitates long-term recall; that is, there is an encoding deficit in early childhood (Wetzler & Sweeney, 1986; White & Pillerman, 1979). Alternatively, it may be that cognitive development results in an increase in the range of situations in which early learning experiences can be retrieved and expressed (Hayne & Rovee-Collier, 1995). Studies of recall *within* the infancy period suggest that memory retrieval is dependent on contexts and cues closely similar to those that applied at the time memories were encoded. Possibly, therefore, infantile amnesia is a consequence both of greater constraints of memory retrieval from the early years and of the increasing disparity between contexts in infancy and later childhood. As part of this general approach, some researchers have emphasized the role of language (e.g., Nelson, 1990), and others the developing sense of self, which is thought to provide a personal frame of reference that makes memory truly autobiographical (Howe & Courage, 1993).

Empirical research findings show that none of these theoretical views are entirely correct (Nelson, 1994; Usher & Neisser, 1993). To begin with, Freud's notion that infantile amnesia extends up to the age of 6 years or so is clearly wrong because most people have some memories, albeit incomplete, from the preschool years (Tessler & Nelson, 1994). Also, the mechanism of repression does not constitute the most plausible explanation for the amnesia (Lewis, 1995). Adults usually recall very little, if anything, from the first 2 years of life; even in the 3rd and 4th years, only a few particular experiences (e.g., the birth of a sibling, a hospital admission) are likely to persist into adult memory; and when memories do begin to appear in the later preschool years, they tend to be relatively incomplete and limited in detail. As already noted, there is evidence of implicit or generic memory from infancy and toddlerhood; the amnesia applies to the explicit recall of specific events. But recent evidence suggests that, at least to some extent, the deficit lies in memory retrieval more than in memory encoding. Young children do remember some events, but as they get older, they become less able to retrieve these memory traces. Functional memory development does seem to have a degree of important discontinuity even though we don't fully understand its basis. It seems highly likely that it has multiple origins. In part, it is likely to involve age-related differences in what is meaningful and memorable. In part, too, the emergence of language makes it possible for people to construct narratives about their past experiences and thereby to form schemata about them. In part, too, during the later years of early childhood, children increasingly share their experiences with other people and come to understand the significance in terms of their own sense of self (Howe, Courage, & Peterson, 1994) and their own social circumstances. These features, however, in themselves, do not seem sufficient to account for the phenomenon. Compared with those of older children and adults, infants' cognitive processes for dealing with memories is different. The neural substrate necessary for long-term recall is almost certainly not in place until the 2nd year of life, and it may well take longer for the cognitive capacity to be fully developed.

∞ RECOVERED OR FALSE MEMORIES

During the last decade, increasing attention has been paid to the possibility that individuals who have experienced some extreme trauma (most characteristically, sexual abuse) can entirely forget about the experience in childhood and then later in adulthood regain memory of the experience under the influence of either psychotherapy or some other form of systematic interviewing that exerts strong pressure to explore early life experiences (Lindsey & Read, 1994; Loftus, 1993; Schooler, 1994). Sharply contrasting views have been expressed on the extent to which such memories are real and the extent to which they are false beliefs that have been suggested as a result of biased interviewing. The controversy has been fueled by the fact that recovered memories have been used in court cases as evidence that sexual abuse occurred many years earlier. There are legitimate grounds for concern both about the interviewing techniques used to elicit such recovered memories and about the safety of some convictions based on such evidence (see Loftus & Ketcham, 1994). The topic is important both with respect to our understanding of memory processes and from a forensic point of view. Several rather different issues are involved in the overall concept.

The first issue is the question of whether people can completely forget about major experiences only to re-remember them later during the course of psychotherapy. Plenty of evidence supports the view that it is common for individuals to forget key experiences partially and to remember them later when questioned via appropriate techniques that contextualize their memories. That is a normal feature of the ways memory processes work, and there is nothing very remarkable about it. By extrapolation, it would seem quite possible that, under certain circumstances, individuals might completely forget what has happened to them, rather than just partially lose the memory. It is difficult to determine how often this occurs, but substantial anecdotal evidence makes it reasonably certain that the phenomenon exists. It is much less clear, however, whether such total amnesia can be resistant to ordinary methods of memory retrieval. In most instances, when people forget about some incident in their past, at least some memory of what happened quickly reemerges if they are asked about the experience. Still, although probably complete amnesia that is resistant to recall is infrequent, sufficient evidence from clinical accounts supports the conclusion that the phenomenon can occur.

The usual explanation for such amnesia is that the experience was such an extremely painful one that it was repressed or blocked out of memory in an active fashion. There is not a very straightforward, unambiguous way of testing the concept of active repression, but again, clinical reports of various kinds contain sufficiently convincing accounts to conclude that repression of painful memories can occur (Ceci, Huffman, Smith, & Loftus, 1994; Lindsey & Read, 1994; Schooler, 1994). But there is no need to invoke the concept of repression for many instances in which memories are temporarily lost. Forgetting about experiences, both painful and nonpainful, is a normal part of what happens with memories. Unless memories are triggered by new events that provide reminders or by discussions about the past, people forget much of what has happened to them. Equally, however, new reminders or new discussions can revive memories of what had hitherto been forgotten.

In that connection, the second issue is whether amnesia is more likely to occur when incidents have been unusually traumatic or frightening or embarrassing. Although it is usually supposed that that is the case, the evidence is not particularly convincing. People exposed to extreme trauma usually do retain some memories of what has happened, and the tendency to forget applies in much the same way to traumatic and nontraumatic events. In many ways, the nearest approach to a systematic investigation is provided by Goodman, Quas, Batterman-Fauce, Riddlesberger, and Kuhn's (1994) study of children's memory of urinary tract catheterization. Most children remembered the experience, but a few denied ever experiencing the medical test, and there is just a hint that such amnesia was more likely when there had been a lack of discussion of the event with the parents and when the procedure was associated with both embarrassment and stress.

A third issue concerning recovered memories is whether such flashback recollections, which may be particularly vivid, are also unusually accurate. The evidence is clear-cut that despite the vividness and the conviction of complete accuracy, recovered memories may be seriously flawed and misleading in absolutely central features of the incident (as well as with respect to more peripheral aspects). Examples of corroboration of recovered memories of trauma, including sexual abuse, are sufficient to accept that the memories can be accurate, but equally, examples of mistaken memories abound, and one cannot rely on the supposed exceptional accuracy of recovered memories. Like any other memories, they can be mistaken (Ceci, 1995; Lindsey & Read, 1994; Loftus & Ketcham, 1994).

In many ways, the most crucial issue is whether biased interviewing can create false memories. It would be a mistake to overestimate the extent to which young children's personal memories are so fragile that they easily incorporate information from other people into their own recall (Fivush, 1994); nevertheless, evidence, both naturalistic and experimental, is good that false memories can be created (Ceci, 1995; Ceci & Huffman, 1997;

Lindsey & Read, 1994; Loftus & Hoffman, 1989; Loftus & Ketcham, 1994). Moreover, with some children, implanted memories can be surprisingly resistent to debriefing. It is important to note, too, that professionals cannot distinguish between implanted (false) memories and true memories. People vary greatly in their suggestibility and in their proneness to develop false memories, but the phenomenon undoubtedly exists. As Schooler (1994) concluded, there is a reasonable foundation for the existence of both recovered and fabricated memories, although we lack evidence on their relative frequency.

∞ FACILITATED COMMUNICATION

A further example of reporting that is open to external manipulation resulting in biases and false information is *facilitated communication,* a technique sometimes used with autistic individuals who cannot communicate through speech or sign language. In essence, the method involves the use of some mode of graphic communication (e.g., pointing to or touching letters on a sheet, or using a keyboard to spell words) in which the facilitator supports (but supposedly does not guide) the autistic individual's arm or hand in some way. This has been used as a teaching technique but also has been employed to enable nonverbal children to report sexual abuse. The key issue is whether the information communicated in this way comes from the autistic individual or from the facilitator.

The question has been examined in several studies using variants of the experimental paradigm in which either the question put to the individual is concealed from the facilitator or the questions put to each of them are different (e.g., Eberlin, McConnachie, Ibel, & Volpe, 1993; Heckler, 1994; Klewe, 1993; Montee, Miltenberger, & Wittrock, 1995; Moore, Donovan, & Hudson, 1993; Moore, Donovan, Hudson, Dykstra, & Lawrence, 1993; Starr, 1994; Wheeler, Jacobson, Paglieri, & Schwartz 1993). Results have been consistent in showing that, under controlled conditions, the content of the autistic individuals' communications tend to be dependent on information available to the facilitator. Most convincing are several examples of correct answers to the wrong questions (the facilitated communication answered the question put to the facilitator, rather than the different question put to the autistic individual). In all instances, it has appeared that the facilitators were unaware of the guidance they were providing (no indication of conscious deception was found), but nevertheless they were indeed determining the answers. The data, of course, do not rule out the possibility that, in individual cases, facilitation could enable a person with a disability to communicate despite being unable to do so on her or his own. The evidence is convincing, however, that in the great majority of cases, this is not what is happening; rather, the reports derive from the facilitator and not from the person with the disability. The example of facilitated communication may seem bizarre, but information obtained only through its use has been given as evidence in court cases of alleged sexual abuse (Myers, 1994). It provides a warning that the unconscious distortion of recall to fit in with prior expectations shown by Radke-Yarrow et al. (1970) for informants may apply also to professionals trying to aid reporting. *Caveat emptor,* indeed!

∞ MENTAL REPRESENTATION OF EARLY EXPERIENCES

The final aspect of retrospective recall to be discussed is quite different in that it focuses, not on efforts to improve the objective validity of the reports, but rather on the use of styles of mental representation of negative experiences as a means of drawing inferences about psychological functioning in adult life. The basic notion is that people's recall of experiences in childhood is influenced by how they think, reflect, and organize their thoughts in relation to such experiences and not simply as a consequence of what is remembered. This emphasis may be said to focus on the *how* rather than the *what* of memories and of attitudes toward those memories. Main et al. (1985) pioneered this approach with respect to adults' recall of attachment experiences in childhood, and this led to the development of the Adult Attachment Interview. Although now reasonable evidence supports the qualities of the Adult Attachment Interview as a satisfactory instrument (Crowell et al, 1996; van IJzendoorn, 1995), evidence is still limited on the extent to which the key features concern the representation of memories as distinct from the experiences themselves that gave rise to the representations (see Fox, 1995, for a critique). Nevertheless, findings are beginning to emerge that suggest the basic notion may have some validity. For example, one of us (Patrick, Hobson, Castle, Howard, & Maughan, 1994) compared adults with borderline personality disorder and adults with dysthymia. The majority of both groups had experienced significant trauma or loss in childhood, but as assessed on Parker's Parental Bonding Instrument (Parker, Tupling, & Brown, 1979), poor maternal care was more frequent in the borderline personality group. On the Adult Attachment Interview, the subjects with borderline personality disorder were much more likely to appear confused, fearful, and overwhelmed in relation to past experiences with attachment figures and to describe their negative experiences in a manner that appeared unresolved, disorganized, and disoriented with respect to their experiences. The data were insufficient to show that the style of representation of early negative experiences, rather than the experiences themselves, were crucial, but findings indicate the potential value of seeking to assess parental representations in a systematic manner. Up to now, the focus has been particularly on the mental representation of attachment relationships, but we have every reason to suppose that the concept applies more broadly than this.

A key question with regard to the mental representation of all experiences is whether the main effects in adult life derive from negative *experiences* in childhood or from maladaptive *representations* of such experiences. Pearson, Cohn, Cowan, and Cowan (1994) addressed this issue by comparing adults with continuous attachment security and those with "earned security" (they had had seriously insecure relationships in childhood but remembered these in a coherent fashion postulated to represent attachment security). Those with earned security were just as likely as the "insecure" to report depression, but they differed in being more likely to report warm parenting. Findings suggest that it may be useful to differentiate between negative experiences and the ways they are thought about, but both may be influential.

∞ CONCLUSIONS

The topic of retrospective recall has grown in both importance and interest in ways that are beyond anything that could have been envisaged at the time of Marian Radke-Yarrow's crucial empirical study and thoughtful conceptual overview of the issues. Nevertheless, it is striking just how accurate she was in her appraisal of the issues. The development of improved interviewing techniques has been useful in improving the quality of retrospective recall. It has also proved possible to diminish the distortions in people's recollections of the past. Interestingly, the main problem does not seem to lie in the biases created by people's current mental state, but rather by the expectations, constructs, and schemata created by their life experiences and their situation at the time of the retrospective recall. Moreover, it is not so much that people with psychopathology and with many negative experiences exaggerate the stresses and adversities they have experienced (indeed, that seems unusual), but rather that normal individuals tend to forget early traumas. Of course, the risk is still significant that these differences in retrospective recall will lead to misleading artifactual conclusions. As the 1970 report adumbrated, the main problem with retrospective recall does not lie in interview techniques, but rather in the ways memory processes operate. A veritable explosion of knowledge has occurred in the field of cognitive psychology during recent decades, and the field now better understands the differences between, say, semantic or implicit memories and explicit or episodic memories; between memory processes in infancy and later; between short-term and long-term memories; and between the encoding of memories and their later retrieval. It would be going too far to claim that cognitive psychology has provided satisfying answers with respect to the mechanisms involved in such phenomena as infantile amnesia or recovered memories, but the field of research has amply documented the value of bringing together basic and applied research as a means of both obtaining a better theoretical understanding and providing a means of dealing with important, real-life problems. That has been a hallmark of Marian Radke-Yarrow's approach to research; her contributions to developmental psychology have been many, and the topic of retrospective recall well illustrates the manifold strengths of her investigative approach.

∞৲∞

COMMENTS ON CHAPTER 10

I am delighted that Michael Rutter, Barbara Maughan, Andrew Pickles, and Emily Simonoff have made us think about a layer of research decisions that precedes a choice of person- or variable-oriented research ventures. They would have us consider the raw data of our research on a dimension that does not have a high profile in critical discussion but that can have a sly influence on our research findings. They remind us that behavioral research is a heavy user of interviews, questionnaires, and self-reports—the parents' and teachers' reports on child behavior, mothers' descriptions of family relationships, and responses to personality inventories and psychiatric interviews. Each of these procedures requires recall.

It takes only a bit of translation to cite points at which issues of recall are issues of findings. Much that is known about the nature of memory encoding and retrieval informs us of the ways data can be influenced. Rutter et al. highlight issues that are particularly relevant in behavioral research: First, recall is best, that is, most congruent with "objective," contemporaneous measures, for clearly defined events. It is less good for material involving inference or judgment. Might this recall difference affect findings regarding developmental continuities of various kinds of behaviors or experiences? Specifically, externalizing disorders are clearly defined events, whereas internalizing (mood, feelings) problems are less so. Are developmental data regarding these two disorders equally valid? For data on relationships, too, where judgment and inference are involved, this feature of recall is relevant. Second, events are brought forward in time. Developmental time tables and developmental sequences are the material of longitudinal research. Are these data subject to a systematic recall distortion? The third issue is the dependence of recollection on the meaning that the recalled events have for the informants. This is a consideration in comparing and combining reports of multiple informants and in comparing responses of children at successive developmental stages.

In these and other ways, the authors remind us that recall is very much with us in our research and that a demanding standard for raw data is as necessary for sound research as sophisticated conceptualization and analysis. Rutter demonstrates this point especially in research on developmental psychopathology. In the exciting growth of this field, Michael Rutter has been at the center— as architect, builder, and critic. Much of the shape of this field, its progress and vitality, stem from the depth and breadth of his contributions. This is a moment to express admiration.

Marian Radke-Yarrow

~ *11* ~

Phenomena Regained

From Configurations to Pathways

Robert B. Cairns
Philip C. Rodkin
University of North Carolina at Chapel Hill

A tension exists in developmental psychology between the richness of its theories on individual ontogeny and the methods available to assess, correct, and revise those theories. Since the emergence of the discipline, one of its most challenging tasks has been to generate methods and analyses that are appropriate for studying the dynamics of lives over time. It has had to be generative; the direct importation of procedures from other areas of psychology has been and continues to be problematic. Experimental psychology—which established the early standards for rigor in psychological research—provided a model for which the strategy of variable isolation and manipulation was the method of choice. According to this model, key variables should be isolated and manipulated independently of the contexts in which they usually occurred. Because ontogenetic phenomena are rarely open to such reductionism, developmental and evolutionary studies were assigned second-class status in the new science (Hall, 1885).

Other developmentalists disagreed with that conclusion. Some critics went ever further to challenge directly the sanctity of the methodological assumptions of experimental psychology. In this regard, Canadian developmental psychobiologist J. W. Mills dismissed as artificial and wrong-headed the experimental procedures devised by Thorndike (1898) to study learning in animals, an experiment that established the prototype for nonhuman learning studies that has endured for a century. Mills argued that

investigations of learning should first be conducted over longitudinal periods in whole organisms in conditions akin to normal
circumstances (Mills, 1898).[1]

In France, Alfred Binet (1903) noted a different but parallel set
of problems in then-dominant procedures for studying children.
He observed, "The Americans, who love to do things big, often
publish experiments made on hundreds or even thousands of
persons. They believe that the conclusive value of a study is
proportional to the number of observations. That is a myth"
(p. 299). For Binet, the key to unlocking the secrets of memory and
intelligence involved not only mapping its gross outlines in large-
scale studies but also in a detailed tracing of its internal features
in individuals. He adopted as a deliberate strategy movement back
and forth in research from a focus on individuals to studies of large
samples. As Binet and Henri (1895) observed, a major problem in
understanding how sensory variables contributed to intelligence
was to determine how they are *combined* to predict cognitive
performance. How are the component elements or variables
weighted in individuals, and what is the nature of the process by
which sensations are translated into cognitions? The solution that
Binet and Henri offered was a wholly pragmatic one: Bypass the
recombination problem and interactions among variables by assessing complex functions directly in individuals.

Four decades into the 20th century, Kurt Lewin (1931) addressed the methodological dilemma from still a different perspective, but he arrived at conclusions not unlike his predecessors. In
the first *Handbook of Child Psychology,* Lewin outlined the need to
study the dynamic relations between the individual and the environment in the concrete particularity of the total situation. Lewin
challenged the then-dominant methodology of psychological inquiry on two counts: (a) its reliance on phenotypic aggregation for
description and statistical analysis and (b) its focus on psychological variables without explicit reference to the milieu of their
operation. On these matters, Lewin observed that sampling methods that attempt to identify the "average child" tend to obscure the
dynamic processes that contribute to the behavior of a specific
child in a specific setting. For Lewin, clumping together children
who were similar with respect to salient extrinsic or demographic
characteristics—but different with respect to key psychological
dynamics—was unlikely to yield generalizable psychological laws.

In a contemporary statement, David Magnusson (1995; this
volume, Chap. 3) has proposed a frame of reference for develop-

mental research and a method that seems appropriate for evaluating the perspective. In brief, Magnusson argues that the configuration of factors that operate in each individual life requires that attention be given to the behavior of each person as an "integrated totality." The action patterns of persons represent unique configurations of biological-interactional-situational factors. To the extent that the elements of these configurations become coalesced over time, a person's status on a single variable is a fallible guide for understanding. Hence, studies of social development call for person-oriented, categorical methods to complement traditional variable-oriented research designs.

So, the method-model tension has been felt in one form or another since the establishment of the field (Cairns, 1983, 1986; Valsiner, 1986). Even today, it seems to be built into the very structure of advanced training (e.g., courses in statistics and methods are typically taught as if they transcended areas of application). Moreover, it has never been politic for researchers to be contentious about gaps that exist in published articles between the introduction and discussion, on the one hand, and methods and results, on the other. Why court displeasure by getting cranky about their procedures, especially if the techniques have been deemed to be models of rigor in other areas of psychology? Why indeed, unless one believes with Marian Radke-Yarrow that methodology is the heart of the science and that "every investigator has a responsibility for excellence" (Radke-Yarrow et al., 1968, p. 168).

∞ TOWARD RAPPROCHEMENT

In a recent comment on the model-method gap, Bronfenbrenner (1996) observed that "the defining properties of the emergent model contradict, almost point for point, the now prevailing conceptual and operational strategies of choice in each specialized field of inquiry" (p. ix). Is a tug-of-war inevitable between the developmental models and the methods and statistics of traditional experimental designs? Perhaps, but a rapprochement may be possible. Amid the contradictions are also examples of productive collaboration wherein the strategies have proved complementary, rather than in conflict. In this regard, experimental, variable-oriented procedures have yielded significant gains in the study of significant population-based features of social development. To be sure, they have been less successful in capturing information about "the child's day-to-day experiences" and how they are coalesced with personal characteristics to produce individual pathways over development. Nor have they been effective in producing advances in our understanding of how complex characteristics of persons and their environments interact and are weighted in the person over time.

With the adoption of longitudinal, multilevel designs, the shortcomings of "prevailing conceptual and operational strategies of choice" have become increasingly difficult to overlook. Nowadays, virtually all developmental researchers agree with the insight of Marian Radke-Yarrow and her colleagues that the discipline should describe the pathways of individual adaptation over time in the concrete context of each life. As they eloquently stated the principle, "The child's day-to-day experiences contribute significantly to his behavior and development and are in many respects the essence of developmental theory" (Radke-Yarrow et al., 1968, p. 152). There is less agreement, however, on how to achieve this objective in research designs and data analyses. In this regard, two different types of analytic solutions have emerged as leading contenders in attempts to maximize information about individual development.

One group of solutions capitalizes on advances in the parametric estimation of individual growth curves, profiles, and trajectories. In this set of solutions, the procedures include the multivariate analysis of individual cases (Nesselroade & Ford, 1987), latent growth analysis (Curran, Harford, & Muthen, 1996), and hierarchical linear modeling (Bryk & Raudenbush, 1992). Although these procedures differ among themselves in assumptions, they provide elegant techniques to estimate the form and type of individual pathways over time. On this count, they represent a qualitative leap toward describing specific features of an individual's developmental course. The techniques also yield conventional information on the pathways of groups (the collection of individuals) and permit direct individual-group comparisons at basic levels.

The other set of solutions involves procedures to preserve the "integrated totality" of individual development at every stage of the design and analysis. This presupposes a shift to classification techniques. Hinde (this volume, Chap. 2) observes that four strategies may be employed to arrive at individual patterns through selection or classification steps and thereby preserve the coherence of the person-in-context system. One strategy is to study individuals from the beginning by using a case study approach, a second is to study extreme cases (Kagan, this volume, Chap. 4), a third is to study categories of children that have been identified by empirical or statistical procedures and then proceed to individual analysis, and the fourth is to employ a priori or theoretical criteria to identify categories and then proceed to individual analysis through an analysis of patterns within categories. Hinde (this volume, Chap. 2) provides a cogent account of the advantages and problems of the four strategies and illustrates how research can proceed by using the fourth strategy.

∞ VARIETIES OF CONFIGURATIONS

The modern developmental framework holds that the actions, emotions, and cognitions of persons are mutually constrained by a network of elements within and without the individual. The upshot is that single variables should not be divorced from the personal and social contexts in which they occur. Moreover, the link among variables is not a passive affair because the network of relationships becomes modified, realigned, and consolidated during the course of development. The proposition that the effects of key variables become mutually constrained, coalesced, and integrated in a child during the course of development has been broadly endorsed in the modern framework.

Although categorical solutions are less common than parametric ones in psychological research, they are common in the concrete affairs of living. For example, some of the most powerful factors in everyday relationships that segregate individuals reflect the operation of simple physical categories (age, gender, ethnic background). Then there are nosological or theoretically relevant categories based on standard empirical criteria or social judgments (e.g., attachment categories, socioeconomic class, depressed parents). When the investigator steps beyond these broadly accepted categories and attempts to disaggregate representative samples of youths into coherent subsets of persons who are reasonably similar to each other, significant problems arise in how to proceed. Cluster analytic procedures constitute one method of identifying subgroups in a sample that are maximally distinct from one another and relatively homogenous within each group on profiles of variables (see Bergman, this volume, Chap. 5; Hinde, this volume,

Chap. 2; Magnusson, this volume, Chap. 3). At an operational level, configuration analyses have been applied in four ways relevant to developmental study. Although they share many features in common, applications can differ among themselves in (a) goals, (b) the time at which the procedures are employed (at the beginning, throughout, or at the end of the investigation), and (c) what information is included in each of the configuration solutions.

Table 11.1 shows four different but related procedures that have been used to analyze longitudinal data sets. The table indicates what have been the goals of the procedures, along with some differential features in when the configurations are determined and the information that needs to be included. It should be noted that the use of cluster analysis to identify subgroups is only one way to identify configurations. Distinctive subgroups or persons who are similar on a pattern of variables can be determined on a priori, theoretical grounds, by the individuals' status on key variables, or by virtue of persons being extreme cases or outliers. Or, alternatively, empirical configurations may be identified through other techniques, such as configural frequency analysis or by splitting groups at the median on two or more variables (see Hinde, this volume, Chap. 2). In this regard, Binet (1903) simply identified persons with distinctive talents. He studied persons with exceptional memories, including chess masters and idiot savants, to better understand the organization of memory processes. In this section, we examine how configurations computed by cluster analyses have been used through progressive steps to identify individual pathways. We also discuss briefly how the configurations of outcomes, profiles, and the stability of configurations have been studied and the distinctive advantages and limitations of these procedures.

Prospective Configuration: Disaggregation, Developmental Comparison, and Prodigal Analysis

When a principal goal of longitudinal study is to identify prospectively the pathways of individuals to specific outcomes, it is useful to determine at the outset whether the sample can be disaggregated into smaller subsets consisting of persons who have relatively similar profiles of characteristics. Depending on the age and circumstances of the subjects, it may be expected that mutual

TABLE 11.1 Types of Configural Analysis in Longitudinal Design

Types	Principal Goals	When Determined	Information Included
Prospective	To preserve integrity of the individual in analysis To provide control comparisons for resilience/ vulnerability To plot individual pathways prospectively	Beginning of the study	Characteristics of individuals and context as they exist at the beginning of the study
Outcome	To preserve integrity of the individual in analysis To relate comorbid outcomes to antecedents To backward-trace dominant paths to comorbidity	End of the study	Characteristics of individuals and the confluence of outcomes at the end of the study
Stability	To preserve integrity of the individual in analysis To establish continuity of clusters and individuals To plot individual paths toward clusters and outcomes	At all assessment points	Characteristics of individuals at each assessment point
Trajectory	To identify types of trajectories To identify factors that account for individual shifts in trajectory	End of the study	Clusters of individual developmental profiles

constraints and correlations among variables will yield a limited number of types of natural configurations. If this expectation is accurate, clustering procedures—or their alternatives, such as configural frequency analysis, correspondence analysis, and network analyses—may be employed to disaggregate the longitudinal sample into homogeneous subgroups of persons at the beginning of the study. Given this beginning, steps can be taken to arrive at individual pathways over time. Each step in itself yields useful data about the nature of subgroups, persons, and variables and their interactions over time. Only at the fourth step, the stage of prodigal analysis, are individual pathways brought from the background to the foreground.

Step 1. Disaggregation and Subgroup Configurations

Given the interdependence of characteristics in persons and contexts, it may be assumed that a finite number of types of configurations of variables exists that may be linked to meaningful outcomes. The number and types of personal configurations that may be identified at the beginning of a longitudinal investigation depend on such factors as (a) the cluster solution adopted, (b) the closeness of relationship among variables selected to be clustered, (c) the number of variables selected to be clustered, (d) the kind of clustering algorithm selected, (e) the proximity measure used in the analysis, (f) the number and diversity of subjects studied, and (g) the criteria employed to establish within-cluster homogeneity. Moreover, the range of variables is crucial. For instance, if the objective is to predict school dropout, decisions must be made at the outset whether to include simply characteristics of the person alone (e.g., academic competence, aggression, popularity) or to include, in addition, characteristics of the person's environment (e.g., socioeconomic class, neighborhood, social group membership). The "range of variables selected" is a strategic decision that reflects, among other things, one's hypothesis about the outcomes to be predicted. In addition, in contrast with multiple logistic regression algorithms that allow nonpredictive variables to be dropped early, superfluous measures in cluster analysis are more difficult (but still possible) to detect and can undermine the quality of the obtained solution.

Is there evidence that this prospective strategy really works? Specifically, what keeps one from being tyrannized by large numbers of ill-defined and poorly described groups of personal configurations? Possibly, it is the nature of human nature. One robust finding to emerge from virtually all cluster solutions conducted is that the solutions are economical. Typically, a small number of common configurations have proved to be sufficient to describe whole samples of persons (e.g., see Cairns, Cairns, & Neckerman, 1989, and Gustafson & Magnusson, 1991). Parsimony in solution occurs even before the prospective solutions are fine-tuned by the removal for further scrutiny of the 1% to 3% of outliers that tend to resist classification (Bergman, this volume, Chap. 5). The economy may reflect the constrained and holistic nature of behavioral organization—the nature of human nature—or it may reflect the nature of the solutions, the limits of measurements, or a combination of all of the above.

Step 2. Subgroup Configurations
to Developmental Outcomes

To the extent that hypotheses underlying the selection of variables at the beginning of the study are correct, the configurations determined at T_o should differ among themselves in targeted outcomes at the end of the study (T_n). We can evaluate this expectation in longitudinal research by determining for each configuration the proportion of children who are classified as positive or negative cases in the targeted outcome (e.g., becoming a teen parent, dropping out of school, graduating with honors from high school, becoming a productive worker). These outcomes were not assessed at T_o because they did not exist in childhood; they emerged in the course of development. Presumably, a "normative" pathway may be described for each configuration. The different pattern of antecedent-outcome contingencies constitute, to the extent that they conform to expectations, evidence for the developmental meaningfulness of the original variable selection and cluster solutions.

But there is a problem of premature closure. If the analysis were left at this stage, as we have done earlier (e.g., Cairns, Cairns, & Neckerman, 1989), it is informative about group configurations and illustrates how higher-order interactions can be retained in the developmental analysis rather than eliminated. The configuration analysis at this stage hardly meets the criterion for tracking individual lives in context over time. Two additional analytic stages seem required to approximate that objective.

Step 3. Developmental Controls
and Developmental Comparisons

Configurations may be used as control procedures to identify and track those resilient or vulnerable children who defy the group odds, for good or for ill. A focus on the persons who do not conform to the longitudinal pattern for the original configuration—the "errors of prediction," whether false positive or false negative—can be especially informative. Specifically, within-configuration comparisons can be made between (a) the persons who conform to the dominant outcome for the configuration and (b) those who do not conform. These "errors" include all persons who were inconsistent with the expectation underlying selection of the original variables and cluster identification. In conventional analyses, they contribute to the within-group error variance or lower predictive correlations. Configuration analyses promote procedures to determine whether these persons differ from other members of the configuration in their initial state (errors of classification) or, rather, whether the differences could not possibly have been predicted a priori because they reflect forces and turning points that arise during development.

This step toward within-configuration analysis over time is a group-based variant of the matched case-control design. That is, developmental comparisons are made among persons who were presumably roughly equivalent to each other at the beginning of the investigation but who proved to be different in outcomes. Although the designs are not identical (e.g., relative within-group homogeneity is not the same as matched-pair homogeneity), they both attempt to ensure high levels of similarity on variables and their interactions that are presumed to be linked to particular outcomes. Relative to matched control procedures, two features of configuration designs are that (a) they potentially include all subjects (without pruning the sample to persons capable of being matched) and (b) they preserve intact natural clusters of characteristics.

How can one determine whether the resilient or vulnerable cases differed in initial condition or differed in turning points in development? The answer to the first part of the question seems straightforward: Standard multivariate ANOVA procedures can be used in within-configuration tests to determine whether the false negative children differed from the true negative children in initial variables despite membership in the same configuration. If children in the configuration who travel the "lesser known path" relative to others in the same configuration also differ from them on key initial variables, the most parsimonious interpretation is that the original cluster was too diffuse and heterogeneous to be meaningful. The slippage may reflect shortcomings of the original cluster solution or the hypothesis that led to variable selection. But what if the individuals did not differ in their status originally? This second possibility—that the original within-group differences are modest and inconsistent—is more challenging because it implies differential effects over the course of development.

All this is to say that focus on between-cluster effects provides information about developmental dynamics that support main trajectories; within-cluster analyses are also valuable for obtaining information about alternative pathways for some members of each cluster. In some important respects, we can learn most about developmental change by the study of individuals who do not conform to the dominant trends or pathways. When this logic is applied to the analysis of longitudinal data sets, it can identify the critical changes over time that are associated with eventual changes in outcomes. For example, Xie and Cairns (1996) reported that "resilient" males, regardless of their original configuration, looked to be buffered against early school dropout if they showed a progressive decrease in aggressive behavior in middle school and high school. Conversely, "vulnerable" boys were those who showed a progressive increase in aggressive behavior over the same years of adolescence. Interestingly, the vulnerable and resilient boys were virtually identical to others in their original configurations at the beginning of the investigation.

Step 4. Prodigal Analysis

The fourth step involves the use of subgroup information to highlight the pathways of the limited number of persons who constitute exceptions to the rule. Depending on the normative pathway of their original subgroup configuration, *prodigal cases* (individuals whose developmental pathways depart significantly from that of their configuration subgroup) may be viewed as either resilient or vulnerable.

In the preceding steps, longitudinal information from hundreds or thousands of individuals was employed to describe the different normative pathways of development for the several configuration subgroups. This information also provides the background from which to identify salient cases who have been deflected from the normative course of development, with the recognition that there are as many normative courses as there are subgroup configurations. A *prodigal analysis* reverses the typical figure-ground relationship between subgroups and individuals. Rather than being buried in the error term, "exceptional" pathways of individuals are projected into the foreground. They become candidates for intense analysis of when and how developmental deflections occur and what their consequences are. The remaining members of the subgroup become the background, or the foundation for interpreting individual contrasts.

Although systematic prodigal analysis has been infrequent in psychology, the logic of the design is broadly represented in sister sciences. For example, research in astronomy depends on a precise description of phenomena and movement patterns throughout the universe to understand specific exceptions or deflections. Detection of change in, say, orbital pathways or spectral frequencies requires enormous amounts of information about the nature of regularities in these domains. Similarly, progress in some areas of high-energy physics depends on the precise analysis of rare events against the background of known patterns.

On this score, prodigal analysis permits investigators to use information from the total longitudinal sample to identify individuals who experience significant turning points in their lives. The normal and expected become the background for identifying change and deflections. Once recognized, the exceptions can become the focus for intensive study. At this stage, hypotheses with respect to possible "turning points" can be evaluated in the person and the context on a case-by-case basis. Standard descriptive and statistical procedures can be employed to determine whether the extent of replication across individuals is sufficient to have confidence in the generality of the relationships. Depending on the probability of exceptions, medium to large samples (500 to 2,000) may be required in order to identify a sufficient number of prodigal cases for quantitative analysis. Each subgroup may be expected to yield prodigal cases, and they may be studied individually or as a special subset to yield generations that transcend personal circumstances.

To illustrate, the Carolina Longitudinal Study was originally designed for the study of only 80 girls and boys. Half of them were at risk for multiple problems, and the remainder were individually matched to risk children on multiple variables. When developed in 1979, the proposal met standard criteria for longitudinal design and went beyond them on some counts (e.g., inclusion of a priori matched case-control comparisons; use of two cohorts in an accelerated longitudinal design). The design was limited, however, because the developmental pathways of children not matchable to risk subjects would be unknown. Within the framework of prodigal analysis, understanding developmental changes in the lives of specially selected children and subgroups presupposes information about the incidence and types of changes in children from the whole population. To address this shortcoming, the study was redesigned to permit "saturated sampling," wherein all children in the designated school grades were invited to participate. This design change permitted the original risk-control subgroups to be embedded in a longitudinal study of the population of which they were a part. Although the design modification required nearly a tenfold expansion in the study, it led to an hundredfold increase in the power and versatility of its analyses.[2]

Is prodigal analysis simply another name for the case study method? Although the two procedures have similar goals—to understand individuals over time—they can be distinguished on four counts: First, in prodigal analysis, whole samples of persons are assessed with common measures and procedures over standard intervals. Second, persons qualify for selection by virtue of the exceptionality of their pathways relative to those of the subgroup or total sample. Third, this systematic form of individual analysis relies on advanced statistical procedures to obtain precise accounts of both individual and group pathways. Fourth, objective guides are available to classify types of pathways across individual cases to clarify the operation of common transitions and turning points.

By contrast, case study may or may not rely on quantification because the method does not presuppose systematic assessment at standard time intervals by common procedures. Accordingly, it is impossible to know whether a given case is an exemplar of an entire subgroup and population or is an exception to the rule. Although case studies typically emphasize the uniqueness of individuals and the contexts in which they have been observed, they are often assumed to represent general principles. Despite the pitfalls of case study, one cannot overestimate the value of the intensive analysis of individual children in the concrete realities of their lives. This was the essential message of Barker and Wright (1951) in their classic monograph *One Boy's Day*. The challenge remains to develop procedures that can capture and quantify such rich descriptions.

In summary, prospective configurations bring organization to medium to large longitudinal data sets by locating persons through disaggregation procedures into natural subgroups. Systematic configuration analyses are guided by hypotheses at each step, from the initial selection of common variables across persons to proposals on what may account for within-cluster variations in pathways. Configurations also provide a refined control for prospective longitudinal comparisons. The intensive study of persons who show deflections from the normative course is assumed to be key in identifying what events are necessary and sufficient to maintain or change developmental patterns. In prodigal analyses, normative, subgroup, and individual information is available on the major events that support an individual's development.

Configurations of Outcomes

In configurations of outcomes, consequent variables (outcomes), rather than antecedent variables (T_n measures rather than T_o measures), are clustered. In this regard, *comorbidity* refers to the finding that problems of adolescence and early adulthood tend to occur in clusters and not as separate or single entities (Jessor, Donovan, & Costa, 1991; Jessor & Jessor, 1977). Accordingly, configurations of outcomes can be identified by clustering persons in terms of the similarity of their profiles on measures associated with problematic developmental outcomes. If end-point configurations are accompanied by longitudinal data extending backward in time, then it becomes possible to explore causal hypotheses. This strategy has been employed by Ensminger and Juon (1996) in a 30-year follow-up of children in the Chicago Woodlawn project (Kellam, Adams, Brown, & Ensminger, 1975). They found common behavioral and familial antecedents to patterns of substance use and that these antecedents differed for males and females. At first blush, it would appear that the backward-tracking involved in the "endpoint" strategy may preclude developmental analyses. To the contrary, the procedures are quite compatible with developmental investigation. For instance, in the Ensminger and Juon (1996) work, children who were identified by the backward-tracking procedure as being at risk but who did not become substance abusers could emerge as a focus for special developmental studies of resilience.

Stability and Change in Configurations

A third use of configural analysis involves clustering on the basis of characteristics of individuals at each sampling interval and then determining whether the clusters remain stable and, if so, whether membership in the clusters was stable. This method involves an examination of stability of the clusters over time and of individual membership within the clusters over time (Bergman, this volume, Chap 5). In a careful illustration of this method, Gustafson and Magnusson (1991) selected the same measures assessing adolescent girls' intelligence, academic achievement, self-judgments concerning ability, and self-judgments concerning school adaptation to create configurations of girls at 13 and at 16 years of age. They found that clusters with similar profiles (e.g., gifted, high-adapted achievers; low-adapted, normal-ability underachievers; moderately adapted, realistic, low achievers) emerged at both time points but that the discriminative power of particular measures varied at 13 and 16 years of age.

In addition, developmental "streams" were identified that indicated the proportion of girls in each age-13 configuration who were placed in each of the age-16 configurations. Proportions greater than that expected by chance were designated as *types,* whereas *antitypes* represented developmental streams that were underpopulated relative to chance proportions. Focused analyses of particular developmental streams of interest enabled a further disaggregation of the sample into subconfigurations, analyses of variability among girls within particular configurations and/or developmental streams, and the determination of relationships between developmental streams with background family characteristics. As with other ways of approaching configural analyses, clustering at multiple time intervals and the determination of developmental streams allow for the identification of common change points for individuals within a cluster and for rare (or antitype) streams embarked upon by a small proportion of individuals.

Trajectory Classification

A fourth way to organize longitudinal information has been to identify for each person in the sample an individual developmental pathway with respect to study-relevant characteristics. Profile configurations can be employed usefully in conjunction with hierarchical linear modeling (HLM) and latent growth analysis. Examination of commonalities of pathways across different persons typically yields a finite subset of reasonably common or homogeneous patterns over time. In this regard, McCall, Appelbaum, and Hagarty (1973) identified common trajectories of intellectual change in the Fels Institute longitudinal study. More recently, Kellam (1995) used HLM procedures to identify common profiles of change over time in response to a well-defined intervention program. Once the common pathways were identified, Kellam (1995) employed the information to identify developmental events associated with year-to-year fluctuations within each identified configurations.

To sum up, several analytic strategies are now available to study configurations of persons and developmental trajectories. They illustrate the methodological implications of the shift from the goal of "disentangling" variables to understanding how variables operate together to produce meaningful outcomes. They also indicate that the study of persons-in-context is now available and that the study of individual developmental pathways is within grasp. To equate configuration or "person-oriented" analyses with any one statistical technique would be an error. Rather, the logic of the configuration procedure is open to a range of statistical and theoretical methods for disaggregating samples into relatively homogeneous subgroups. Once this step is taken, avenues are opened to promote the developmental study of individuals.

∞ TRANSITIONS, TURNING POINTS, AND STABILITY

Transitions and turning points have special relevance for plotting and understanding the prodigal analysis of individual change over time. The term *turning point* has been broadly employed in the recent literature. It has been the title of a compendium on education and adolescence (Carnegie Council on Adolescent Development, 1990), a concept applied to business cycles (Ayres, 1969), a term used in accounts of world history (Barraclough, 1979), and a term used to describe life course transitions (Elder, Caspi, & Burton, 1988; Pickles & Rutter, 1991; Rutter, 1989). Terms that are used so broadly in the sciences and society become candidates for projective interpretations, so efforts have been made to delineate the term with precision.

How can one recognize a turning point when one sees it? The establishment of turning points requires longitudinal methods to determine change over time in psychological functioning. In this regard, an apparent change potentially could not be a turning point so much as it is the continuation of an earlier-determined pattern. How does one know whether or not an event or action represents momentary adaptation or major deflection in the life course? Whether or not a turn is deemed to be stable depends, in part, on the time intervals involved. To head off problems of interpretation, criteria must be established for defining turning points and for recognizing them when they occur. Accordingly, membership in reasonably homogeneous configurations provides a control for taking into account preexisting developmental differences. Such homogeneity at the onset can help the researcher determine whether individuals remain in the mainstream of their configuration or have made a sharp and enduring turn from it.

To this end, Pickles and Rutter (1991) equated turning points with life course transitions. Specifically, "there has been a growing interest in what have been termed transitions or 'turning points' in a person's development or life course. . . . The focus is upon two main types of everyday events or happenings that bring about a potential for long-term psychological change" (p. 133). Accordingly, one type of everyday experience refers to opening up or closing down opportunities, such as "going to university and dropping out of school" (p. 133). The other type refers to those that involve a "radical lasting change in life circumstances." Subsumed by this second class are such events as transition to parenthood, marriage and divorce, moving, having children, or "becoming redundant in mid-life." The events that are excluded by these two classes may be as important as those included. On this score, Pickles and Rutter explicitly omit three classes of events: (a) "rare dramatic 'internal events' " such as religious conversions; (b) "rare dramatic 'external experiences' " such as earthquakes, shipwrecks, or being taken hostage; and (c) "universal, age-defined transitions" such as the hypothesized mid-life crisis.[3]

Pickles and Rutter (1991) require that two criteria be met in order for an event or change to qualify as a turning point:

1. *Turning points* refer to major life transitions that may be identified independently of the individual. Hence, idiosyncratic developmental events are excluded, and certain normative opportunities and circumstances are included (e.g., entering school, graduating from high school or school dropout, joining the military, university enrollment, very early menarche, marriage, and beginning a career). Such turning points are typically correlated with differences in opportunities, social networks, and social reference groups.

2. Shifts that occur in the individual's life must endure. To satisfy this individual-based criterion, longitudinal and/or retrospective tracking procedures are required. The enduring shift may involve movement away from a well-established behavior pattern, or it may involve the establishment and long-term adoption of a novel pattern.

So far, so good. The occurrence of a major life event (e.g., getting married) and a dramatic shift in behavior or lifestyle do not, in themselves, qualify as turning points. Longitudinal assessment of any change is required to establish its durability, and only lasting changes qualify as turning points (Pickles & Rutter, 1991). One problem in fulfilling these criteria is that short-term shifts occur daily, yet few of these changes are maintained in the long term (Cairns & Cairns, 1994). Why are most changes short term, and why do certain changes endure? Moreover, even some "major" life course transitions are reversible. For instance, getting married to a nondeviant spouse may be correlated with a change in the behavior of high-risk adolescents. But this change may endure only as long as they remain married. In this case, the turning point was a roundabout. Finally, longitudinal analyses tend to obscure the difference between sequence and causality in the establishment of turning points. For example, marrying a "good spouse" may be a determinant of rehabilitation, or it may simply mark the changes that are already under way (Quinton & Rutter, 1988).

More broadly, conservation in social behavior may be supported by the correlations between events that occur within and outside of individuals (e.g., Cairns, 1995; Magnusson & Cairns, 1996). Biological states of the individual tend to be brought into line with the environmental context and social actions and vice versa. These normal conditions of development yield what we have termed elsewhere *correlated constraints* (Cairns, McGuire, & Gariépy, 1993). The result is that behavior organization tends to be continuous and conservative over time despite the fluidity and change. In ontogeny, correlated constraints establish the conditions such that (a) variables occur in packages, not as independent elements, (b) similarities evolve among individuals in that only a limited number of configurations of characteristics are possible, and (c) commonalities in developmental pathways will occur, given the parallel constraints that become active over time.

One legitimate concern about the holistic proposal is that systems of social behavior become so complicated that they lie beyond the limits of contemporary science. This concern seems misplaced, however. Rather than complicate the analysis, the networks of correlated relationships across variables may simplify the analytic task. They reduce the degrees of freedom and the range of possibilities. The correlated constraints in development place limits on the pathways possible and provide direction for further development. These considerations are consistent with the general proposition that social behaviors constitute the leading edge for contextual adaptations and biological change (Bateson, 1991; Cairns, 1986). Once interactions prove effective, they create the scaffolding for further changes in neurobiology and social contexts. Interchanges affect the internal conditions of both organisms and their environments and provide the directions for future development. As von Bertalanffy (1933/1962) argued, no vitalistic assumptions of *entelechy*—or assumptions of fixation by early experience—are required if future directions are an outcome of the developmental processes themselves.

∞ CONCLUDING COMMENT

Throughout her career, Marian Radke-Yarrow has emphasized that an essential challenge for behavioral research has been to bring methodology into better alignment with theory. Her commitment to excellence in methodology has held regardless of domain, from investigations of prejudice in children to the developmental of empathy and the complexities of child-parent interactions. In the course of this work, she discovered that many primary procedures routinely employed in developmental study—retrospective interviews and survey reports by parents, self-reports that have no confirmation from independent agents—often provide faulty foundations for a science. More broadly, failure to address the compelling issues of methodology has been perhaps the largest shortfall of the emergent science. Rather than make methodological concerns the first priority of the discipline, they seem to have been relegated to applied statistics and experimental psychology. Fundamental issues of measures and methods, including the functional meaning of self-reports and reconstructive memories, are sometimes acknowledged but are soon forgotten as an unpleasant memory, or are ignored (see Rutter, Maughan, Pickles, & Simonoff, this volume, Chap. 10).

That state of affairs creates a dilemma for researchers who aspire to Radke-Yarrow's challenge for excellence in the study of development. One option has been to confine the scope of research to problems that seem compatible with the limits of existing methods and analyses (Aslin, 1993). Unfortunately, the empirical information obtained may be only remotely relevant to the questions the researcher sought to answer. This was the complaint of Mills (1898) and Binet (1903) about the application of nondevelopmental methods to developmental phenomena, and their points seem to remain valid.

Ideas on correlated constraints and the procedures of disaggregation through subgroup configurations cannot be viewed as panacea for the multiple needs of developmental research. That would be a fanciful and misleading conclusion, given the different problems and phenomena explored in developmental studies of behavior, emotion, and cognition. Prodigal analysis offers a technique to bridge between large-sample longitudinal designs and accounts of the lives of individual children over time. Now that longitudinal research has become a design of choice, one hazard is that the richness of individual and subgroup information may be aborted by standard statistical procedures. Data tyranny invites surrender to large-sample statistical models. Configuration procedures and their parametric counterparts provide fresh ways to clarify how variables within and without the individual interact and become coalesced over time.

William James (1890) predicted that "biographies will never be written in advance no matter how 'evolved' psychology may become" (pp. 576-577). After a century of technological advance, developmental prediction remains a probabilistic affair. Still, the science has evolved, and the results of modern longitudinal studies indicate that behavioral continuities are not simply self-serving illusions. Despite the plasticity of persons and of environmental contingencies, prospective studies indicate a reasonable lawfulness in some—but not all—domains of social behavior. And precision is enhanced if meaningful configurations of correlated constraints can be identified at successive stages of development. So what might we expect in the future? Although developmental science will never write biographies in advance, its procedures may be adequate to outline contents of the main chapters.

∞ℒ∞

COMMENTS ON CHAPTER 11

Throughout his career, Robert Cairns has devoted his energies to making developmental research a stronger enterprise, conceptually and methodologically. He has done so, not as a theorist remote from the realities of research, but as a scientist—worker and theorist—investigating processes of development in vastly diverse areas—from studies of mice and lambs and dogs to troubled adolescents. All of which is a sound recommendation for listening to his conclusions.

In 1986, Cairns wrote the article "Phenomena Lost," in which he presented a penetrating evaluation of the prevailing methods of research. He reviewed them in relation to advances in developmental theory and conceptualizations of behavioral processes. He noted distressing contradictions and discrepancies between the practice of research and conceptual sophistication. He concluded that, in many instances, conventional research methods obscure the problem; in the research process, the phenomenon of interest is lost.

*In this chapter, Cairns and Rodkin elaborate this position.
Several themes run through their concerns and advocacy: (a) that
recognition of the complexity of development is a first step toward
understanding its coherence, (b) that the individual-in-context must
be the unit of analysis, and (c) that it is not a matter of seeking the
separate and unique contribution of single variables to the behavioral outcome, but rather of determining how variables function
together in influencing behavior. They summarize the position so
well—as variables within and outside the individual cohering in
clusters, mutually constraining development, and providing direction in pathways.*

*For longitudinal studies to provide the route to understanding
individual development, they stress, investigation of subgroups of
individuals homogeneous in variable-clusters is necessary. There
will be exceptions in the findings from this route. Investigation of the
exceptions is an essential step in this process.*

*They mark also a companion guide for successful developmental studies: attending to time and timing in individual development.
The behavior system that is being studied has an individual course.
It emerges, becomes organized, and perhaps wanes. Research imposes itself on this ongoing process. Knowing where research enters
is essential for understanding the individual's course and the factors
affecting the trajectory.*

*Cairns and Rodkin lay out guides and warnings and challenges
that spell out the exacting tasks for developmental researchers using
a holistic approach.*

Marian Radke-Yarrow

References

ACHENBACH, T. M., & EDELBROCK, C. S. (1983). *Manual for the Child Behavior Checklist and revised Child Behavior Profile.* Burlington: University of Vermont.

AF KLINTEBERG, B., ANDERSSON, T., MAGNUSSON, D., & STATTIN, H. (1993). Hyperactive behavior in childhood as related to subsequent alcohol problems and violent offending: A longitudinal study of male subjects. *Personality and Individual Differences, 15,* 381-388.

AINSWORTH, M. D. S., BLEHAR, M. C., WATERS, E., & WALL, T. (1978). *Patterns of attachment.* Mahwah, NJ: Lawrence Erlbaum.

ALLPORT, G. W. (1937). *Personality: A psychological interpretation.* New York: Holt, Rinehart & Winston.

AMERICAN PSYCHIATRIC ASSOCIATION (APA). (1983). *Diagnostic and statistical manual of mental disorders* (3rd ed.). Washington, DC: Author.

AMERICAN PSYCHIATRIC ASSOCIATION (APA). (1987). *Diagnostic and statistical manual of mental disorders* (3rd ed., rev.). Washington, DC: Author.

AMERICAN PSYCHIATRIC ASSOCIATION (APA). (1994). *Diagnostic and statistical manual of mental disorders* (4th ed.). Washington, DC: Author.

ANDERSSON, T. (1988). *Alkoholvanor i ett utvecklingsperspektiv* (Drinking habits in a developmental perspective). Unpublished doctoral dissertation, University of Stockholm, Department of Psychology.

ANDERSSON, T., BERGMAN, L. R., & MAGNUSSON, D. (1989). Patterns of adjustment problems and alcohol abuse in early childhood: A prospective longitudinal study. *Development and Psychopathology, 1,* 119-131.

ANGOLD, A., & COSTELLO, E. J. (1995). A test-retest reliability study of child-reported psychiatric symptoms and diagnoses using the Child and Adolescent Psychiatry Assessment (CAPA-C). *Psychological Medicine, 25,* 755-762.

ANGOLD, A., PRENDERGAST, M., COX, A., HARRINGTON, R., SIMONOFF, E., & RUTTER, M. (1995). The Child and Adolescent Psychiatric Assessment (CAPA). *Psychological Medicine, 25,* 739-753.

ARCUS, D., & KAGAN, J. (1995). Temperament and craniofacial variation in the first 2 years. *Child Development, 66,* 1529-1540.

ASENDORPF, J. B., & VAN AKEN, M. A. G. (1991). Correlates of the temporal consistency of personality patterns in childhood. *Journal of Personality, 4,* 689-703.

ASLIN, R. N. (1993). Commentary: The strange attractiveness of dynamic systems to development. In L. Smith & E. Thelen (Eds.), *A dynamic systems approach to development: Application* (pp. 385-399). Cambridge: MIT Press.

AYRES, L. P. (1969). *Turning points in business cycles.* New York: A. M. Kelley.

BACKMAN, C. W. (1988). The self: A dialectical approach. In L. Berkowitz (Ed.), *Advances in experimental social psychology* (pp. 229-260). San Diego: Academic Press.

BADDELEY, A. D. (1990). *Human memory: Theory and practice.* Mahwah, NJ: Lawrence Erlbaum.

BAICKER-McKEE, C. (1990). *Saints, sinners, and prodigal sons: An investigation of continuities and discontinuities in antisocial development.* Unpublished Doctoral Dissertation, University of Virginia, Charlottesville.

BAKAN, D. (1966). *The duality of human existence: Isolation and communion in Western man.* Boston: Beacon Press.

BANDURA, A., & WALTERS, R. H. (1959). *Adolescent aggression.* New York: Ronald Press.

BARKER, R. G., & WRIGHT, H. F. (1951). *One boy's day.* New York: Harper.

BARLOW, D. H., & HERSEN, D. H. (1984). *Single-case experimental designs.* New York: Pergamon.

BARRACLOUGH, G. (1979). *Turning points in world history.* London: Thames and Hudson.

BARTLETT, F. C. (1932). *Remembering, a study in experimental and social psychology.* Cambridge, UK: Cambridge University Press.

BARTON, S. (1994). Chaos, self-organization, and psychology. *American Psychologist, 49,* 5-14.

BASAR, E. (1990). *Chaos in brain function.* Berlin: Springer Verlag.

BATESON, P. P. G. (Ed.). (1991). *The development and integration of behavior: Essays in honor of Robert Hinde.* Cambridge, UK: Cambridge University Press.

BAUMRIND, D. (1971). Current patterns of parental authority. *Developmental Psychology Monographs, 4*(1&2).

BEKERIAN, D. A., & DENNETT, J. L. (1985). Assessing the truth in children's statements. In T. Ney (Ed.), *Allegations of sexual abuse: Assessment and management* (pp. 163-175). New York: Brunner/Mazel.

BEKERIAN, D. A., & DENNETT, J. L. (1992). The truth in content analyses of a child's testimony. In F. Lösel, D. Bender, & T. Bliesner (Eds.), *Psychology & law—International perspectives* (pp. 335-344). Berlin, Germany: Walter de Gruyte.

BELBIN, L., FAITH, D. P., & MILLIGAN, G. W. (1992). A comparison of two approaches to beta-flexible clustering. *Multivariate Behavioral Research, 27,* 417-433.

BEM, D. J., & FUNDER, D. C. (1978). Predicting more of the people more of the time. *Psychological Review, 85,* 485-501.

BERGMAN, L. R. (1972). Change as the dependent variable. *Reports from the Psychological Laboratories,* University of Stockholm, Suppl. 14.

BERGMAN, L. R. (1973). Parent's education and mean change in intelligence. *Scandinavian Journal of Psychology, 14,* 273-281.

BERGMAN, L. R. (1988a). Modeling reality: Some comments. In M. Rutter (Ed.), *Studies of psychosocial risk* (pp. 354-366). Cambridge, UK: Cambridge University Press.

BERGMAN, L. R. (1988b). You can't classify all of the people all of the time. *Multivariate Behavioral Research, 23,* 425-441.

BERGMAN, L. R. (1993). Some methodological issues in longitudinal research: Looking ahead. In D. Magnusson & P. Casaer (Eds.), *Longitudinal research on individual development: Present status and future perspectives* (pp. 217-241). Cambridge, UK: Cambridge University Press.

BERGMAN, L. R. (1995a). Describing individual development using i-state sequence analysis (ISSA). *Reports from the Department of Psychology,* Stockholm University, No. 805.

BERGMAN, L. R. (1995b). Describing individual development using i-states as objects analysis (ISOA). *Reports from the Department of Psychology,* Stockholm University, No. 806.

BERGMAN, L. R., & EL-KHOURI, B. M. (1987). EXACON-a Fortran 77 program for the exact analysis of single cells in a contingency table. *Educational and Psychological Measurement, 47,* 155-161.

BERGMAN, L. R., & EL-KHOURI, B. M. (1992). M-PREP: A Fortran 77 computer program for the preparatory analysis of multivariate data. *Reports from the Department of Psychology,* Stockholm University, No. 751.

BERGMAN, L. R., & EL-KHOURI, B. M. (1995). *SLEIPNER: A computer package for person-oriented analyses of developmental data* (Version A manual). Stockholm: Stockholm University, Department of Psychology.

BERGMAN, L. R., & MAGNUSSON, D. (1983). *The development of patterns of maladjustment* (Report from the project Individual Development and Adjustment, No. 50). Stockholm: University of Stockholm.

BERGMAN, L. R., & MAGNUSSON, D. (1984a). *Patterns of adjustment problems at age 10: An empirical and methodological study* (Report from the Department of Psychology, No. 615). Stockholm: University of Stockholm.

BERGMAN, L. R., & MAGNUSSON, D. (1984b). *Patterns of adjustment problems at age 13: An empirical and methodological study* (Report from the Department of Psychology, No. 620). Stockholm: University of Stockholm.

BERGMAN, L. R., & MAGNUSSON, D. (1986, September). *RESCLUS methodology in longitudinal research.* Paper presented at the International Conference on Longitudinal Methodology in Budapest.

BERGMAN, L. R., & MAGNUSSON, D. (1987). A person approach to the study of development and adjustment problems: An empirical example and some research strategy considerations. In D. Magnusson & A. Ohman (Eds.), *Psychopathology: An interactional perspective* (pp. 383-401). San Diego: Academic Press.

BERGMAN, L. R., & MAGNUSSON, D. (1991). Stability and change in patterns of extrinsic adjustment problems. In D. Magnusson, L. R. Bergman, G. Rudinger, & B. Törestad (Eds.), *Problems and methods in longitudinal research: Stability and change* (pp. 323-346). Cambridge, UK: Cambridge University Press.

BERGMAN, L. R., & MAGNUSSON, D. (1997). A person-oriented approach in research on developmental psychopathology. *Develpmental Psychopathology, 9,* 291-319.

BERGMAN, L. R., & WÅNGBY, M. (1995). The teenage girl: Patterns of self-reported adjustment problems and some correlates. *International Journal of Methods in Psychiatric Research, 5,* 171-188.

BIFULCO, A., BROWN, G. W., LILLIE, A., & JARVIS, J. (1997). Memories of childhood neglect and abuse: Corroboration in a series of sisters. *Journal of Child Psychology and Psychiatry, 38,* 365-374.

BINET, A. (1903). *L'étude experimentale de l'intelligence.* Paris: Schleicher.

BINET, A., & HENRI, V. (1895). La psychologie individuelle. *L'Annee Psychologique, 2,* 411-465.

BISHOP, Y. M. M., FEINBERG, S. E., & HOLLAND, P. W. (1975). *Discrete multivariate analysis: Theory and practice.* Cambridge: MIT Press.

BLASHFIELD, R. K (1980). The growth of cluster analysis: Tryon, Ward, and Johnson. *Multivariate Behavioral Research, 15,* 439-458.

BLOCK, J. (1971). *Lives through time.* Berkeley, CA: Bancroft.

BLOCK, J. (1977). Advancing the psychology of personality: Paradigmatic shift or improving the quality of research? In D. Magnusson & N. S. Endler (Eds.), *Personality at the crossroads: Current issues in interactional research.* Mahwah, NJ: Lawrence Erlbaum.

BLOCK, J. (1978). *The Q-sort method in personality assessment and psychiatric research.* Palo Alto, CA: Consulting Psychologists Press. (Original work published 1961)

BLOCK, J., & KREMEN, A. (in press). *Ego-resiliency and intelligence: Differential personality implications.*

BLOCK, J. H., & BLOCK, J. (1980). The role of ego-control and ego-resiliency in the organization of behavior. In W. A. Collins (Ed.), *Minnesota Symposium on Child Psychology* (Vol. 13, pp. 39-101). Mahwah, NJ: Lawrence Erlbaum.

BOCK, H. H. (1987). *Classification and related methods of data analysis.* Amsterdam: North-Holland.

BOTHE, H. G., EBELING, W., KURZHANSKI, A. B., & PESCHEL, M. (1987). *Dynamic systems and environmental models.* Berlin: Akademie-Verlag.

BOWLBY, J. (1973). *Separation.* New York: Basic Books.

BRADBURN, N. M., RIPS, L. J., & SHEVELL, S. K. (1987). Answering autobiographical questions: The impact of memory and inference on surveys. *Science, 236,* 157-161.

BRECKENRIDGE, J. N. (1989). Replicating cluster analysis: Method, consistency, and validity. *Multivariate Behavioral Research, 24,* 147-161.

BRESLOW, R., KOCSIS, J., & BELKIN, B. (1980). Memory deficits in depression: Evidence utilizing the Wechsler Memory Scale. *Perceptual and Motor Skills, 51,* 541-542.

BRETON, J.-J., BERGERON, L., VALLA, J.-P., LÉPINE, S., HOUDE, L., & GAUDET, N. (1995). Do children aged 9 to 11 years understand the DISC version 2.25 questions? *Journal of the American Academy of Child & Adolescent Psychiatry, 34,* 946-954.

BREWER, W. F. (1986). What is autobiographical memory? In D. C. Rubin (Ed.), *Autobiographical memory* (pp. 25-49). New York: Cambridge University Press.

BREWIN, C. R., ANDREWS, B., & GOTLIB, I. H. (1993). Psychopathology and early experience: A reappraisal of retrospective reports. *Psychological Bulletin, 113,* 82-98.

BROMET, E. J., DUNN, L. O., CONNELL, M. M., DEW, M. A., & SCHULBERG, H. C. (1986). Long-term reliability of diagnosing lifetime major depression in a community sample. *Archives of General Psychiatry, 43,* 435-440.

BRONFENBRENNER, U. (1996). Foreword. In R. B. Cairns, G. H. Elder, Jr., & E. J. Costello (Eds)., *Developmental science*. New York: Cambridge University Press.

BROWN, G. W., & RUTTER, M. (1966). The measurement of family activities and relationships: A methodological study. *Human Relations, 19,* 241-263.

BRUNSWIK, E. (1929). Prinzipenfragen der Gestalttheorie. In E. Brunswik, C. Buhler, H. Hetzer, L. Kardos, E. Köhler, J. Krug, & A. Willwoll (Eds.), *Beiträge zur Problemgeschichte der Psychologie* (pp. 78-149). Jena: Verlag von Gustav Fischer.

BRYK, A. S., & RAUDENBUSH, S. W. (1992). *Hierarchical linear models: Applications and data analysis*. Newbury Park, CA: Sage.

BUDESCU, D. V. (1980). Some new measures of profile dissimilarity. *Applied Psychological Measurement, 4,* 261-272.

BUSS, A. H., & PLOMIN, R. (1984). *Temperament: Early developing personality traits*. Mahwah, NJ: Lawrence Erlbaum.

CAIRNS, R. B. (1979). *Social development: The origins and plasticity of interchanges*. San Francisco: Freeman.

CAIRNS, R. B. (1983). The emergence of developmental psychology. In P. H. Mussen (Gen. Ed.) & W. Kessen (Vol. Ed.), *Handbook of child psychology: Vol. 1. History, theory, and methods* (4th ed., pp. 41-102). New York: John Wiley.

CAIRNS, R. B. (1986). Phenomena lost: Issues in the study of development. In J. Valsiner (Ed.), *The individual subject and scientific psychology* (pp. 97-112). New York: Plenum.

CAIRNS, R. B. (1995). Aggression from a developmental perspective: Genes, environments, and interactions. In M. Rutter (Ed.), *Genetics of criminal and antisocial behavior* (Ciba Foundation Symposium No. 194, pp. 45-60). New York: John Wiley.

CAIRNS, R. B., & CAIRNS, B. D. (1994). *Lifelines and risks: Pathways of youth in our time*. Cambridge, UK: Cambridge University Press.

CAIRNS, R. B., CAIRNS, B. D., & NECKERMAN, H. J. (1989). Early school dropout: Configurations and determinants. *Child Development, 60,* 1437-1452.

CAIRNS, R. B., CAIRNS, B. D., NECKERMAN, H. J., FERGUSON, L. L., & GARIÉPY, J. L. (1989). Growth and aggression: I. Childhood to early adolescence. *Developmental Psychology, 25,* 320-330.

CAIRNS, R. B., McGUIRE, A. M., & GARIÉPY, J.-L. (1993). Developmental behavior genetics: Fusion, correlated constraints, and timing. In D. F. Hay & A. Angold (Eds.), *Precursors and causes in development and psychopathology* (pp. 87-122). New York: John Wiley.

CARLSON, M., EARLS, F., & TODD, R. D. (1988). The importance of regressive changes in the development of the nervous system: Toward a neurobiological theory of child development. *Psychiatric Developments, 1,* 1-22.

CARLSSON, R. (1971). Where is the person in personality research? *Psychological Bulletin, 75,* 203-219.

CARNEGIE COUNCIL ON ADOLESCENT DEVELOPMENT, TASK FORCE ON EDUCATION. (1990). *Turning points: Preparing American youth for the 21st century: Recommendations for transforming middle grade schools*. Washington, DC: Author.

CARROLL, J. B. (1993). *Human cognitive abilities: A survey of factor analytic studies*. New York: Cambridge University Press.

CASPI, A., & BEM, D. J. (1990). Personality continuity and change across the life course. In L. A. Pervin (Ed.), *Handbook of personality: Theory and research* (pp. 549-575). New York: Guilford.

CASPI, A., ELDER, G. G., JR., & HERBENER, E. S. (1990). Childhood personality and the prediction of life-course patterns. In L. Robins & M. Rutter (Eds.), *Straight and devious pathways from childhood to adulthood* (pp. 13-35). Cambridge, UK: Cambridge University Press.

CASPI, A., MOFFITT, T., THORNTON, A., FREEDMAN, D., AMELL, J. W., HARRINGTON, H., SMEIJERS, J., & SILVA, P. A. (1996). The life history calendar: A research and clinical assessment method for collecting retrospective event-history data. *International Journal of Methods in Psychiatric Research, 6,* 101-114.

CASPI, A., & SILVA, P. A. (1995). Temperamental qualities at age 3 predict personality traits in young adulthood: Longitudinal evidence from a birth cohort. *Child Development, 66,* 486-498.

CATTELL, R. B., CATTELL, A. K. S., & RHYMER, R. M. (1947). P-technique demonstrated in determining psycho-physiological source traits in a normal individual. *Psychometrika, 12,* 267-288.

CECI, S. J. (1995). False beliefs: Some developmental and clinical considerations. In D. L. Schacter, J. T. Coyle, G. D. Fischbach, M. M. Mesuklam, & L. E. Sullivan (Eds.), *Memory distortion: How minds, brains, and society reconstruct the past* (pp. 91-125). Cambridge, MA: Harvard University Press.

CECI, S. J., & BRUCK, M. (1993). Suggestibility of the child witness: A historical review and synthesis. *Psychological Bulletin, 113,* 403-439.

CECI, S. J., & HUFFMAN, M. L. (1997). How suggestible are preschool children? Cognitive and social factors. *Journal of the American Academy of Child and Adolescent Psychiatry, 36,* 948-958.

CECI, S. J., HUFFMAN, M. L. C., SMITH, E., & LOFTUS, E. F. (1994). Repeatedly thinking about a non-event: Source misattributions among preschoolers. *Consciousness and Cognition, 3,* 388-407.

CECI, S. J., ROSS, D. F., & TOGLIA, M. P. (1987). Suggestibility of children's memory: Psycholegal implications. *Journal of Experimental Psychology: General, 116,* 38-49.

CHESS, S., THOMAS, A., & BIRCH, H. G. (1966). Distortions in developmental reporting made by parents of behaviorally disturbed children. *Journal of the American Academy of Child Psychiatry, 5,* 226-234.

CHILCONT, H. D., & BRESLAU, N. (1997). Does psychiatric history bias mothers' reports? An application of a new analytic approach. *Journal of the American Academy of Child and Adolescent Psychiatry, 36,* 971-979.

CICCHETTI, D., & TOTH, S. L. (1991). A developmental perspective on internalizing and externalizing disorders. In D. Cicchetti & S. L. Toth (Eds.), *Internalizing and externalizing expressions of dysfunction. Rochester Symposium on Developmental Psychopathology* (Vol. 2, pp. 1-19). Mahwah, NJ: Lawrence Erlbaum.

CLOGG, C. C., ELIASON, S. R., & GREGO, J. M. (1990). Models for the analysis of change in discrete variables. In A. von Eye (Ed.), *Statistical methods in longitudinal research: Vol. II. Time series and categorical longitudinal data* (pp. 409-441). San Diego: Academic Press.

CLONINGER, C. R., SIGVARDSSON, S., & BOHMAN, M. (1988). *Childhood personality predicts alcohol abuse in young adults.* Unpublished manuscript, University of Umeå, Department of Child and Youth Psychiatry.

COIE, J. D., DODGE, K., & KUPERSMIDT, J. B. (1990). Peer group behavior and social status. In S. R. Asher & J. D. Coie (Eds.), *Peer rejection in childhood* (pp. 17-59). Cambridge, UK: Cambridge University Press.

COLEMAN, J. (1986). Social theory, social research, and a theory of action. *American Journal of Sociology, 91,* 1309-1335.

COLINVAUX, P. (1980). *Why big fierce animals are rare.* Gretna, LA: Pelican.

COLLINS, L. M., & WUGALTER, S. E. (1992). Latent class models for stage-sequential dynamic latent variables. *Multivariate Behavioral Research, 27,* 131-157.

COSTELLO, A. J., EDELBROCK, C. S., DULCAN, M. K., KALAS, R., & KLARIC, S. H. (1984). *Report on the NIMH Diagnostic Interview Schedule for Children (DISC).* Unpublished manuscript, University of Pittsburgh, School of Medicine, Western Psychiatric Institute and Clinic.

COVINGTON, M. V. (1992). *Making the grade: A self-worth perspective on motivation and school reform.* Cambridge, UK: Cambridge University Press.

COX, A. D. (1994). Interviews with parents. In M. Rutter, E. Taylor, & L. Hersov (Eds.), *Child and adolescent psychiatry: Modern approaches* (3rd ed., pp. 34-50). Oxford, UK: Blackwell.

CRICK, F. (1988). *What mad pursuit: A personal view of scientific discovery.* New York: Basic Books.

CRONBACH, L. J. (1975). Beyond the two disciplines of scientific psychology. *American Psychologist, 30,* 116-127.

CRONBACH, L. J., & GLESER, G. C. (1953). Assessing similarity between profiles. *Psychological Bulletin, 50,* 456-473.

CROWELL, J. A., WATERS, E., TREBOUX, D., O'CONNOR, E., COLON-DOWNS, C., & FEIDER, O. (1996). Discriminant validity of the Adult Attachment Interview. *Child Development, 67,* 2584-2599.

CRUTCHFIELD, J. P., FARMER, J. D., PACKARD, N. H., & SHAW, R. B. (1986). Chaos. *Scientific American, 252,* 38-49.

CURRAN, P. J., HARFORD, T. C., & MUTHEN, B. O. (1996). The relation between heavy alcohol use and bar patronage: A latent growth model. *Journal of Studies of Alcohol, 57,* 410-418.

DAMASIO, A. R., & DAMASIO, H. (1996). Advances in cognitive neuroscience. In D. Magnusson (Ed.), *The life-span development of individuals: Behavioral, neurobiological, and psychosocial perspectives* (pp. 265-274). Cambridge, UK: Cambridge University Press.

DARLINGTON, R. B. (1968). Multiple regression. *Psychological Bulletin, 69,* 161-182.

DE LEON, M. K. P. (1995). *Parenting in long-term perspective: Modeling longitudinal data.* Unpublished doctoral dissertation, University of London.

DEWEY, J. (1896). The reflex arc concept in psychology. *Psychological Review, 3,* 357-370.

DONOVAN, J., JESSOR, R., & JESSOR, L. (1983). Problem drinking in adolescence and young adulthood: A follow-up study. *Journal of Studies on Alcohol, 44,* 109-138.

EBERLIN, M., McCONNACHIE, G., IBEL, S., & VOLPE, L. (1993). Facilitated communication: A failure to replicate the phenomenon. *Journal of Autism and Developmental Disorders, 23,* 507-530.

EDELBROCK, C. (1979). Mixture model tests of hierarchical clustering algorithms: The problem of classifying everybody. *Multivariate Behavioral Research, 14,* 367-384.

EDELBROCK, C., & ACHENBACH, T. (1980). A typology of child behavior profile patterns: Distribution and correlates for disturbed children aged 6-16. *Journal of Abnormal Child Psychology, 8*, 441-470.

EIGEN, M. (1971). Self-organization of matter and the evolution of biological macromolecules. *Die Naturwissenschaften, 58*, 265-523.

EISENBERG, N., PASTERNACK, J. F., CAMERON, E., & TRYON, K. (1984). The relation of quantity and mode of prosocial behavior to moral cognitions and social style. *Child Development, 55*, 1479-1485.

EKMAN, G. (1951). On typological and dimensional systems of reference in describing personality. *Acta Psychologica, 8*, 1-24.

EKMAN, G. (1952). *Differentiell psykologi (Differential psychology)*. Uppsala, Sweden: Almqvist & Wiksell.

ELDER, G. H., JR., CASPI, A., & BURTON, L. M. (1988). Adolescent transitions in developmental perspective: Historical and sociological insights. In M. Gunnar (Ed.), *Minnesota Symposia on Child Psychology* (Vol. 21), pp. 151-179. Mahwah, NJ: Lawrence Erlbaum.

ELLIOTT, D. S. (1994). Serious violent offenders: Onset, developmental course, and termination—The American Society of Criminology 1993 Presidential address. *Criminology, 32*, 1-21.

ELLIOTT, D. S., HUIZINGA, D., & AGETON, S. S. (1985). *Explaining delinquency and drug use*. Beverly Hills, CA: Sage.

ENDLER, N. S., & MAGNUSSON, D. (Eds.). (1976). *Interactional psychology and personality*. Washington, DC: Halsted-Wiley.

ENSMINGER, M. E., & JUON, H-S. (1996, June). *Transition to adulthood among high-risk youth*. Paper presented at the Conference on New Perspectives on Adolescent Risk Behavior, Beverly Hills, CA.

EVERETT, J. E. (1983). Factor congruence as a criterion for determining the number of factors. *Multivariate Behavioral Research, 18*, 197-218.

EVERITT, B. (1974). *Cluster analysis*. London: Heinemann.

FALLON, T., & SCHWAB-STONE, M. (1994). Determinants of reliability in psychiatric surveys of children aged 6-12. *Journal of Child Psychology and Psychiatry, 35*, 1391-1408.

FARRINGTON, D. P., LOEBER, R., ELLIOTT, D. S., HAWKINS, J. D., KANDEL, D. B., KLEIN, M. W., McCORD, J., ROWE, D. C., & TREMBLAY, R. E. (1990). Advancing knowledge about the onset of delinquency and crime. In B. B. Lahey & A. E. Kazdin (Eds.), *Advances in clinical child psychology* (Vol. 13, pp. 283-342). New York: Plenum.

FENDRICH, M., WEISSMAN, M. M., WARNER, V., & MUFSON, L. (1990). Two-year recall of lifetime diagnoses in offspring at high and low risk for major depression: The stability of offspring reports. *Archives of General Psychiatry, 47*, 1121-1127.

FERGUSSON, D. M., HORWOOD, L. J., & LYNSKEY, M. T. (1994). Structure of *DSM-III-R* criteria for disruptive childhood behaviors: Confirmatory factor models. *Journal of the American Academy of Child and Adolescent Psychiatry, 33*, 1145-1157.

FILSINGER, E. E., & KAROLY, P. (1985). Taxonomic methods in health psychology. In P. Karoly (Ed.), *Measurement strategies in health psychology*. New York: John Wiley.

FISHER, P., SHAFFER, D., PIACENTINI, J., LAPKIN, J., KAFANTARIS, V., LEONARD, H., & JERZOG, D. (1993). Sensitivity of the Diagnostic Interview Schedule for Children, 2nd edition (DISC-2.1) for specific diagnoses of children and adolescents. *Journal of the American Academy of Child and Adolescent Psychiatry, 32,* 666-673.

FIVUSH, R. (1993). Developmental perspectives on autobiographical recall. In G. Goodman & B. Bottoms (Eds.), *Child victims, child witnesses: Understanding and improving testimony* (pp. 1-24). New York: Guilford.

FIVUSH, R. (1994). Young children's event recall: Are memories constructed through discourse? *Consciousness and Cognition, 3,* 356-373.

FIVUSH, R., & HUDSON, J. A. (1990). *Knowing and remembering in children.* New York: Cambridge University Press.

FLIN, R., & SPENCER, J. R. (1995). Children as witnesses: Legal and psychological perspectives. *Journal of Child Psychology and Psychiatry, 36,* 171-189.

FOGEL, A., & THELEN, E, (1987). Development of early expressive and communicative action: Reinterpreting the evidence from a dynamic systems perspective. *Developmental Psychology, 23,* 747-761.

FOMBONNE, E. (1995). Depressive disorders: Time trends and possible explanatory mechanisms. In M. Rutter & D. J. Smith (Eds.), *Psychosocial disorders in young people: Time trends and their causes* (pp. 544-615). Chichester, UK: Wiley.

FOX, N. A. (1995). Of the way we were: Adult memories about attachment experiences and their role in determining infant-parent relationships: A commentary on van IJzendoorn (1995). *Psychological Bulletin, 117,* 404-410.

FREUD, S. (1953). Three essays on the theory of sexuality. In J. Strachey (Ed. and Trans.), *The standard edition of the complete psychological works of Sigmund Freud* (Vol. 7, pp. 135-243). London: Hogarth. (Original work published 1905)

FREUD, S. (1963). Introductory lectures on psycho-analysis. In J. Strachey (Ed. and Trans.), *The standard edition of the complete psychological works of Sigmund Freud* (Vols. 15-16). London: Hogarth. (Original work published 1916-1917)

FRICK, P. J., LAHEY, B. B., LOEBER, R., TANNENBAUM, L., VAN HORN, Y., CHRIST, M. A. G., HART, E. A., & HANSON, K. (1993). Oppositional defiant disorder and conduct disorder: A meta-analytic review of factor analyses and cross-validation in a clinic sample. *Clinical Psychology Review, 13,* 319-340.

FRIEDMAN, W. J. (1993). Memory for the time of past events. *Psychological Bulletin, 113,* 44-66.

GANGESTAD, S., & SNYDER, M. (1985). To carve nature at its joints: On the existence of discrete classes in personality. *Psychological Review, 92,* 317-349.

GARRETT, H. E. (1946). A developmental theory of intelligence. *American Psychologist, 1,* 372-378.

GAUL, W., & SCHADER, M. (1986). Classification as a tool of research. *Proceedings of the 9th Annual Meeting of the Classification Society.* Karlsruhe: University of Karlsruhe, June 1985.

GEISELMAN, R. E., SAYWITZ, K. J., & BORNSTEIN, G. K. (1993). Effects of cognitive questioning techniques on children's recall performance. In G. Goodman & B. Bottoms (Eds.), *Child victims, child witnesses: Understanding and improving testimony* (pp. 71-93). New York: Guilford.

GIBSON, W. A. (1959). Three multivariate models: Factor analysis, latent structure analysis, and latent profile analysis. *Psychometrica, 24,* 229-252.

GIUFFRA, L. A., & RISCH, N. (1994). Diminished recall and the cohort effect of major depression: A simulation study. *Psychological Medicine, 24,* 375-383.

GLEICK, J. (1987). *Chaos: Making a new science.* New York: Penguin.

GLEN, S., SIMPSON, A., DRINNAN, D., McGUINNESS, D., & SANDBERG, S. (1993). Testing the reliability of a new measure of life events and experiences in childhood: The psychosocial assessment of childhood experiences (PACE). *European Journal of Child and Adolescent Psychiatry, 2,* 98-110.

GOFFMAN, E. W. (1959). *The presentation of the self in everyday life.* New York: Doubleday Anchor.

GOLDSMITH, H., BUSS, A. H., PLOMIN, R., ROTHBART, M. K., THOMAS, A., CHESS, S., HINDE, R. A., & McCALL, R. B. (1987). What is temperament? Four approaches. *Child Development, 58,* 505-529.

GOODMAN, G., & BOTTOMS, B. (Eds.). (1993). *Child victims, child witnesses: Understanding and improving testimony.* New York: Guilford.

GOODMAN, G. S., QUAS, J. A., BATTERMAN-FAUCE, J. M., RIDDLESBERGER, M., & KUHN, J. (1994). Predictors of accurate and inaccurate memories of traumatic events experienced in childhood. *Consciousness & Cognition, 3,* 269-294.

GOODWIN, B. (1994). *How the leopard changed its spots.* New York: Scribner.

GORDON, A. D. (1981). *Classification: Methods for the exploratory analysis of multivariate data.* London: Chapman & Hall.

GRAMER, M., & HUBER, H. P. (1994). Individual variability in task-specific cardiovascular response patterns during psychological challenge. *German Journal of Psychology, 18,* 1-17.

GREENWALD, N. G., PRATKANIS, A. R., LIEPPE, M. R., & BAUMGARDNER, M. H. (1986). Under what conditions does theory obstruct research progress? *Psychological Review, 93,* 216-229.

GUSTAFSON, S. B., & MAGNUSSON, D. (1991). *Female life careers: A pattern approach.* Mahwah, NJ: Lawrence Erlbaum.

HALL, D. F., LOFTUS, E. F., & TOUSIGNANT, J. P. (1984). Postevent information and changes in recollection for a natural event. In G. L. Wells & E. F. Loftus (Eds.), *Eye-witness testimony: Psychological perspectives* (pp. 124-141). New York: Cambridge University Press.

HALL, G. S. (1885). The new psychology. *Andover Review, 3,* 120-135.

HALL, N. (1991). *The new scientist guide to chaos.* New York: Penguin.

HAMMERSLEY, R. (1994). A digest of memory phenomena for addiction research. *Addiction, 89,* 283-293.

HÄRNQVIST, K., GUSTATSSON, J.-E., MUTHÉN, B. O., & NELSON, G. (1994). Hierarchical models of ability at individual and class levels. *Intelligence, 18,* 166-187.

HARRIS, C. W. (1963). *Problems in measuring change.* Madison: University of Wisconsin Press.

HART, D., HOFMANN, V., EDELSTEIN, W., & KELLER, M. (1997). The relation of childhood personality types to adolescent behavior and development: A longitudinal study of Icelandic children. *Developmental Psychology, 33,* 195-205.

HART, E. L., LAHEY, B. B., LOEBER, R., APPLEGATE, B., & FRICK, P. J. (1995). Developmental change in attention-deficit hyperactivity disorder in boys: A 4-year longitudinal study. *Journal of Abnormal Child Psychology, 23,* 729-749.

HARTUP, W. W., & VAN LIESHOUT, C. F. M. (1995). Personality development in social context. *Annual Review of Psychology, 46,* 665-687.

HAYNE, H., & ROVEE-COLLIER, C. (1995). The organization of reactivated memory in infancy. *Child Development, 66,* 893-906.

HECKLER, S. (1994). Facilitated communication: A response by child protection. *Child Abuse & Neglect, 18,* 495-503.

HELLVIK, O. (1988). *Introduction to causal analysis: Exploring survey data by cross-tabulation.* Oslo: Norwegian University Press.

HENRY, B., MOFFITT, T. E., CASPI, A., LANGLEY, J., & SILVA, P. A. (1994). On the "remembrance of things past": A longitudinal evaluation of the retrospective method. *Psychological Assessment, 6,* 92-101.

HESS, B., & MIKHAILOV, A. (1994). Self-organization in living cells. *Science, 264,* 223-224.

HESSELBROOK, M. N., HESSELBROOK, V. M., BABOR, T. F., STABENAU, J. R., MEYER, R. E., & WEIDENMAN, M. (1984). Antisocial behavior, psychopathology, and problem drinking in the natural history of alcoholism. In D. W. Goodwin, K. T. van Dusen, & A. Mednick (Eds.), *Longitudinal research in alcoholism* (pp. 197-214). Boston: Kluwer-Nijhoff.

HILL, J., FUDGE, H., HARRINGTON, R., PICKLES, A., & RUTTER, M. (1995). The Adult Personality Functioning Assessment (APFA): Factors influencing agreement between subject and informant. *Psychological Medicine, 25,* 263-275.

HILL, J., HARRINGTON, R., FUDGE, H., RUTTER, M., & PICKLES, A. (1989). Adult Personality Functioning Assessment (APFA): An investigator-based standardized interview. *British Journal of Psychiatry, 155,* 24-35.

HINDE, R. A. (1987). *Individuals, relationships, and culture.* Cambridge, UK: Cambridge University Press.

HINDE, R. A. (1997). *Relationships: A dialectical perspective.* Hove, UK: Psychology Press.

HINDE, R. A., & DENNIS, A. (1986). Categorizing individuals: An alternative to linear analysis. *International Journal of Behavioral Development 9,* 105-119.

HINDE, R. A., TAMPLIN, A., & BARRETT, J. (1993a). Home correlates of aggression in pre-school. *Aggressive Behavior, 19,* 85-105.

HINDE, R. A., TAMPLIN, A., & BARRETT, J. (1993b). Social isolation in 4-year-olds. *British Journal of Developmental Psychology, 11,* 211-36.

HINDE, R. A., TAMPLIN, A., & BARRETT, J. (1995). Consistency within and between relationships. *Czlowiek i Spoleczenstwo, 12,* 7-18.

HOCKEY, G. R., GAILLARD, A. W. K., & COLES, M. G. H. (1986). *Energetic and human information processing.* Dordrecht, The Netherlands: Martin Nijhoff.

HOFFMAN, M. L. (1960). Power assertion by the parent and its impact on the child. *Child Development, 31,* 129-143.

HOLMSHAW, J., & SIMONOFF, E. (1996). Retrospective recall of childhood psychopathology. *International Journal of Methods in Psychiatric Research, 6,* 79-88.

HOWE, M. L., & COURAGE, M. L. (1993). On resolving the enigma of infantile amnesia. *Psychological Bulletin, 113,* 305-326.

HOWE, M. L., COURAGE, M. L., & PETERSON, C. (1994). How can I remember when "I" wasn't there: Long term retention of traumatic experiences and emergence of the cognitive self. *Consciousness and Cognition, 3,* 327-355.

HOYLE, R. H. (1995). The structural equation modeling approach: Basic concepts and fundamental issues. In R. H. Hoyle (Ed.), *Structural equation modeling: Concepts, issues, and applications* (pp. 1-15). Thousand Oaks, CA: Sage.

HUBERT, L., & ARABIE, P. (1985). Comparing partitions. *Journal of Classificaiton, 2,* 193-218.

HUIZINGA, D. H. (1995). Developmental sequences in delinquency. In L. Crockett & A. Crouter (Eds.), *Pathways through adolescence* (pp. 15-34). Mahwah, NJ: Lawrence Erlbaum.

HUTTENLOCHER, J., HEDGES, L., & PROHASKA, V. (1988). Hierarchical organization in ordered domains: Estimating the dates of events. *Psychological Review, 95*, 471-484.

JACOB, F. (1989). *The logic of life: A history of heredity and the possible and the actual.* New York: Penguin.

JAMES, W. (1890). *The principles of psychology* (Vol. 1). New York: Macmillan.

JESSOR, R., DONOVAN, J. E., & COSTA, F. M. (1991). *Beyond adolescence: Problem behavior and young adult development.* New York: Cambridge University Press.

JESSOR, R., & JESSOR, S. L. (1977). *Problem behavior and psychosocial development.* San Diego: Academic Press.

JOHN, O. P. (1990). The "Big Five" factor taxonomy: Dimensions of personality in the natural language and questionnaires. In L. A. Pervin (Ed.), *Handbook of personality: Theory and research* (pp. 66-100). New York: Guilford.

JOHN, O. P., & OSTROVE, J. (1994). *Personality types in adult women: Longitudinal evidence for four distinct life trajectories.* Berkeley: University of California, Institute of Personality and Social Research.

JONES, C. J., & NESSELROADE, J. R. (1990). Multivariate, replicated, single-subject, repeated measures designs and P-technique factor analysis: A review of intraindividual change studies. *Experimental Aging Research, 16*, 171-183.

JONES, M. G. (1968). Personality correlates and antecedents of drinking patterns in adult males. *Journal of Consulting and Clinical Psychology, 32*, 2-12.

KAGAN, J. (1969). The three faces of continuity in human development. In D. A. Goslin (Ed.), *Handbook of socialization theory and research* (pp. 983-1002). Chicago: Rand McNally.

KAGAN, J. (1989). The concept of behavioral inhibition to the unfamiliar. In J. S. Reznick (Ed.), *Perspectives on behavioral inhibition* (pp. 1-23). Chicago: University of Chicago Press.

KAGAN, J. (1992). Yesterday's premises, tomorrows promises. *American Psychologist, 28*, 990-997.

KAGAN, J. (1994). *Galen's prophecy: Temperament in human nature.* New York: Basic Books.

KAGAN, J., REZNICK, J. S., & SNIDMAN, N. (1987). The physiology and psychology of behavioral inhibition in children. *Child Development, 58*, 1459-1473.

KAGAN, J., & SNIDMAN, N. (1991). Infant predictors of an inhibited profile. *Psychological Science, 2*, 40-44.

KAPLAN, M. L., & KAPLAN, N. R. (1991). The self-organization of human psychological functioning. *Behavioral Science, 36*, 161-179.

KAUFFMANN, S. A. (1993). *The origins of order.* New York: Oxford University Press.

KEENAN, K., LOEBER, R., ZHANG, Q., STOUTHAMER-LOEBER, M., & VAN KAMMEN, W. B. (1995). The influence of deviant peers on the development of boys' disruptive and delinquency behavior: A temporal analysis. *Development and Psychopathology, 7*, 715-726.

KELLAM, S. (1995, October). *Testing developmental paths through parallel preventive trials.* Presentation given at the Carolina Consortium on Human Development, Center for Developmental Science, Chapel Hill, NC.

KELLAM, S. G., ADAMS, R. G., BROWN, C. H., & ENSMINGER, M. E. (1975). *Mental health and going to school: The Woodlawn program of assessment, early intervention, and evaluation.* Chicago: University of Chicago Press.

KENDLER, K. S., SILBERG, J. L., NEALE, M. C., KESSLER, R. C., HEATH, A. C., & EAVES, L. J. (1991). The family history method: Whose psychiatric history is measured? *American Journal of Psychiatry, 148,* 1501-1504.

KESSLER, R. C., McGONAGLE, K. A., ZHAO, S., NELSON, C. B., HUGHES, M., ESHLEMAN, S., WITTCHEN, H. U., & KENDLER, K. S. (1994). Lifetime and 12-month prevalence of *DSM-III-R* psychiatric disorders in the United States: Results from the National Comorbidity Survey. *Archives of General Psychiatry, 51,* 8-19.

KLEWE, L. (1993). Brief report: An empirical evaluation of spelling boards as a means of communication for the multihandicapped. *Journal of Autism and Developmental Disorders, 23,* 559-566.

KLOHNEN, E. C., & BLOCK, J. (1996). Unpublished data, University of California, Department of Psychology, Berkeley.

KOHNSTAMM, G. A., BATES, J. E., & ROTHBART, M. K. (Eds.). (1989). *Temperament in childhood.* New York: John Wiley.

KRAUTH, J., & LIENERT, G. A. (1982). Fundamentals and modifications of configural frequency analysis (CFA). *Interdisciplinaria, 3*(1).

LAMBERT, N. M. (1988). Adolescent outcomes for hyperactive children: Perspectives on general and specific patterns of childhood risk for adolescent educational, social, and mental health problems. *American Psychologist, 43,* 786-799.

LASZLO, E. (1972). *The systems view of the world.* New York: Braziller.

LAUDEMAN, I. V., & JOHN, O. P. (1995). *Neural network modeling and fuzzy clustering techniques applied to multivariate personality data.* Poster presented at the annual convention of the American Psychological Association, New York.

LE BLANC, M., CÔTÉ, G., & LOEBER, R. (1991, January). Temporal paths in delinquency: Stability, regression, and progression analyzed with panel data from an adolescent and a delinquent male sample. *Canadian Journal of Criminology,* 23-44.

LE BLANC, M., & KASPY, N. (1995). *Trajectories of delinquency and problem behavior: Comparison of synchronous and nonsynchronous paths on social and personal control characteristics of adolescents.* Paper presented at the annual meeting of the American Society of Criminology, Boston.

LE COUTEUR, A., RUTTER, M., LORD, C., RIOS, P., ROBERTSON, S., HOLDGRAFEN, M., & McLENNAN, J. (1989). Autism Diagnostic Interview: A standardized investigator-based instrument. *Journal of Autism and Developmental Disorders, 19,* 363-387.

LERNER, R. M. (1984). *On the nature of human plasticity.* Cambridge, UK: Cambridge University Press.

LEWIN, K. (1931). Environmental forces in child behavior and development. In C. Murchison (Ed.), *A handbook of child psychology* (2nd ed., pp. 590-625). Worcester, MA: Clark University Press.

LEWIN, K. (1935). *A dynamic theory of personality.* New York: McGraw-Hill.

LEWIS, M. (1995). Memory and psychoanalysis: A new look at infantile amnesia and transference. *Journal of the American Academy of Child & Adolescent Psychiatry, 34,* 405-417.

LIENERT, G. A., & BERGMAN, L. R. (1985). Longisectional interaction structure analysis (LISA) in psychopharmacology and developmental psychopathology. *Neuropsychobiology, 14,* 27-34.

280   METHODS AND MODELS FOR STUDYING THE INDIVIDUAL

LIENERT, G. A., & ZUR OEVESTE, H. (1985). CFA as a statistical tool for developmental research. *Educational & Psychological Measurement, 45,* 301-307.

LINDSEY, D. S., & READ, J. D. (1994). Psychotherapy and memories of sexual abuse: A cognitive perspective. *Applied Cognitive Psychology, 8,* 281-338.

LOCKMAN, J. J., & THELEN, E. (1993). Developmental biodynamics: Brain, body, behavior connections. *Child Development, 64,* 953-959.

LOEBER, R. (1990). Development and risk factors of juvenile antisocial behavior and delinquency. *Clinical Psychology Review, 10,* 1-41.

LOEBER, R. (1991). Questions and advances in the study of developmental pathways. In D. Cicchetti & S. Toth (Eds.), *Rochester Symposium on Developmental Psychopathology* (Vol. 3, pp. 97-115). Rochester, NY: Rochester University Press.

LOEBER, R., & DISHION, T. J. (1983). Early predictors of male delinquency: A review. *Psychological Bulletin, 94,* 68-99.

LOEBER, R., GREEN, S. M., KEENAN, K., & LAHEY, B. B. (1995). Which boys will fare worse? Early predictors of the onset of conduct disorder in a 4-year longitudinal study. *Journal of the American Academy of Child and Adolescent Psychiatry, 34,* 499-509.

LOEBER, R., GREEN, S. M., & LAHEY, B. B. (1990). Mental health professionals' perception of the utility of children, mothers, and teachers as informants on childhood psychopathology. *Journal of Clinical Child Psychology, 19,* 136-143.

LOEBER, R., GREEN, S. M., LAHEY, B. B., & STOUTHAMER-LOEBER, M. (1989). Optimal informants on childhood disruptive behaviors. *Development and Psychopathology, 1,* 317-337.

LOEBER, R., KEENAN, K., & ZHANG, Q. (1997). Boys' experimentation and persistence in developmental pathways toward serious delinquency. *Journal of Child and Family Studies, 6,* 321-357.

LOEBER, R., RUSSO, M. F., STOUTHAMER-LOEBER, M., & LAHEY, B. B. (1994). Internalizing problems and their relation to the development of externalizing behaviors in adolescence. *Journal of Research on Adolescence, 4,* 615-637.

LOEBER, R., & SCHMALING, K. (1985). Empirical evidence for overt and covert patterns of antisocial conduct problems. *Journal of Abnormal Child Psychology, 13,* 337-352.

LOEBER, R., STOUTHAMER-LOEBER, M., & GREEN, S. M. (1991). Age at onset of problem behavior in boys, and later disruptive and delinquent behavior. *Criminal Behavior and Mental Health, 1,* 229-246.

LOEBER, R., STOUTHAMER-LOEBER, M., VAN KAMMEN, W. B., & FARRINGTON, D. P. (1989). Development of a new measure of self-reported antisocial behavior in young children: Prevalence and reliability. In M. W. Klein (Ed.), *Self-report methodology in criminologic research* (pp. 203-225). Boston: Kluwer-Nijhoff.

LOEBER, R., STOUTHAMER-LOEBER, M., VAN KAMMEN, W. B., & FARRINGTON, D. P. (1991). Initiation, escalation, and desistance in juvenile offending and their correlates. *Journal of Criminal Law and Criminology, 82,* 36-82.

LOEBER, R., & WIKSTRÖM, P.-O. (1993). Individual pathways to crime in different types of neighborhood. In D. P. Farrington, R. J. Sampson, & P. O. Wikström (Eds.), *Integrating individual and ecological aspects of crime* (pp. 169-204). Stockholm, Sweden: Liber Forlag.

LOEBER, R., WUNG, P., KEENAN, K., GIROUX, B., STOUTHAMER-LOEBER, M., VAN KAMMEN, W. B., & MAUGHAN, B. (1993). Developmental pathways in disruptive child behavior. *Development and Psychopathology, 5,* 101-133.

LOEHLIN, J. C. (1992). *Genes and environment in personality development.* Newbury Park, CA: Sage.

LOFTUS, E. F. (1993). The reality of repressed memories. *American Psychologist, 48,* 518-537.

LOFTUS, E. F., & HOFFMAN, H. G. (1989). Misinformation and memory: The creation of new memories. *Journal of Experimental Psychology: General, 118,* 100-104.

LOFTUS, E. F., & KETCHAM, K. (1994). *The myth of repressed memories.* New York: St Martin's.

LOFTUS, E. F., & MARBURGER, W. (1983). Since the eruption of Mt. St. Helens, has anyone beaten you up? Improving the accuracy of retrospective reports with landmark events. *Memory and Cognition, 11,* 114-120.

LORD, C., RUTTER, M., GOODE, S., HEEMSBERGEN, J., JORDAN, H., MAWHOOD, L., & SCHOPLER, E. (1989). Autism Diagnostic Observation Schedule: A standardized observation of communicative and social behavior. *Journal of Autism and Developmental Disorders, 19,* 185-212.

LORD, C., RUTTER, M., & LE COUTEUR, A. (1994). Autism Diagnostic Interview-Revised: A revised version of a diagnostic interview for caregivers of individuals with possible pervasive developmental disorders. *Journal of Autism and Developmental Disorders, 24,* 659-685.

LYKKEN, D. T., McGUE, M., TELLEGEN, A., & BOUCHARD, P. J. (1992). Emergenesis. *American Psychologist, 47,* 1565-1577.

MACCOBY, E. E., & MARTIN, J. A. (1983). Socialization in the context of the family parent-child interaction. In P. Mussen (Series Ed.) & E. M. Hetherington (Vol. Ed.), *Handbook of child psychology: Vol. 4. Socialization, personality, and social development* (pp. 1-102). New York: John Wiley.

MAGNUSSON, D. (1976). The person and the situation in an interactional model of behavior. *Scandinavian Journal of Psychology, 17,* 253-271.

MAGNUSSON, D. (1985). Implications of an interactional paradigm for research on human development. *International Journal of Behavioral Development, 8,* 115-137.

MAGNUSSON, D. (1988). *Individual development from an interactional perspective.* Mahwah, NJ: Lawrence Erlbaum.

MAGNUSSON, D. (1990). Personality development from an interactional perspective. In L. Pervin (Ed.), *Handbook of personality* (pp. 193-222). New York: Guilford.

MAGNUSSON, D. (1992). Back to the phenomena: Theory, methods, and statistics in psychological research. *European Journal of Personality, 6,* 1-14.

MAGNUSSON, D. (1995). Individual development: A holistic integrated model. In P. Moen, G. H. Elder, Jr., & K. Lüscher (Eds.), *Examining lives in context: Perspectives on the ecology of human development* (pp. 19-60). Washington, DC: American Psychological Association.

MAGNUSSON, D. (Ed.). (1996a). *The life-span development of individuals: Behavioral, neurobiological, and psychosocial perspectives.* Cambridge, UK: Cambridge University Press.

MAGNUSSON, D. (1996b). The patterning of antisocial behavior and autonomic reactivity. In D. M. Stoff & R. B. Cairns (Eds.), *The neurobiology of clinical aggression* (pp. 291-308). Mahwah, NJ: Lawrence Erlbaum.

MAGNUSSON, D., & ALLEN, V. L. (1983). Implications and applications of an interactional perspective for human development. In D. Magnusson & V. L.

Allen (Eds.), *Human development: An interactional perspective* (pp. 369-387). San Diego: Academic Press.

MAGNUSSON, D., ANDERSSON, T., & TÖRESTAD, B. (1993). Methodological implications of a peephole perspective on personality. In D. C. Funder, R. D. Parke, C. Tomlinson-Keasey, & K. Widaman (Eds.), *Studying lives through time: Personality and development* (pp. 207-220). Washington, DC: American Psychological Association.

MAGNUSSON, D., & BERGMAN, L. (1988). Individual and variable-based approaches to longitudinal research on early risk factors. In M. Rutter (Eds.), *Studies of psychosocial risk: The power of longitudinal data* (pp. 45-61). Cambridge, UK: Cambridge University Press.

MAGNUSSON, D., & BERGMAN, L. R. (1990). A pattern approach to the study of pathways from childhood to adulthood. In L. N. Robins & M. Rutter (Eds.), *Straight and devious pathways from childhood to adulthood* (pp. 101-115). Cambridge, UK: Cambridge University Press.

MAGNUSSON, D., BERGMAN, L. R., RUDINGER, G., & TÖRESTAD, B. (1991). *Problems and methods in longitudinal research: Stability and change.* Cambridge, UK: Cambridge University Press.

MAGNUSSON, D., & CAIRNS, R. B. (1996). Developmental science: Toward a unified framework. In R. B. Cairns, G. H. Elder, Jr., & J. Costello (Eds.), *Developmental science* (pp. 7-30). New York: Cambridge University Press.

MAGNUSSON, D., & CASAER, P. (1992). *Longitudinal research on individual development: Present status and future perspectives.* Cambridge, UK: Cambridge University Press.

MAGNUSSON, D., DUNÉR, A., & ZETTERBLOM, G. (1975). *Adjustment: A longitudinal study.* Stockholm, Sweden: Almqvist & Wiksell.

MAGNUSSON, D., & STATTIN, H. (1998). Person-context interaction theories. In R. M. Lerner (Ed.), *Theoretical models of human development: Handbook of child psychology* (Vol. 1, 5th ed.), pp. 685-759. New York: John Wiley.

MAGNUSSON, D., & TÖRESTAD, B. (1993). A holistic view of personality: A model revisited. *Annual Review of Psychology, 44*, 427-452.

MAIN, M., KAPLAN, N., & CASSIDY, J. (1985). Security in infancy, childhood, and adulthood: A move to the level of representation. In I. Bretherton & E. Waters (Eds.), Growing points in attachment theory and research (pp. 66-106). *Monographs of the Society for Research in Child Development, 50*(Serial no. 209).

MANLY, B. F. (1994). *Multivariate statistical methods: A primer* (2nd ed.). London: Chapman & Hall.

MARTIN, R. P. (1988). The Temperament Assessment Battery for Children. Brandon, VT: Clinical Psychology Publishing.

MAUGHAN, B., PICKLES, A., & QUINTON, D. (1995). Parental hostility, childhood behavior, and adult social functioning. In J. McCord (Ed.), *Coercion and punishment in long-term perspectives* (pp. 34-58). New York: Cambridge University Press.

MAUGHAN, B., & RUTTER, M. (1997). Retrospective reporting of childhood adversity: Some methodological considerations. *Journal of Personality Disorders, 11*, 19-33.

McADAMS, D. P. (1988). Personal needs and personal relationships. In S. Duck (Ed.), *Handbook of personal relationships* (pp. 7-22). Chichester, UK: Wiley.

McADAMS, D. P. (1993). *The stories we live by: Personal myths and the making of the self.* New York: Morrow.

McCALL, G. J. (1974). A symbolic interactionist approach to attraction. In T. L. Huston (Ed.), *Foundations of interpersonal attraction* (pp. 217-235). San Diego: Academic Press.

McCALL, R. B., APPELBAUM, M. I., & HAGARTY, P. S. (1973). Developmental changes in mental performance. *Monographs of the Society for Research in Child Development, 38*(3, Whole No. 150).

McCORD, W., & McCORD, J. (1960). *Origins of alcoholism.* Stanford, CA: Stanford University Press.

McKEOWN, B., & THOMAS, D. (1988). *Q methodology.* Newbury Park, CA: Sage.

MEEHL, P. E. (1979). A funny thing happened to us on the way to the latent entities. *Journal of Personality Assessment, 43*, 564-581.

MEEHL, P.E. (1992). Factors and taxa, traits and types, differences of degree and differences in kind. *Journal of Personality, 60*, 117-174.

MEEHL, P. E., & GOLDEN, R. R. (1982). Taxometric methods. In J. N. Butcher & P. C. Kendall (Eds.), *The handbook of research methods in clinical psychology* (pp. 127-181). New York: John Wiley.

MENARD, S., & ELLIOTT, D. S. (1990). Longitudinal and cross-sectional data collection and analysis in the study of crime and delinquency. *Justice Quarterly, 7*(19), 11-55.

MENDELSOHN, G. A., WEISS, D., & FEIMER, N. (1982). Conceptual and empirical analysis of the typological implications of patterns of socialization and femininity. *Journal of Personality and Social Psychology, 42*, 1157-1170.

MILLER, J. G. (1978). *Living systems.* New York: McGraw-Hill.

MILLIGAN, G. W. (1980). An examination of the effect of six types of error perturbation on 15 clustering algorithms. *Psychometrika, 45*, 325-342.

MILLIGAN, G. W. (1981a). A Monte Carlo study of 30 internal criterion measures for cluster analysis. *Psychometrika, 46*, 187-199.

MILLIGAN, G. W. (1981b). A review of Monte Carlo tests of cluster analysis. *Multivariate Behavioral Research, 16*, 379-407.

MILLIGAN, G. W., & COOPER, M. C. (1985). An examination of procedures for determining the number of clusters in a data set. *Psychometrika, 50*(2), 159-179.

MILNER, B., CORKIN, S., & TEUBER, H.C. (1968). Further analysis of the hippocampal amnesic syndrome. *Neuropsychologia 6*, 215-234.

MILLS, J. W. (1898). *The nature and development of animal intelligence.* London: Unwin.

MILLS, P., DIMSDALE, J. E., NELESEN, R. A., JASIEVICZ, J., ZIEGLER, G., & KENNEDY, B. (1994). Patterns of adrenergic receptors and adrenergic agonists underlying cardiovascular responses to a psychological challenge. *Psychological Medicine, 56*, 70-56.

MISCHEL, W. (1973). Toward a cognitive social learning reconceptualization of personality. *Psychological Review, 80*, 252-283.

MISIAK, H., & SEXTON, V. (1966). *History of psychology.* New York: Grune & Stratton.

MOFFITT, T. E. (1993). Adolescence-limited and life-course persistent antisocial behavior: A developmental taxonomy. *Psychological Review, 100*, 674-701.

MOFFITT, T. E., & SILVA, P. A. (1988). Self-reported delinquency, neuropsychological deficit, and history of attention deficit disorder. *Journal of Abnormal Child Psychology, 16*, 553-567.

MONTEE, B. B., MILTENBERGER, R. G., & WITTROCK, D. (1995). An experimental analysis of facilitated communication. *Journal of Applied Behavior Analysis, 28*, 189-200.

MOORE, S., DONOVAN, B., & HUDSON, A. (1993). Brief report: Facilitator-suggested conversational evaluation of facilitated communication. *Journal of Autism and Developmental Disorders, 23,* 541-552.

MOORE, S., DONOVAN, B., HUDSON, A., DYKSTRA, J., & LAWRENCE, J. (1993). Brief report: Evaluation of eight case studies of facilitated communication. *Journal of Autism and Developmental Disorders, 23,* 531-539.

MOREY, L. C., BLASHFIELD, R. K., & SKINNER, H. A. (1983). A comparison of cluster analysis techniques within a sequential validation framework. *Multivariate Behavioral Research, 18,* 309-329.

MORTON, J., HAMMERSLEY, R. H., & BEKERIAN, D. A. (1985). Headed records: A model for memory and its failures. *Cognition, 20,* 1-23.

MUMFORD, M. D., & OWENS, W. A. (1984). Individuality in a developmental context: Some empirical and theoretical considerations. *Human Development, 27,* 84-108.

MURRAY, H. A. (1938). *Explorations in personality.* New York: Oxford University Press.

MYERS, I. B., & McCAULLEY, M. H. (1985). *Manual: A guide to the development and use of the Myers-Briggs Type Indicator.* Palo Alto, CA: Consulting Psychologists Press.

MYERS, J. E. B. (1994). Commentary: The tendency of the legal system to distort scientific and clinical innovations: Facilitated communication as a case study. *Child Abuse & Neglect, 18,* 505-513.

NAUGHTON, M., OPPENHEIM, A., & HILL, J. (1996). Assessment of personality functioning in the transition from adolescent to adult life: Preliminary findings. *British Journal of Psychiatry, 168,* 33-37.

NEISSER, U. (1982). Snapshots or benchmarks? In U. Neisser (Ed.), *Memory observed: Remembering in natural contexts* (pp. 43-48). San Francisco: Freeman.

NEISSER, U., & WINOGRAD, E. (Eds.). (1988). *Remembering reconsidered: Ecological and traditional approaches to the study of memory.* Cambridge, UK: Cambridge University Press.

NELSON, K. (1990). Remembering, forgetting, and childhood amnesia. In R. Fivush & J. A. Hudson (Eds.), *Knowing and remembering in young children* (pp. 301-316). New York: Cambridge University Press.

NELSON, K. (1994). Long-term retention of memory for preverbal experience: Evidence and implications. *Memory, 2,* 467-475.

NESSELROADE, J. R., & FORD, D. H. (1987). Methodological considerations in modeling living systems. In M. E. Ford & D. H. Ford (Eds.), *Humans as self-constructing living systems: Putting the framework to work* (pp. 47-79). Mahwah, NJ: Lawrence Erlbaum.

NICOLIS, G., & PRIGOGINE, I. (1977). *Self-organization in non-equilibrium systems.* New York: John Wiley.

OLSSON, U., & BERGMAN, L. R. (1977). A longitudinal factor model for studying change in ability structure. *Multivariate Behavioral Research, 12,* 221-242.

OZER, D. J. (1993). The Q-sort method and the study of personality development. In D. C. Funder, R. D. Parke, C. Tomlinson-Keasey, & K. Widaman (Eds.), *Studying lives through time: Personality and development* (pp. 147-168). Washington, DC: American Psychological Association.

OZER, D. J., & GJERDE, P. F. (1989). Patterns of personality consistency and change from childhood through adolescence. *Journal of Personality, 57,* 483-507.

PACKER, M., MEDINA, N., YUSHAK, M., & MELLER, J. (1983). Hemodynamic patterns of response during long-term captopril therapy for severe chronic heart failure. *Circulation, 68,* 103-112.

PARKER, G., TUPLING, H., & BROWN, L. B. (1979). A parental bonding instrument. *British Journal of Medical Psychology, 52,* 1-10.

PATRICK, M., HOBSON, P., CASTLE, D., HOWARD, R., & MAUGHAN, B. (1994). Personality disorder and the mental representation of early social experience. *Development and Psychopathology, 6,* 375-388.

PATTERSON, G. R. (1980). Children who steal. In T. Hirschi & M. Gottfredson (Eds.), *Understanding crime: Current theory and research* (pp. 73-90). London: Sage.

PATTERSON, G. R. (1982). *A social learning approach: Vol. 3. Coercive family process.* Eugene, OR: Castalia.

PATTERSON, G. R. (1992). Developmental changes in antisocial behavior. In R. deV. Peters, R. J. McMahon, & V. L. Quinsey (Eds.), *Aggression and violence throughout the life span* (pp. 52-82). Newbury Park, CA: Sage.

PATTERSON, G. R., DEBARYSHE, B. D., & RAMSEY, E. (1989). A developmental perspective on antisocial behavior. *American Psychologist, 44,* 329-335.

PEARSON, J. L., COHN, D. A., COWAN, P. A., & COWAN, C. P. (1994). Earned- and continuous-security in adult attachment: Relation to depressive symptomatology and parenting style. *Development and Psychopathology, 6,* 359-375.

PICKLES, A., PICKERING, K., & TAYLOR, C. (1996). Reconciling recalled dates of developmental milestones, events, and transitions: A mixed GLM with random mean and variance functions. *Journal of the Royal Statistical Society, Series A, 159,* 225-234.

PICKLES, A., & RUTTER, M. (1991). Statistical and conceptual models of "turning points" in developmental processes. In D. Magnusson, L. R. Bergman, G. Rudinger, & B. Törestat (Eds.), *Problems and methods in longitudinal research: Stability and change* (pp. 133-165). Cambridge, UK: Cambridge University Press.

PILLEMER, D. B., & WHITE, S. H. (1989). Childhood events recalled by children and adults. In H. W. Reese (Ed.), *Advances in Child Development and Behavior, 21,* 297-340.

PLOMIN, R., & DANIELS, D. (1987). Why are children in the same family so different from each other? *Behavioral and Brain Sciences, 10,* 1-16.

PULKKINEN, L. (1982). Self-control and continuity from childhood to adolescence. In B. P. Baltes & O. G. Brim, Jr. (Eds.), *Life-span development and behavior* (Vol. 4, pp. 63-105). San Diego: Academic Press.

PULKKINEN, L. (1992a). Lifestyles in personality development. *European Journal of Personality, 6,* 139-155.

PULKKINEN, L. (1992b). The path to adulthood for aggressively inclined girls. In K. Björkqvist & P. Niemelä (Eds.), *Of mice and women: Aspects of female aggression* (pp. 113-121). San Diego: Academic Press.

PULKKINEN, L. (1995). Behavioral precursors to accidents and resulting physical impairment. *Child Development, 66,* 1660-1679.

PULKKINEN, L. (1996). Female and male personality styles: A typological and developmental analysis. *Journal of Personality and Social Psychology, 70,* 1288-1306.

PULKKINEN, L., & HÄMÄLÄINEN, M. (1995). Low self-control as a precursor to crime and accidents in a Finnish longitudinal study. *Criminal Behavior and Mental Health, 5,* 578-587.

PULKKINEN, L., & HURME, H. (1984). Aggression as a predictor of weak self-control. In L. Pulkkinen & P. Lyytinen (Eds.), Human action and personality (pp. 172-189). Jyvaskyla, Finland: University of Jyvaskyla.

PULKKINEN, L., & PITKÄNEN, T. (1994). A prospective study on the precursors to problem drinking in young adulthood. Journal of Studies on Alcohol, 55, 578-587.

PULKKINEN, L., & TREMBLAY, R. (1992). Patterns of boys' social adjustment in two cultures and at different ages: A longitudinal perspective. International Journal of Behavioral Development, 15, 527-553.

QUINTON, D., & RUTTER, M. (1988). Parental breakdown: The making and breaking of intergenerational links. Aldershot, The Netherlands: Avebury.

QUINTON, D., RUTTER, M., & ROWLANDS, O. (1976). An evaluation of an interview assessment of marriage. Psychological Medicine, 6, 577-586.

RADKE-YARROW, M. (1991). The individual and the environment in human behavioral development. In P. Bateson (Ed.), The development and integration of behavior (pp. 389-410). Cambridge, UK: Cambridge University Press.

RADKE-YARROW, M., CAMPBELL, J. D., & BURTON, R. V. (1968). Child rearing: An inquiry in research and methods. San Francisco: Jossey-Bass.

RADKE-YARROW, M., CAMPBELL, J. D., & BURTON, R. V. (1970). Recollections of childhood: A study of the retrospective method. In M. C. Templin (Ed.), Monographs for the Society for Research in Child Development, 35(5, Serial No. 138).

RADKE-YARROW, M., RICHTERS, J., & WILSON, W. E. (1988). Child development in a network of relationships. In R. A. Hinde & J. Stevenson-Hinde (Eds.), Relationships within families (pp. 48-67). Oxford, UK: Clarendon.

RADKE-YARROW, M., & WAXLER, C. Z. (1979). Observing interaction: Confrontation with methodology. In R. B. Cairns (Ed.), The analysis of social interactions: Methods, issues, and illustrations. Mahwah, NJ: Lawrence Erlbaum.

RAPHAEL, K. G., & CLOITRE, M. (1994). Does mood-congruence or causal search govern recall bias? A test of life event recall. Journal of Clinical Epidemiology, 47, 555-564.

REZNICK, J. S. (Ed.). (1989). Perspectives on behavioral inhibition. Chicago: University of Chicago Press.

REZNICK, J. S., KAGAN, J., SNIDMAN, N., GERSTEN, M., BAAK, K., & ROSENBERG, A. (1986). Inhibited and uninhibited children: A follow-up study. Child Development, 57, 660-680.

RICHTERS, J. E. (1992). Depressed mothers as informants about their children: A critical review of the evidence for distortion. Psychological Bulletin, 112, 485-499.

RICHTERS, J. E., & CICCHETTI, D. (1993). Mark Twain meets DSM-III-R, conduct disorder, development, and the concept of harmful dysfunction. Development and Psychopathology, 5, 5-29.

ROBBINS, L. C. (1963). The accuracy of parental recall of aspects of child development and of child rearing practices. Journal of Abnormal and Social Psychology, 66, 261-270.

ROBINS, L. N. (1966). Deviant children grown-up: A sociological and psychiatric study of sociopathic personality. Baltimore: Williams & Wilkins.

ROBINS, L. N., BATES, W. M., & O'NEILL, P. (1962). Adult drinking patterns of former problem drinking children: Society culture and drinking patterns. New York: Wiley.

ROBINS, L. N., SCHOENBERG, S. P., HOLMES, S. J., RATCLIFF, K. S., BENHAM, A., & WORKS, J. (1985). Early home environment and retrospective recall: A test for concordance between siblings with and without psychiatric disorders. *American Journal of Orthopsychiatry, 55*, 27-41.

ROBINS, R. W., JOHN, O. P., CASPI, A., MOFFITT, T. E., & STOUTHAMER-LOEBER, M. (1996). Resilient, overcontrolled, and undercontrolled boys: Three personality types in early adolescence. *Journal of Personality and Social Psychology, 70*, 157-171.

ROGLER, L. H., MALGADY, R. G., & TYRON, W. W. (1992). Evaluation of mental health: Issues of memory in the Diagnostic Interview Schedule. *Journal of Nervous and Mental Disease, 180*, 215-222.

ROGOFF, B. (1996). Developmental transitions in children's participation in sociocultural activities. In A. J. Sameroff & M. M. Haith (Eds.), *The 5- to 7-year shift* (pp. 273-294). Chicago: University of Chicago Press.

ROSE, S. (1995). The rise of neurogenetic determinism. *Nature, 373*, 380-382.

ROSS, M. (1989). Relation of implicit theories to the construction of personal histories. *Psychological Review, 96*, 341-357.

ROTHBART, M. K. (1989). Behavioral approach and inhibition. In J. S. Reznick (Ed.), *Perspectives on behavioral inhibition* (pp. 139-157). Chicago: University of Chicago Press.

RUBIN, D. C., & BADDELEY, A. D. (1989). Telescoping is not time compression: A model of the dating of autobiographical events. *Memory & Cognition, 17*, 653-661.

RUBIN, K. H. (1982). Nonsocial play in preschoolers. Necessary evil? *Child Development, 53*, 651-657.

RUBIN, K. H., & ASENDORPF, J. B. (Eds.). (1993). *Social withdrawal, inhibition, and shyness in childhood.* Mahwah, NJ: Lawrence Erlbaum.

RUBIN, K. H., LEMARE, L. J., & LOLLIS, S. (1990). Social withdrawal in childhood: Developmental pathways to peer rejection. In S. R. Asher & J. D. Coie (Eds.), *Peer rejection in childhood* (pp. 217-252). Cambridge, UK: Cambridge University Press.

RUSSELL, R. W. (1970). "Psychology": Noun or adjective? *American Psychologist, 25*, 211-218.

RUTTER, M. (1989). Pathways from childhood to adult life: Jack Tizard Memorial Lecture. *Journal of Child Psychology and Psychiatry, 30*, 23-51.

RUTTER, M. (1994a). Psychiatric genetics: Research challenges and pathways forward. *American Journal of Medical Genetics (Neuropsychiatric Genetics), 54*, 185-198.

RUTTER, M. (1994b). Stress research: Accomplishments and tasks ahead. In R. J. Haggerty, L. R. Sherrod, N. Garmezy, & M. Rutter (Eds.), *Stress, risk, and resilience in children and adolescents: Processes, mechanisms, and interventions* (pp. 354-385). New York: Cambridge University Press.

RUTTER, M., & BROWN, G. W. (1966). The reliability and validity of measures of family life and relationships in families containing a psychiatric patient. *Social Psychiatry, 1*, 38-53.

RUTTER, M., & COX, A. (1981). Psychiatric interviewing techniques: Methods and measures. *British Journal of Psychiatry, 138*, 273-282.

RUTTER, M., COX, A., EGERT, S., HOLBROOK, D., & EVERITT, B. (1981). Psychiatric interviewing techniques: V. Experimental study: Eliciting information. *British Journal of Psychiatry, 139*, 29-37.

RUTTER, M., & RUTTER, M. (1993). *Developing minds: Challenge and continuity across the lifespan.* New York: Basic Books.

RUTTER, M., & SMITH, D. J. (Eds.). (1995). *Psychosocial disorders in young people: Time trends and their causes.* Chichester, UK: Wiley.

SAMEROFF, A. J. (1982). Development and the dialectic: The need for a systems approach. In W. A. Collins (Ed.), *The concept of development* (pp. 83-103). Mahwah, NJ: Lawrence Erlbaum.

SANDBERG, S., RUTTER, M., GILES, S., OWEN, A., CHAMPION, L., NICHOLLS, J., PRIOR, V., MCGUINNESS, D., & DRINNAN, D. (1993). Assessment of psychosocial experiences in childhood: Methodological issues and some illustrative findings. *Journal of Child Psychology and Psychiatry, 34,* 879-897.

SAPOLSKY, R. M. (1994). On human nature. *Science, 34,* 14-16.

SATTERFIELD, J. H., HOPPE, C. M., & SCHELL, A. M. (1982). A prospective study of delinquency in 110 adolescent boys with attention deficit disorder and 88 normal adolescent boys. *American Journal of Psychiatry, 139,* 795-798.

SCHACHTEL, E. G. (1947). On memory and childhood amnesia. *Psychiatry, 10,* 1-26.

SCHOOLER, J. W. (1994). Seeking the core: The issues and evidence surrounding recovered accounts of sexual trauma. *Consciousness and Cognition, 3,* 452-469.

SCHULKIN, J., McEWEN, B. S., & GOLD, P. W. (1994). Allostasis, amygdala, and anticipatory angst. *Neuroscientific Biobehavioral Review, 18,* 385-396.

SCHWAB-STONE, M., FALLON, T., BRIGGS, M., & CROWTHER, B. (1994). Reliability of diagnostic reporting for children aged 6 to 11 years: A test-retest study of the Diagnostic Interview Schedule for Children-Revised. *American Journal of Psychiatry, 151,* 1048-1054.

SCHWAB-STONE, M., FISHER, P., PIACENTINI, J., SHAFFER, D., DAVIES, M., & BRIGGS, M. (1993). The Diagnostic Interview Schedule for Children-Revised Version (DISC-R): II. Test retest reliability. *Journal of the American Academy of Child and Adolescent Psychiatry, 32,* 651-657.

SEARS, R. R., MACCOBY, E. E., & LEVIN, H. (1957). *Patterns of child rearing.* Evanston, IL: Row, Peterson.

SEARS, R. R., WHITING, J. W. M., NOWLIS, V., & SEARS, P. S. (1953). Some child-rearing antecedents of aggressive and dependency in young children. *Genetic Psychology Monographs, 47,* 135-234.

SHAFFER, D., SCHWAB-STONE, M., FISHER, P., COHEN, P., PIACENTINI, J., DAVIES, M., CONNERS, C. K., & REGIER, D. (1993). The Diagnostic Interview Schedule for Children-Revised Version (DISC-R): I. Preparation, field testing, interrater reliability, and acceptability. *Journal of the American Academy of Child and Adolescent Psychiatry, 32,* 643-650.

SIMON, G. E., & VONKORFF, M. (1995). Recall of psychiatric history in cross-sectional surveys: Implications for epidemiologic research. *Epidemiologic Reviews, 17,* 221-227.

SKINNER, H. A., & BLASHFIELD, R. K (1982). Increasing the impact of cluster analysis research: The case of psychiatric classification. *Journal of Consulting and Clinical Psychology, 50,* 727-735.

SNEATH, P. H. A., & SOKAL, R. R. (1973). *Numerical taxonomy: The principles and practice of numerical classification.* New York: Freeman.

SNIDMAN, N., KAGAN, J., RIORDAN, L., & SHANNON, D. C. (1995). Cardiac function and behavioral reactivity during infancy. *Psychophysiology, 32,* 199-207.

SNYDER, M. (1984). When belief creates reality. In L. Berkowitz (Ed.), *Advances in experimental social psychology* (Vol. 18, pp. 248-305). San Diego: Academic Press.

SQUIRE, L. R. (1989). On the course of forgetting in very long-term memory. *Journal of Experimental Psychology: Learning, meaning, and cognition, 15*, 241-245.

SROUFE, L. A. (1979). The coherence of individual development: Early care, attachment, and subsequent developmental issues. *American Psychologist, 34*, 834-841.

STARR, E. (1994). Commentary: Facilitated communication: A response by child protection. *Child Abuse & Neglect, 18*, 515-527.

STATTIN, H., & MAGNUSSON, D. (1990). *Pubertal maturation in female development.* Mahwah, NJ: Lawrence Erlbaum.

STEVENSON-HINDE, J. (1989). Behavioral inhibition: Issues of context. In J. S. Reznick (Ed.), *Perspectives on behavioral inhibition* (pp. 125-138). Chicago: University of Chicago Press.

STEVENSON-HINDE, J., & GLOVER, A. (1996). Shy girls and boys: A new look. *Journal of Child Psychology & Psychiatry, 37.*

STEVENSON-HINDE, J., & HINDE, R. A. (1986). Changes in associations between characteristics and interactions. In R. Plomin & J. Dunn (Eds.), *The study of temperament: Changes, continuities, and challenges* (pp. 115-129). Mahwah, NJ: Lawrence Erlbaum.

STEVENSON-HINDE, J., & SHOULDICE, A. (1993). Wariness to strangers: A behavior systems perspective revisited. In K. H. Rubin & J. B. Asendorpf (Eds.), *Social withdrawal, inhibition, and shyness in childhood* (pp. 101-116). Mahwah, NJ: Lawrence Erlbaum.

STEVENSON-HINDE, J., & SHOULDICE, A. (1995). 4.5 to 7 years: Fearful behavior, fears, and worries. *Journal of Child Psychology & Psychiatry, 36*, 1027-1038.

STRUBE, M. J. (1989). Evidence for the type in Type A behavior: A taxometric analysis. *Journal of Personality and Social Psychology, 56*, 972-987.

TEASDALE, J. D. (1993). Selective effects of emotion on information processing. In A. Baddeley & L. Weiskrantz (Eds.), *Attention: Selection, awareness, and control* (pp. 374-389). Oxford, UK: Oxford University Press.

TEASDALE, J. D., & BARNARD, P. J. (1993). *Affect, cognition, and change.* Hove, UK: Erlbaum.

TELLEGEN, A., & LUBINSKI, D. (1983). Some methodological comments on labels, traits, interaction, and types in the study of "femininity" and "masculinity": A reply to Spence. *Journal of Personality and Social Psychology, 44*, 447-455.

TESSLER, M., & NELSON, K. (1994). Making memories: The influence of joint encoding on later recall by young children. *Consciousness and Cognition, 3*, 307-326.

THELEN, E. (1989). Self-organization in developmental processes: Can systems approaches work? In M. R. Gunnar & E. Thelen (Eds.), *Systems and development* (pp. 77-117). Mahwah, NJ: Lawrence Erlbaum.

THEOPHRASTUS. (1960). *The characters of Theophrastus* (R. G. Ussher, Ed.). London: Macmillan.

THOMAE, H. (1988). *Das Individuum und seine Welt: Eine Personlichkeitstheorie (The individual and his world: A theory of personality).* Gottingen, Germany: Hogrefe.

THOMAS, A., & CHESS, S. (1977). *Temperament and development.* New York: Brunner/Mazel.

THOMPSON, C. P., SKOWRONSKI, J. J., & LEE, D. J. (1988). Telescoping in dating naturally occurring events. *Memory & Cognition, 16*, 461-468.

THORNDIKE, E. L. (1898). Animal intelligence: An experimental study of the associative processes in animals. *Psychological Monographs, 2*(whole No. 8).

TULVING, E. (1983). *Elements of episodic memory.* New York: Oxford University Press.

USHER, J. N. A., & NEISSER, U. (1993). Childhood amnesia and the beginnings of memory for four early life events. *Journal of Experimental Psychology: General, 122*, 155-165.

VALSINER, J. (Ed.). (1986). *The individual in scientific psychology.* New York: Plenum.

VALSINER, J. (1994). "Vygotskian dynamics of development": Comment. *Human Development, 37*, 366-369.

VAN AKEN, M. A. G., & ASENDORPF, J. B. (1994, July). *A person-oriented approach to development: The temporal consistency of personality and self-concept.* Paper presented at the International Conference on Longitudinal Study on the Genesis of Individual Competencies, Ringberg Castle, Germany.

VAN GEERT, P. (1994). Vygotskian dynamics of development. *Human Development, 37*, 346-345.

VAN KAMMEN, W. B., LOEBER, R., & STOUTHAMER-LOEBER, M. (1991). Substance use and its relationship to conduct problems and delinquency in young boys. *Journal of Youth & Adolescence, 20*, 399-414.

VAN IJZENDOORN, M. H. (1995). Adult attachment representations, parental responsiveness, and infant attachment: A meta-analysis on the predictive validity of the adult attachment interview. *Psychological Bulletin, 117*, 387-403.

VAN LIESHOUT, C. F. M., HASELAGER, G. J. T., RIKSEN-WALRAVEN, J. M., & VAN AKEN, M. A. (1995, April). *Personality development in middle childhood.* Paper presented at the Society for Research in Child Development, Indianapolis, IN.

VON BERTALANFFY, L. (1962). *Modern theories of development: An introduction to theoretical biology.* New York: Harper & Brothers. (Original work published 1933)

VON BERTALANFFY, L. (1968). *General system theory.* New York: Braziller.

VON EYE, A. (1990a). Configural frequency analysis of longitudinal multivariate responses. In A. von Eye (Ed.), *Statistical methods in longitudinal research* (Vol. 2, pp. 545-570). San Diego: Academic Press.

VON EYE, A. (1990b). *Introduction to configural frequency analysis: The search for types and antitypes in cross-classifications.* New York: Cambridge University Press.

VON EYE, A., & CLOGG, C. C. (1994). *Latent variables analysis: Applications for developmental research.* London: Sage.

VON EYE, A., SPIEL, C., & WOOD, P. K. (1996). Configural frequency analysis in applied psychological research. *Applied Psychology: An International Review, 45*(4).

VYGOTSKY, L. (1978). *Mind in society: The development of higher psychological processes.* Cambridge, MA: Harvard University Press.

WALLACHER, R. B., & NOWAK, A. (1994). *Dynamical systems in social psychology.* San Diego: Academic Press.

WALLER, N. G., & MEEHL, P. E. (1997). *Multivariate taxometric procedures: Distinguishing types from continua.* Thousand Oaks, CA: Sage.

WAPNER, S., & KAPLAN, B. (1983). *Toward a holistic developmental psychology.* Mahwah, NJ: Lawrence Erlbaum.

WARD, J. H. (1963). Hierarchical grouping to optimize an objective function. *Journal of the American Statistical Association, 58,* 236-244.

WEINER, H. (1989). The dynamics of the organism: Implications of recent biological thought for psychosomatic theory and research. *Psychosomatic Medicine, 51,* 608-635.

WEISS, R. S. (1974). The provisions of personal relationships. In Z. Rubin (Ed.), *Doing unto others.* Upper Saddle River, NJ: Prentice Hall.

WELLS, G. L., & LOFTUS, E. F. (Eds.). (1984). *Eyewitness testimony: Psychological perspectives.* New York: Cambridge University Press.

WETZLER, S. E., & SWEENEY, J. A. (1986). Childhood amnesia: A conceptualization in cognitive-psychological terms. *Journal of the American Psychoanalytic Association, 34,* 663-685.

WHEELER, D. L., JACOBSON, J. W., PAGLIERI, R. A., & SCHWARTZ, A. A. (1993). An experimental assessment of facilitated communication. *Mental Retardation, 31,* 49-59.

WHITE, S., & PILLERMAN, D. (1979). Childhood amnesia and the development of a socially accessible memory system. In J. F. Kihlstrom & F. J. Evans (Eds.), *Functional disorders of memory* (pp. 29-73). Mahwah, NJ: Lawrence Erlbaum.

WHITING, B. D. (1963). *Six cultures: Studies of child rearing.* New York: Wiley.

WIDOM, C. S., & MORRIS, S. (1997). Accuracy of adult recollections of childhood victimization: Part 2. Childhood sexual abuse. *Psychological Assessment, 9,* 34-46.

WIDOM, C. S., & SHEPARD, R. L. (1996). Accuracy of adult recollections of childhood victimization: Part 1. Childhood physical abuse. *Psychological Assessment, 8,* 412-421.

WIENER-EHRLICH, W. K. (1981). Hierarchical vs. generally overlapping models in psychiatric classification. *Multivariate Behavioral Research, 16,* 455-482.

WILLIAMS, J. E., & BEST, D. L. (1982). *Measuring sex stereotypes.* Beverly Hills, CA: Sage.

WISHART, D. (1987). CLUSTAN user manual [Cluster analysis software manual]. University of St. Andrews, Computing Laboratory.

WOHLWILL, J. F. (1973). *The study of behavioral development.* San Diego: Academic Press.

WOLFF, P. H. (1981). Normal variation in human maturation. In K. J. Conolly & H. F. R. Prechtl (Eds.), *Maturation and development: Biological and psychological maturation* (pp. 1-12). London: Heinemann Medical.

WOOD, P. (1990). Applications of scaling to developmental research. In A. von Eye (Ed.), *Statistical methods in longitudinal research* (Vol. 1, pp. 225-256). San Diego: Academic Press.

XIE, H.-L., & CAIRNS, R. B. (1996, August). *The development of aggression: Antecedents and pathways of early school dropout.* Poster presentation at the biennial meeting of the International Society for the Study of Behavior Development; Québec City, PQ.

YORK, K., & JOHN, O. P. (1992). The four faces of Eve: A typological analysis of women's personality at midlife. *Journal of Personality and Social Psychology, 63,* 494-508.

YORK, K., & JOHN, O. P. (1994). *Three paths into adulthood: A longitudinal study of the antecedents of personality types in adult women.* Manuscript submitted for publication.

YUILLE, J. C., HUNTER, R., JOFFE, R., & ZAPARNIUK, J. (1993). Interviewing children in sexual abuse cases. In G. Goodman & B. Bottoms (Eds.), *Child victims, child witnesses: Understanding and improving testimony* (pp. 95-115). New York: Guilford.

ZEEMAN, E. C. (1976). Catastrophe theory. *Scientific American, 234,* 65-83.

ZOCCOLILLO, M., PICKLES, A., QUINTON, D., & RUTTER, M. (1992). The outcome of childhood conduct disorder: Implications for defining adult personality disorder and conduct disorder. *Psychological Medicine, 22,* 971-986.

ZUBIN, J. (1937). The determination of response patterns in personality adjustment inventories. *Journal of Educational Psychology, 28,* 401-413.

Author Index

Subject Index

❈

Accuracy of retrospective recall, 224
ADHD (attention-deficit hyperactivity
    disorder), 193, 203-207, 214-215
Adolescent research, 51, 47-50, 90,
    103-114, 146-153, 164-174, 195,
    214, 220, 227, 232, 252, 256-258,
    260, 262
Adult outcomes, 48-50, 55-60, 151, 153,
    164-181, 253-257
African American children, 148-151,
    194-195, 197, 199
Aggression, 7, 67, 78, 167-168, 172-183,
    186, 189-191, 206, 212
    alcohol and, 170
    clustering, 54, 58-59
    cross-cultural, 130
    evolution, 124
    latent and manifest, 42-44
    impulsive, 162
    preschool, 16-22
Alcohol use, 6, 44, 47-49, 55-59, 163,
    167-168, 170-171, 175-177, 179,
    181-184
Allostasis, 36
Altruism, 132
Anomic extroverts, 145
ANOVA insensitivity to interactions, 50
Antitype, 7, 56-58, 85, 99-100, 174, 259
Assumptions on individual
    development, 84
Atomistic approach, 34
Attachment:
Adult attachment, 240-241

Attachment categories, 16
Attachment theorists, 4, 12
Attachment types, 157
Atypical emotional responses, 70
Autobiographical memory, 224

Behavioral inhibition, 125, 127
Behavioral system, 33
Belated adjusters, 145
Big Five, 147-148, 153, 156
Blood pressure, 39-42
Brown vs. Board of Education, 5

Captopril therapy, 39-42
Cardiovascular system, 33, 38-42
Carolina Longitudinal Study (CLS),
    256-257
Case study, 65-66, 249, 257
Catastrophe theory, 35
Categorical analyses, 6, 8, 11-31, 41-42,
    60, 79-80, 85-86, 100, 126-128,
    131, 136-138, 140-143, 154, 162,
    247-249
CFA (configural frequency analysis), 52,
    56-57, 85, 87, 99-100, 109
    illustration, 108-111
    profile extremes, 101, 109-111
Chaos theory, 35
Chaotic families, 13
Character, 15
Child Behavior Checklist (CBCL), 194

About the Authors

❦

Doreen Arcus
Department of Psychology, Harvard University

Lars R. Bergman
Department of Psychology, Stockholm University

Robert B. Cairns
Center for Developmental Science, University of North Carolina

Avshalom Caspi
Department of Psychology, University of Wisconsin

Mary S. DeLamatre
University of Pittsburgh Medical Center

Robert A. Hinde
Sub-Department of Animal Behaviour, Madingley
St. John's College, Cambridge

Oliver P. John
Department of Psychology, University of California at Berkeley

Jerome Kagan
Department of Psychology, Harvard University

Kate Keenan
Department of Psychiatry, University of Chicago

Rolf Loeber
School of Medicine, University of Pittsburgh

David Magnusson
Department of Psychology, Stockholm University

Barbara Maughan
Institute of Psychiatry, University of London

Andrew Pickles
Institute of Psychiatry, University of London

Lea Pulkkinen
Department of Psychology, University of Jyväskylä, Finland

Marian Radke-Yarrow
Scientist Emerita
National Institute of Mental Health, Bethesda, Maryland

Richard W. Robins
Department of Pyschology, University of California at Davis

Philip C. Rodkin
Center for Developmental Science, University of North Carolina

Sir Michael Rutter
Institute of Psychiatry, University of London

Emily Simonoff
Institute of Psychiatry, University of London

Nancy Snidman
Department of Psychology, Harvard University

Joan Stevenson-Hinde
Sub-Department of Animal Behaviour, University of Cambridge

Quanwu Zhang
Center for Law and Justice, Rutgers University, Newark, New Jersey